SOME PEOPLE CALL US CLAUS

Mike Claus

Illustrations by Jake Donovan

Copyright © 2024 by Michael D. Claus.

All rights reserved. No portion of this book may be reproduced in any form without written permission from the author, except as permitted by U.S. copyright law.

Some names and identifying details of people described in this book have been altered to protect their privacy.

Illustrations by Jake Donovan.

For rights and permissions, please contact:
Michael Claus
mdclaus@gmail.com

Dedicated to the memories of

Mary Jane, Jerome, Ruth, Ralph, and Walt

With great gratitude to my wife for her patience and encouragement, my mother for her many hours of editing and proofreading (with special attention to comma placement), and my brother-in-law, Jake, whose illustrations have, predictably, stolen the show.

Introduction
On Legacies

We use a unique expression at the Claus family dinner table. When someone asks for salt to be passed (or butter or gravy or whatever), if the passing party first helps themselves to the requested item before sending it along, the maneuver is known as "pulling an A.C."

The phrase comes from my mom's family, named for her aunt. For years Aunt Catherine (A.C.) would crowd into the kitchen with the rest of the Murphy clan to break bread. And for years she would dutifully pass dishes and seasonings around the large table to the gathered masses. Somewhere along the way, someone noticed a slight delay whenever Aunt Catherine was asked to pass an item. Without fail, she would sprinkle some salt and then pass; butter some bread and then pass; ladle some gravy and then pass. She simply could not pass an item without using it first. It became a family curiosity, then a phenomenon, and then a legend.

It sounds silly, but for a long time this was the only piece of information I knew about my Grandpa Murphy's twin sister. Despite her lifetime of experiences—the triumphs and sorrows and everything in between—all I could tell you about the dear woman is that she compulsively swiped the salt before passing it. Her little habit didn't hurt anyone. I'm sure she didn't even know she was doing it. It is a completely inconsequential footnote in the story of her life. Yet here I am, *sixty years later*, writing about it in a book.

Legacies can be a peculiar thing.

The unhappy reality is that memories of our loved ones fade with the passing years and generations. Our own legacies will do the same, until one day all that is left of us, in this life at least, are a name and some dates on a page. We're fortunate if we know a couple of anecdotes about the relatives we never met.

I have since learned more about Aunt Catherine. She was a reserved, somewhat anxious person who grew quirkier with age. She never married and lived with her parents as an adult until their deaths. She was a kind soul who probably would have benefited from modern antidepressants. Her twin brother, Jerome, was the complete opposite in personality and looked after her like a father. And, yes, she helped herself to the salt before passing it. That's not so bad as far as legacies go. We know virtually nothing about other branches of the family tree. Most of our ancestors are indeed reduced to mere names on a page and—barring some extraordinary discovery in grandma's attic or the time capsule buried in the old churchyard—will stay that way.

This is a book of family stories. The earlier chapters come from original letters and other documents that were tucked away in boxes, in some cases more than a hundred years ago. Such source materials are invaluable, but also imperfect. The letters we have are from a moment in time, written to a particular audience that is not us. For example, I learned a lot about my great-grandfather, Charles Dwyer, through letters he wrote to his young wife when he was 20 years old. But Charles was a much different man at 35, so the picture is incomplete. Seriously, take a gander at some of your own writing from fifteen years ago. I recently re-read some emails from my college days and I want to hop in the nearest time machine and smack myself.

Naturally, the available information increases as we move forward in time. But even first-hand accounts are distilled, exaggerated, or misremembered. Sometimes a few embellishments (I call them "narrative enhancers") here and there make for a better story, and before you know it, the "better story" becomes the only version we know. "When the legend becomes fact, print the legend," observes that great line from *The Man Who Shot Liberty Valance*. The point is, we should tell our stories, but we can never know the *full* story.

With those lawyerly caveats, the reader should be assured that I have strived for accuracy. I can just about say that almost everything in these pages is nearly 100% true, for the most part, except when it isn't.

As much as anything, this undertaking is about honoring the legacy of my grandparents: Mary Jane (Dwyer) and Jerome Murphy, and Ruth (Wahrow) and Walt Kresge, as well as Ralph Claus, who I never had the chance to meet. Each had a lasting (eternal, actually) impact on the family in their own unique way. I hope that future generations will gain an appreciation of what made these people so inspiring, so hilarious, and so worthy of remembering. That they are more than names on a page.

Not that my motives are completely altruistic. I have my *own* legacy to protect. I don't want to look down from my apartment beyond the Pearly Gates eighty years from now and hear the following, very realistic conversation:

Future Great-Granddaughter: "Who is this, Mommy?"

Future Granddaughter: "That is your Great-Grandpa Mike. I don't remember too much about him, except that he mumbled a lot. He was real mumbler, that guy."

Future Great-Granddaughter: "Oh! That's why in our family when someone is mumbling, we always say, 'Speak up! Don't pull a Grandpa Mike.'"

Future Granddaughter: "That's exactly right, Sweetie! Now run along, I need to veto some bills. I *am the President of the United States*, after all."

No, sir. Now when they talk about old Grandpa Mike, they'll have to say:

Future Granddaughter: "My sweet child, Great-Grandpa Mike did more than mumble. He actually wrote a book of family stories. Not a soul read it, but he wrote the thing."

Future Great-Granddaughter: "Golly! Great-Grandpa Mike sounds like a brilliant man. But I have another question, Mommy. What is a ... *book?*"

3

None of this could have happened without my parents, Chuck and Kerry, who, (1) love and appreciate their families, (2) taught us to love and appreciate our families, and (3) saved a lot of old junk in boxes that we could review decades later. Mom has done the yeoman's (yeolady's?) work, painstakingly organizing and labeling old documents and photographs. Dad is the storyteller of the family and never too proud to self-deprecate. You will see that a lot of these stories feature him playing the role of the fool. The buffoon. The chump. The clod and the clown. The dope and the dunce. The imbeci—well, you get the picture. (A note to future generations: my dad is a man of great intelligence, integrity, and generosity. The foregoing was hyperbole for humorous effect. He's not even half of those nasty things I called him.)

Which leads me to the title: *Some People Call Us Claus*. You might be thinking to yourself, "What the heck is that supposed to mean? Why do only *some* people call them Claus? Is that some weird reference? I don't get it. This book is confusing and stupid."

Some People Call Us Claus is actually a "rap" song written and recorded by one of the most celebrated hip-hop artists of his generation: my dad. This was back in the days of landline telephones (for the younger reader, the communication device that came between the telegraph and the smartphone.) When someone called your home and no one answered, the caller would hear an answering machine recording. Most folks had fairly *pro forma* messages:

"You have reached the Smiths. We're not available. Please leave your name and number. Have a nice day."

Dad, on the other hand, realized that our answering machine, with the captive audience on the other end of the call, would be the perfect opportunity to showcase his vocal and lyrical stylings. When people called the Claus House, they were greeted by the energetic voice of my father, performing a rap which is forever etched into the brains of his children. (The opening line is a riff on the frequent mispronunciation of our last name. The first usage of "Clause" sounds like "claws," while the second, correctly pronounced "Claus" rhymes with "mouse.") It went:

Some people call us Clause, some people call us Claus,
But now that you have called, there is no one at the house.
You can leave yourself a message, you can leave one for us too,
And if you will be patient, we'll be getting back to you.
Now I know you want to cheer, and I know you want to clap!
So this will be the ending of my tele-phony rap!

And ... it was a hit! As God as my witness, a bona fide hit. We went from two or three missed calls a day to dozens. People called and then called back twice more to hear the song again. They had their friends call. We would get the craziest voicemails.

"*<Laughing> Hi, this is Dawn from the proctologist's office. One of our other nurses just called you about your examination. She started laughing hysterically and said I HAD to hear your answering machine. Another nurse is about to call too, so don't pick up.*"

It got to the point where if one of us answered the phone, the caller would sound disappointed, sometimes scrambling to think of a pretext as to why they were calling, but often not even trying to hide it.

"*Oh, sorry. I was, er, actually hoping to get your answering machine. If I call back, do you mind just letting it ring?*"

The whole episode reinforced that our family is, in my estimation, uncommonly goofy. Whether people were laughing with Dad or at him is an open question, but he couldn't have cared less. It's a trait that he and Mom passed onto us. Not caring if we look goofy is one of our better qualities, actually. Hopefully some of that goofiness comes through in these pages.

Before we proceed: some names you should know. First, the Clauses. My dad is Ralph Charles Claus. He goes by Chuck. His father was Ralph Claus. He went by Ralph. Names associated with the Claus line are the Wahrows, the Wahrowskys (which happens to be the same family as the Wahrows), the Hausers, the Hausers (which happens to be a different family than the other Hausers), the Danberts, and throw in the Kresges for good measure. Broadly speaking, these families settled in New York City and Michigan. I have dubbed these folks: The Lutherans.

Before she was Kerry Claus, my mom was Kerry Murphy. Other names associated with the Murphy line are the Dwyers, the Oswalds, the Primassings, and the Sheehans. These folks settled in Chicago, Iowa, and Canada. This proud lot shall heretofore be known as: The Catholics.

With that background, let's beg—

"WAIT!!" the future generations shout. "Aren't we only getting half the story? I'm all for the Clauses and the Murphys, but what about your better half? Have you forgotten the family of the mother of your children? You haven't mentioned the Donovans! Not one word about the Piros? The Martinos?! And *just where* are the Hungerfords, I'd like to know!?!"

Fear not, future generations. My father-in-law, Mark Donovan, has already published the authoritative history of Mother's side of the family (I am assuming that in the future I will refer to my wife Cortney as "Mother," because it will annoy her). It is called *7 Brides for 2 Brothers* and is available from fine booksellers somewhere. You absolutely must read it, and if you have already read it, read it again.

I first read *7Bf2B* on an airplane flying to New York City to visit Cortney. We were dating at the time and things were "getting serious." The thought crossed my mind that the book I held in my hands might contain the origin stories of my future in-laws. Beyond that, I specifically remember being motivated and inspired by Mark's call to action in the closing words of the book's introduction (reproduced here *without* express written consent of the author—go ahead and sue me).

> So herein lie my family stories. I don't know what will become of them in the years to come, but at least I will know that I have done my duty to family and to Western Civilization. That's right, my duty. So for anyone who might happen upon these words in the future I have a message for you. First, 'Hello, future!' Second, you have the same duty. You cannot let your stories die and turn to dust. Get going! Start writing, or recording, or telling your own stories.

To which I now respond, "Hello, voice from the past! You old relic! You ancient windbag, you! Thank you for your transmission. Message received, loud and clear!"

So, onward to the business at hand! Pour yourself a drink, settle in, pass the salt, and let's get started.

PART I

The Lutherans

WE IMAGINE THESE LITTLE TOWNS IN THE OLD COUNTRY
AS IDYLLIC. LIKE SOMETHING OUT OF A FAIRY TALE.

1
Das Leiden

New Year's Eve, 1827. In the tiny German village of Tuningen, Andreas Hauser was born. He was my great-great-great-grandfather.

Tuningen is tucked among the gently sloping hills of southern Germany, near the edge of the Black Forest to the west and the border of Switzerland to the south. Even today, it appears to be a charming little farming community with a total population of less than 3,000. Most buildings in the village are painted bright white and covered by orange roofs, providing a striking contrast to the green fields that issue from the town center. The tower of protestant Michael's Church reaches just slightly above the homes and civic buildings that surround it, modest and unassuming.

We imagine these little towns in the Old Country as idyllic. Like something out of a fairy tale. For most of our ancestors, however, their lives in Europe were marked by a never-ending cycle of war, poverty, famine, political upheaval, economic collapse, disease, and early death. For all its quaint beauty, Tuningen in the 19th century was a wretched place to live. It was indeed like a fairy tale—not the sanitized cartoon versions, but the creepy originals where every character is devoured by a wolf or cooked in a boiling cauldron.

Andreas Hauser was a mason, perhaps of the stone-laying variety, and the family owned a farm. In 1855, he married Anna Christina (Hansmann) who gave birth to 14 children. Let's briefly pause to appreciate that—14 separate labors and deliveries, all without an epidural. God bless you, Grandma Anna.

Two of Andreas and Anna's children were named Matthieas. The first Matthieas died as a baby. The second Matthieas moved to America as a young man and from the looks of the photographs grew to be, in contrast to his father, a rather rotund old man. More on the second Matthieas in the next chapter.

Tragically, the first Matthieas was not the only child Andreas and Anna lost. Of the 14, six of them, all sons, died before reaching age 2. As incredible as that sounds, this was in line with the average at the time. In Germany during the 1850s, a staggering 47% of children did not reach the age of five.[1]

It is tempting to downplay these losses as "just a part of life back then." Maybe parents were more resigned, having seen so many children among them perish. They tried not to grow too attached, too soon. But these were living, breathing, crying, giggling kids—babies who never had a chance to flourish—and Andreas and Anna naturally agonized over losing them.

Late in his life, Andreas handwrote a family register documenting the critical information for his 14 children—their dates of births, baptisms, and for the six, their dates of death. Other than his notes, I doubt the names of these poor souls are recorded anywhere other than, perhaps, dusty church and cemetery records buried away somewhere in Tuningen. To honor these six departed children and their tormented parents, Andreas' words are reprinted here.

> Matthieas, born on August 11th, 1856, between 9 and 10 o'clock in the morning, baptized on August 13th by pastor Schmidgall in the Lutheran church in Tuningen. This child, Matthieas, died on September 1st, 1857, at the age of 1 year, 21 days.

> Marx, born on October 21st, 1861, at 8:30 in the evening, baptized on October 23rd in the Lutheran church at Tuningen by pastor Schlager. This child, Marx, died on June 11th, 1863, at 4 o'clock in the afternoon, at the age of 1 year, 8 months, and 12 days.

---

1 Child mortality in Germany 1825-2020; Published by Aaron O'Neill (2019), *available at* https://www.statista.com/.

Johan Georg, born on August 2nd, 1863, between 4 and 5 o'clock in the morning, he received emergency baptism within 5 hours of his birth by the midwife Münger, however he was brought into the church and blessed by pastor Schlager, and 7 hours after his birth he died.

Richard, born on November 1st, 1871, at 7:30 in the evening, baptized on November 2nd in the church at Tuningen by pastor Schlager. This child, Richard, died on February 15th, 1872, at the age of 3 months and 12 days.

Richard, born on January 27th, 1873, baptized by pastor Schlager. This child, Richard, died on April 22nd, 1873, at the age of 3 months and 5 days.

Christian, born on April 18th, 1875, baptized by pastor Schlager. This child died on September 1st, 1875, at the age of 4 months, 12 days.

There was no respite for Andreas. Anna Christina died in 1876 at age 48, leaving Andreas with sole responsibility of caring for four young children, ages 11, 9, 8, and 6. The oldest four children had already left home, or soon would. Indeed, nearly 1.5 million Germans migrated to America in the 1880s—more than any other decade in history. Among them were three of Andreas' sons, including Matthieas. It appears that at least two of his daughters moved away from Tuningen, either to America or elsewhere with their husbands. Now in his fifties, with four youngsters to care for and no wife, leaving Germany was not a realistic option. He would stay in Tuningen and work the farm, hoping to pass it to his youngest son, Jakob.

Now comes the part where I brighten things up with a surprise twist and happy ending, right? Time to charge in with that promised goofiness? Would that I could. Sadly, the last decade of Andreas' life was marked by new variations on the themes of sorrow and misery. His wife was gone and most of his children had moved away. He knew that he would never see them again. He wrote to them, all but begging them to write back. He worried about them constantly, and the scarce news from America was not encouraging. Just as the influx of German immigrants arrived, the country entered a horrible recession, putting millions out of work.

In 1885, Andreas wrote to his son in America:[2]

Dear Matthieas,

It's been a long time since I received news from you, and I thought I wouldn't write earlier because it was your turn first, but now I could no longer hold back. It's really been upsetting to me, day and night my thoughts are with you, especially since we're always hearing that things are going so badly, all the reports and letters depict such a significant business crisis as has not existed in many years. ... Write to me how things are going, for better or worse, I would be less nervous knowing what the situation is. ...

Andreas' health was also failing. His feet were horribly swollen and he could barely breathe or sleep at night. The combination of his feet and the bitter cold kept him homebound for the winter. He was alone and depressed. His letters note that he would gladly sell the farm if he could, but the fields were poor and there were no buyers.

In another 1885 letter Andreas wrote:

Dearly beloved Matthieas!

We've had quite a cold winter, which has also had a big influence on my health, but now things are a little bit better. Since the weather has gotten more mild, I'm confident that things will be looking up for me, as I've had badly swollen feet, so that I wasn't able to walk any more. I couldn't wear any normal shoes anymore, but now thank God it's already somewhat better. I can also go back out into the neighbors' houses here and there, and also to the bookbinder's. I was often frightfully bored and wept after you when I felt so completely alone. I had to stay at home for days and nights, as Christine and Jakob didn't want to stay with me, nor did I expect it of them. ...

The next letter to Matthieas was from his brother Jakob, enclosing a copy of the sermon given at Andreas' funeral. There was no mention of a

---

[2] The letters are written in German Sütterlin, an old form of German-language handwriting based on medieval cursive writing, so the translation is imperfect.

feel-good "Celebration of Life" like we see today. No, in true German spirit, Jakob wrote, "Here we send to you the funeral sermon of our dear father, so that you can also hear how his final days of suffering were." Andreas Hauser died on August 19, 1885.

Das leiden is German for "the suffering" and Andreas did enough leiden-ing for all of us. I do not envy his life, but I greatly admire the man. Through misery, *pure misery,* he continued to love his children and keep his faith. He told the folks gathered at his deathbed, "Always keep God in front of your eyes and in your hearts. See that you don't willingly commit any sin and continue to do God's bidding." Wise words from Great-Great-Great-Grandpa.

Not the most uplifting tale to kick things off, but *das leiden* was Andreas' reality, and the reality of so many who came before. Stories like his are a reminder of just how much things have improved. The child mortality rate in Western countries is now less than one percent. We can chat with our friends and family any time we want, even on video if we feel like it. We can turn up the heat in the winter and blast the air conditioning in the summer. The bookbinder delivers right to our front door. We can buy orthopedic shoes for our swollen feet. Somehow, we still find plenty to complain about.

Let us raise a glass, or a stein if you have one, to our long-suffering Grossvater Andreas. His temporary agony on earth is ended, and I believe he is reunited with his wife, his children, and his Savior for eternity. He may not have gained fortune or fame, but he still achieved everything.

Der Tod ist ihm zuf Schlaf geworden,
Aus dem er zu neuem Leben arwacht.

Death has become his sleep,
From which he awakens to new life.

"You earned this, Billy! Let me pin it on!"

2
Keeping it in the Family

My, what a jolly little paperback this is. Some light reading for a day at the beach? A perfect companion to a picnic lunch? You probably haven't laughed this hard since the end of *Old Yeller*.

After the previous chapter, I acknowledge that I ought to lighten things up a bit. Can't risk the audience putting down the book, shaken and in existential crisis. So, I suppose now is a good time to talk about folks marrying their cousins.

First, consider this: Everyone in the world has two parents, four grandparents, eight great-grandparents, and so on. With each generation, the number of direct ancestors doubles. For example, Andreas Hauser was one of my 32 great-great-great (shorthanded as "3x") grandparents. Of course, Andreas had 32 (3x) great-grandparents of his own—those folks are among my (8x) great-grandparents. We have more than a thousand (8x) great-grandparents, all of whom are directly related to us. The number of our direct ancestors adds up quickly. In fact, it adds up exponentially.

Here is something to ponder, but before you ponder it, I recommend going out on a clear night and looking up at the sky. I'll give you a moment … Are you looking? Do you feel like a speck of dust as you gaze at the starry expanse? Here we go.

If you were to trace your family tree back to the Middle Ages—not even ancient history, only to around the year 1000 AD—you would arrive at your (28x) great-grandparents. And, here's the crazy thing … we all have more than *a billion* direct (28x) great-grandparents. A billion ancestors, just in that single generation living in 1000 AD! It's unfathomable, but it's true. Is your mind sufficiently boggled?

It's not quite as simple as that, however. Astute readers will note that the population of the entire world in the Middle Ages was far less than a billion. So, how can it be that we had a billion (28x) great-grandparents roaming around primitive villages in the year 1000 AD? The answer is: shared ancestors. That is, the same individuals occupying multiple slots on the family tree. To use a basic example, a child of two "kissing cousins" would share a set of great-grandparents, and therefore would have only six individuals accounting for eight great-grandparents positions in his lineage. Your family tree includes all sorts of shared ancestors—the math simply will not work any other way. We're all a little inbred.

Arriving (mercifully) at the point. There is absolutely no concrete evidence that my Great-Great-Grandfather Matthieas Hauser married his cousin. Anyone who tells you otherwise is just speculating, based on the teeny-tiny coincidence that he married a local gal from the same village with the same last name. (Truth be told, they kind of look alike, too.) But if Anna Hauser *was* somehow related to Matthieas Hauser, it's really not a big deal!

Some experts in the field of Cousin Love estimate that 80% of marriages throughout human history were between second cousins or closer. And if the mathematical case doesn't sway you, consider some of the esteemed historical figures who found their happily-ever-after with relatives:

- Marie Antoinette (They were a good couple. She let him eat as much cake as he wanted).
- Edgar Allen Poe (His cousin stole his tell-tale heart).
- Charles Darwin (A cousin marrier who considered himself *very* evolved).
- Albert Einstein (He said that $E=mc^2$, where E = "enjoying," and mc = "my cousin").

We know little of Matthieas Hauser's childhood. Andreas' handwritten family register tells us that Matthias "was born on October 17th, 1859, in the morning at half past one, baptized on October 18th in the church at Tuningen by pastor Schlager." German men at age 20 were obligated to report for three years of military service. Matthieas served in a mounted cavalry unit, the 25th Dragoon Regiment of Queen Olga. He saw no combat and was discharged in 1882, "having served and conducted himself well," according to his service papers.

Matthieas came to America with his lady love (possible cousin) soon after, and, as far as we know, never returned to Germany. They lived in New York City, where he worked as a harness-maker. At some point, Matthieas adopted the more Americanized name, "Matthew." He died in 1939, having outlived Anna by more than a decade. A portion of his modest savings went to the "Bethlehem Orphan and Half-Orphan Asylum," an institution with a terrible name but a good mission, providing housing and care for German-American children who had lost parents to influenza and cholera outbreaks in New York City.[1] I think Andreas would have been proud of him.

Matthew and Anna had four children, including a daughter, Julia—my great-grandmother. Julia married a man named William Wawrosky. The Wawrosky clan is largely a mystery. William's father, Charles, was from Germany. His mother, Anna (Witte), was born in a town that no longer exists, West Hoboken, New Jersey. We think that Anna died when William was young and that Charles remarried. Names on a page.

Speaking of names, in 1914 William Wawrosky filed a petition to legally change his. William wanted to swap Wawrosky for Wahrow, probably because he thought the former sounded "too ethnic." William's petition for name change was brought before—I promise I am not making this up—the Honorable Judge Peter Schmuck. Yes, the guy with the legal authority to change names was himself named Schmuck!

Believe me when I tell you that my interest was absolutely piqued by this information. As piqued as piqued can be. I temporarily backburnered the Wawrosky research and devoted my studies to Schmuck. As it turns out, Judge Schmuck was something of a celebrity, known not only for his amusing name, but for his legal mind and the clever turns of phrase and witticisms he delivered from the bench. "He is the funniest and most popular judge in New York," said one profile in *Vanity Fair*.[2]

---

[1] https://lssny.org/about-us/history/
[2] Walker, Stanley, *Tammany Judge: Peter Schmuck*, Vanity Fair (1934).

Wild stuff, but it gets even wilder. There are legends, told as recently as 2009 in an article in the UCLA Law Review,[3] that Judge Schmuck refused any and all applications for a name change. Several versions of the story float around out there, but all involve Judge Schmuck telling the petitioner something along the lines of, "I was born a Schmuck and I'm going to die a Schmuck and if my name is good enough for me, your name is good enough for you. Petition denied."

Well, in what may be my only actual contribution to the field of History, I can positively debunk the legend that Judge Schmuck denied all applications for a name change. We have the proof—a copy of Schmuck's order *granting* William Wawrosky's request to change his name. Myth Busted! My guess is that the good judge engaged in some playful ribbing with the petitioners before granting their applications and the legend grew from that. In any event, with the stroke of a Schmuck's pen, Wawrosky became Wahrow.

If Judge Schmuck did try to razz William, he found a poor target. Julia Wahrow née Hauser was, by unanimous vote of those who knew her, a certified sweetheart. Her husband, William Wahrow née Wawrosky, in contrast, was a stern man. Dour, even. In fact, the quality people seem to remember most about Great-Grandpa Wahrow was his temper, which was directed especially at kids, often with scary results.

By coincidence—and I bet a psychologist could explain if there's a connection here—his own childhood was unhappy. As the story goes, Charles' second wife resented Anna's children, assuming the archetypical role of the evil stepmom with gusto. Just one example: William, perhaps five or six years old, woke in the middle of the night during a loud thunderstorm. Seeking comfort, he ran to his father's room, but his stepmom intercepted him, whereupon she locked him in a pitch-black closet until morning. Gee, do you think that event had any lasting impact on young William?

William also had rotten luck in business. In 1920, he was a salesman of office furniture—seemingly a very promising career path in booming New York City. Then the stock market crashed in 1929. The last thing businesses

---

3 Julia Shear Kushner, Comment, *The Right to Control One's Name*, 57 UCLA L. Rev. 313 (2009).

needed were fancy new rolltop desks. William ended up working as a grocery store clerk for most of his career and the family never had much money. So, if William was grumpy, I think we can show him some grace.

We should also resist the urge to caricaturize these people. Humans are complex creatures. There is persuasive evidence to suggest that William wasn't all salt and vinegar. One photograph we have shows William absolutely beaming. His grin is textbook—ear to ear and toothy. He appears entirely at ease whilst lounging in some sort of ceramic tub, feet raised, completely nude. Looks to be about nine months old. Of course, in the remaining two-dozen photos spanning the rest of William's life he wears the familiar frown, but he did enjoy that bath in 1891.

Truthfully, to focus on William's serious manner tells only part of the story. He managed to stay happily married for more than fifty years and, with Julia, raised two brilliant girls, Lillian, and my grandmother, Ruth. His surviving letters to his daughter are full of warmth and affection, and, in one instance, a brief moment of legitimate comedy.

It seems that a pair of newlyweds had moved into the apartment above the Wahrows and were most enthusiastic in their, shall we say, "enjoyment of the rights and privileges of marriage." They took to the task with as much gusto as Charles Wawrosky's second wife took to evil step-momming. Those thin-walled New York City apartments didn't hold many secrets. William and Julia, now in their eighties, had just about enough of the racket. But in a letter to his daughter, William reported a happy development:

> Our friends upstairs have quieted down considerably. If they do "engage," it does not last too long. I have met them on the street and they seem willing to cooperate.

We also know that William Wahrow was a hero. We know this because he had an official medal that says so. This was back in the 1920s and the sands of time have buried the exact details of what occurred, but in synopsis, an automobile had caught fire on the busy city streets and William sprinted to the scene and extinguished it. (Depending on who you ask, he may have also pulled the driver from the wreckage.) It was not a major inferno, but significant enough to warrant a story in the newspaper. The writer even interviewed William, who no doubt rushed to the newsstand to buy the early edition the next morning. As promised, there was a story about the fire. But, incredibly, William was unmentioned. His comments, and his heroic role, had been cut by the editor.

The snub did not go unnoticed by William's pals and they resolved to make things right. One imagines a group of them gathered in a crowded saloon on a Friday evening in jovial mood, celebrating the end of the work week. One of the ringleaders calls for the group's attention.

"Listen here, Will. We heard about you putting out that blaze. And, well, we all felt real sore about that newspaper article. So, uh, we passed a hat and we [snickering], we got you something ..."

"What's this all about?"

"... we got you something that we think you're really going to like."

"Ahh, you're all wet."

The ringleader reveals a velvet pouch. Contained within is a medal, of sorts. Its overall appearance is something between kitschy and ludicrous.

On top is a brass plaque that reads: Fire Chief – William Wahrow. Suspended from the name plate by two chains is the fireman's cross—with an automobile engraved in the center, surrounded by the words, FORD FIRE and HERO. Silliest of all, a tin firefighter's helmet hangs on the bottom of the apparatus. No doubt the craftsman commissioned to make it was urged to add plenty of gaud, and to not spare the tawd.

"You earned this, Billy! Let me pin it on!"

"Go chase yourself!"

"No, no, no. Put it on! There ya go, Chief!"

To great applause, William affixes the trinket to his jacket. And to conclude the ceremony, the group begins a rousing chorus of *For He's a Jolly Good Fellow*, as their serious-minded friend permits himself a smile.

A complete grouch would have trashed the thing. But William kept it—his major award safely stored in the velvet pouch, where it has remained in the family's possession a century later. Behind that solemn veneer, William had, I'm confident in saying, a hint of a sense of humor.

With that, we temporarily leave the Wahrows and Hausers in Twentieth Century New York City, and return to the 1800s, to Michigan and the world of Danberts and Clauses. And as we continue this journey, you may be relieved to hear that there are no more suspected cousin-marriages—even if, it bears repeating, it's really not a big deal!

On top of a tall pedestal stands a soldier loading his rifle and wearing the distinctive hat of the Iron Brigade.

3
The Forgotten Danbert

John Danbert may have read the announcement in the *Detroit Free Press:*

> To ARMS! The Union is now in its greatest peril. Unless the people rush to the flag, the days of American glory will be gone forever. Let the meeting be marked by harmony, enthusiasm, patriotism. Let every man forget party and behold only his imperiled country. The federal union must be preserved. The folds of the flag must wave forever over all the territory the fathers left us or which we have acquired by the blood and treasure of the nation.

The notice went on to declare that a public meeting would be held on the Campus Martius in downtown Detroit the evening of July 15, 1862. Mayor William Duncan would lead the rally, joined by an impressive roster of the era's political bigwigs. Their goal was to recruit more soldiers into the Union army.

In the first year of the Civil War, the secessionist Confederates delivered a series of unexpected setbacks to the Federals, prompting President Abraham Lincoln to call on the governors of loyal states to send 300,000 new volunteers. The Detroit contingent planned a spirited ceremony, like dozens of others successfully held across the Midwest, brimming with rousing speeches and songs to whip up patriotic fervor and encourage the assembled men to sign their lives over to their country. So, risers were built. Laurels were pruned. Flags were pressed, and the bunting draped, just so. The political bigwigs readied their speeches.

It ended in a riot. A group of Southern sympathizers infiltrated the crowd, shouted down the speakers, and disrupted the proceedings. Part of their strategy was to start rumors that the government would impose an unpopular draft and force men into service—even though the stated purpose of the meeting was strictly to call for volunteers. When one of the speakers stepped forward and asked the committee to "draft resolutions" to form a regiment, a secessionist in the crowd shouted, *"Did ye hear that, boys? Didn't I tell ye they are going to draft?!"*[1]

Now, you know, and I know, and the speaker knew, and I'll bet even those Southern sympathizers knew, that "draft" is just a fancy word for "write." When preceding the word "resolutions," it invariably refers to a committee drawing up some declarations for a vote. But context did not matter to the Southern sympathizers. They were just waiting for the D-word. Upon hearing it, the infiltrators rushed the stage, destroyed the podium, and chased after the carriage of 80-year-old Lewis Cass, Michigan's most famous statesman, apparently with designs to hang him. Having failed that, the rioters roamed the streets looking for other lesser statesmen to hang, until darkness finally dispersed them.

Detroit's patriotic rally was a flop. The city was humiliated. Abraham Lincoln probably rolled his eyes. The political bigwigs regrouped. A second announcement appeared in the newspaper several days later.

> MEN OF DETROIT! The fair fame of your city is at stake. Come forth in your might and prove your patriotism to meet the crisis. Your friends from many a stricken field call you to the rescue. Shall a few pestilent sympathizers with treason neutralize your patriotic effort? Let an expression go forth which shall rebuke the traitors and vindicate the patriotism of the city. All who favor an energetic prosecution of the war are requested to meet on the Campus Martius on Tuesday afternoon at 3 o'clock, July 22, 1862.

Translation: "MEN OF DETROIT! For real this time. Get your act together and form a gol-derned regiment!"

---

[1] This account, along with most of the information for this chapter, comes from O.B. Curtis's, *History of the Twenty-Fourth Michigan of the Iron Brigade, Known as the Detroit and Wayne County Regiment* (1891). Along with being a detailed historian and beautiful writer, Corporal Curtis was a member of the regiment and lost his left arm due to battle injuries. Unless otherwise noted, assume historical references come from Curtis.

The men of Detroit met the task. In the weeks following the second rally, they raised not only the regiment the governor requested, but an extra one on top of that. More than 1,000 men gathered at the old State Fair Grounds on August 15, 1862, to officially enlist and begin their training. Among them was a 20-year-old gasfitter and plumber named John Danbert.

You probably have deduced already that John Danbert is a relative—another great-great-great grandfather from my dad's side. He was born in Switzerland in 1844 and emigrated to the United States as a young child. Twenty years later he was marching southward toward the Potomac, a member of the brand new 24th Michigan regiment.

A brief primer on Civil War terminology is helpful here. A regiment was the basic building block of the army. A thousand soldiers, usually from the same city or area, made up a regiment. Within a regiment were ten companies, each with 100 soldiers. John Danbert joined the twenty-fourth infantry regiment formed in Michigan ("the 24th Michigan") and was assigned to Company D.

The next step up after regiment was a brigade. In the Union army, a brigade was a group of three to six regiments. Above that was a division, then a corps, then an army, but for purposes of John Danbert's story, we may content ourselves to focus on the regiment and brigade. That is because Grandpa Danbert was a member of arguably the most famous of all brigades in the entire Civil War—and definitely the one with the coolest name. The exceptional group of fighters, originally from the "Western" states of Wisconsin and Indiana, had famously earned the designation: The Iron Brigade.

The nickname came from General George McClellan, who observed the Western men advancing under relentless fire during the Battle of South Mountain. McClellan exclaimed, "They must be made of iron!" The Union won the battle and the name stuck.[2] The newly-formed 24th

---

2 The nickname of the 3rd New Jersey cavalry was "The New Jersey Butterflies." Nobody ever talked about those guys being made of iron. Too bad. They could have been the Iron Butterflies.

Michigan would be added as reinforcements to the veteran Indiana and Wisconsin regiments of the Iron Brigade.

Of the 1,000 men to join the 24th, about half were farmers. Most of the rest, like John Danbert, were a variety of tradesmen. Their number also included ten students, six lawyers, five doctors, four journalists, three preachers, and one coffin maker. The average age of the recruits was 25, though this figure is inflated by some outliers, including a 70-year-old farmer. One third, again like John Danbert, had been born in foreign lands.

The men trained for two weeks then headed east, drilling as they went. By the end of September, they were in Washington and encamped one night in the shadow of the United States Capitol building—its dome still under construction. They then proceeded into Maryland where they joined the battle-hardened troops from Wisconsin and Indiana. John Danbert's first impression of the meeting may well have mirrored that of Corporal Curtis, who described it this way:

> Our suits were new; theirs were army-worn. Our Colonel extolled our qualities, but the brigade was silent. Not a cheer. A pretty cool reception, we thought. We had come out to reinforce them, and supposed they would be glad to see us. Neither was satisfied with the other.

The 24th would see their first combat two months later at the Battle of Fredericksburg. The regiment performed well, successfully dislodging a group of Confederates from a dense group of trees and withstanding hellacious artillery barrage. They won the respect of their peers, but the Union lost the battle. The regiment also fought at Chancellorsville and some secondary engagements—but the audience is getting restless.

"Get to Gettysburg!!" they shout. So, to Gettysburg we shall go.

The three-day battle from July 1 to July 3, 1863, was the bloodiest of the war and the most famous battle in American history. Accounts of valor on both sides are numerous, but history most remembers the celebrated bayonet charge of the 20th Maine on July 2, and the doomed charge of Confederate General Pickett's division on July 3 that left the rebel army obliterated. The 24th Michigan was involved in neither—its only combat action was on the first day of the battle. Yet, the 24th suffered more casualties than any Union regiment at Gettysburg. Of the 496 men who went into battle on July 1, only 99 remained able to fight by the end of the day.

The most ferocious fighting on July 1 was between the 24th Michigan and the 26th North Carolina in an area called Herbst Woods (now known as Reynolds Woods, in honor of General John Reynolds who died there). The two regiments engaged in what has been described as a one-on-one "brutal battle of mutual annihilation."[3] At times, the foes were within forty yards of each other, in an open field with no cover. The North Carolina regiment lost 588 of their 800 men—the most of any Confederate regiment at Gettysburg. Though the Tar Heels eventually forced the Wolverines back, the Michigan men heroically repelled the attack long enough to give the rest of the Union troops time to set up defensive positions that would be so critical on July 2 and 3. What was left of the 24th fell back and regrouped as the sun set.

One newspaper reporting shortly after the battle observed the fearlessness of the Iron Brigade, and the 24th Michigan in particular:

> It was to the Iron Brigade more than any other that the nation owes its salvation at Gettysburg, and we say not more than history will verify, that of all the heroic regiments which fought there, the Twenty-fourth Michigan stands preeminent for its devotion and valor. Against the overwhelming hordes of the enemy, it stood for hours, a wall of granite, which beat back, again and again, the resolute but baffled foe.

We believe that John Danbert was probably among those who rallied with his comrades one final time as darkness fell on the Pennsylvania hills on July 1. I use the qualifiers "believe" and "probably" because, as is often the case with research, the historical records disagree. A newspaper article quoting Danbert himself states that he survived the Battle of Gettysburg. Government pension records appear to conflict, however, placing him in a Washington D.C. hospital, sick with bronchitis until September 1863. I would be inclined to credit the official records except they regularly contain

---

3 26th North Carolina Infantry Regiment, *available at* https://gettysburg.stonesentinels.com/.

basic errors—Danbert's birthplace, age, and the year of his marriage are incorrect in the "official" account, to name but a few examples. Either way he was in a bad spot—pneumonia, including influenza and bronchitis, accounted for 45,000 deaths on the Union side alone—a greater number than died at Gettysburg.[4] If he was indeed present at Gettysburg, John Danbert, along with the remainder of the battered 24th, were witnesses to the historic events of the second and third days but were not engaged for the remainder of the battle.

While the Union victory at Gettysburg was the most critical moment of the war, fighting persisted for nearly two more years. Danbert suffered an unspecified wound at Laurel Hill[5] in May 1864 but recovered and returned to duty a month later. The regiment's final battle came at Hatcher's Run (also called Dabney's Mill) in Virginia on February 6 and 7, 1865. It was there, on the very last day the 24th Michigan ever saw combat, that a cannon blast nearly killed Grandpa Danbert and would have erased any of his future kin from existence. Curtis describes the fateful engagement:

Tuesday, February 7.

The weather was terribly cold. It began to rain in the morning and there was a cold sleet all day. Crawford's Division moved out again and formed its lines further to the right, joining the Second Corps. The line advanced into some woods and met the enemy, who opened a severe artillery fire. A solid shot passed directly under Sergeant Augustus Pomeroy, which stunned him and covered him with mud. The same shot ricocheting, killed Sergeant George H. Canfield and George Wallace, both of Company I; wounded Sergeant Walter Morley and took a leg off of John Danbert of Company D.

---

4 *The Devastating Effects of Diseases on the Civil War Battlefield*, Gary Gallagher, Ph.D., (April 17, 2020), *available at* https://www.wondriumdaily.com/the-devastating-effects-of-diseases-on-the-civil-war-battlefield/.

5 The fighting on Laurel Hill was a major phase of the Battle of Spotsylvania Court House, fought from May 9 – 21, 1864.

He was inches away from death. Two men standing right next to him were not spared that fate. But John Danbert survived. His leg mutilated, he lay on the battlefield in freezing rain for seven hours until the firing finally stopped. Field medics amputated his right leg below the knee and took a chunk of his left big toe for good measure. He then rode in an ambulance (a wagon) over twelve miles of uneven log road to the emergency hospital. That he survived the ordeal seems, in a word, miraculous.

Curtis employs his usual evocative prose in describing what wounded soldiers like Grandpa Danbert would have endured:

> Hospital experience formed a peculiar part of soldier life, known only to such as the chances of battle or disease contracted in the field compelled to endure. As soon as possible after or during a fight, the surgeons began their work. A place was selected near the field to which the wounded were brought on stretchers if unable to walk. The amputating table was put to use and soon a pile of hands, feet, arms and legs accumulated. A row of dead forms might be seen nearby, of such as had died during the operation. Chloroform, the greatest physical blessing to mankind, was used, and limbs were severed without the knowledge of the patient, often needlessly, no doubt.

> If possible, the wounded were taken by ambulance, railroad or boat to some town or city when the real hospital life began. Churches, schoolhouses, colleges and public halls were occupied with the wounded, if within a few miles even of a battlefield. Each soldier was placed upon a cot and for the first time for months had an easy bed. He was among strangers whom he had never seen before and a myriad of wounded, numbers of whom were dying, for though removed from the front, death was still around. He must keep up his spirits or homesickness and depression would send him to the grave more surely than his wound.

John Danbert's fighting days were finished, and with the Confederate surrender at Appomattox two months later, so was the war. After several months in the hospital, Danbert received a medical discharge on May 16, 1865. The remainder of the 24th Michigan was officially discharged that

June—but not before serving as escort and honor guard for the funeral procession of Abraham Lincoln.

Returning home to Michigan, Danbert married a Detroit girl named Clara Sussanna Karrer. Clara's family was also from Switzerland, arriving in America when she was just an infant. They named their first son John and had at least five more children. The second John Danbert is, for his own reasons, a legendary figure in the Claus family mythos. But John Danbert of the Iron Brigade has been, until recently, largely forgotten.

Anyone who knows the Clauses will tell you that we have an above-average fascination with (1) family history, (2) the Civil War, and (3) all things Michigan. Go ahead and ask them.

"The Clauses?" they will say to you. "I know the family well. Their fascination with family history is matched only by their fascination with the Civil War and all things Michigan."

Of course, John Danbert checks all three boxes, so you would expect his name to be among the first off the lips of a grandparent bouncing a tiny Claus on his knee. Yet somehow, I was completely unaware of any of the tales of John Danbert, hero of the Civil War. In the course of researching, I couldn't help wondering if I had the right guy.

How did I not know this? I asked again and again. *This can't be right. Can it?*

Imagine my excitement when I discovered an article from a 1932 Niagara Falls newspaper,[6] profiling my great-great-great grandfather! The case was cracked. The puzzle was solved. And oh!, what glorious new insights each sentence revealed about this incredible man. I here attempt to reconstruct my mind's spinning thoughts as I read the account.

> "Born in Switzerland on December 17, 1844, Mr. Danbert emigrated to the United States when a young child and lived in Flint, Michigan for a number of years."

The dates check out. That's him! That's our man!

---

[6] *Available at* https://www.oocities.org/24th_michigan/jdart.html. Details of Danbert's injury are from this article as well.

32

"The only surviving veteran of the American Civil War residing in Canada at the present time is John Danbert, who lives on Main Street in Chippawa."

Wow, he was almost 90 years old when this was written. This is incredible!

"He enlisted with the 24th Michigan, Company D under Col. Henry A. Morrow in 1862, and three years later, after escaping injury in the Battle of Gettysburg, had his leg blown off at the Battle of Hatcher's Run."

That confirms Curtis' account. Excellent.

"When he was demobilized from the army, Mr. Danbert returned to Flint and later ... moved to Chippawa and established a plumbing business, retiring some time ago."

So that's how he ended up in Canada. Fascinating!

"Playing Solitaire and collecting old pipes, some of them 25 years old, are hobbies of Mr. Danbert."

He collects old pipes! Sweet!

"He keeps pace with developments in this area by reading a medley of newspapers daily."

I too read the news! I'm just like him!

"Although a resident of Canada, he is not forgotten by the American government and every month receives a pension cheque. Every three years he is allowed a new leg or the equivalent in cash. In 65 years, Mr. Danbert has had only three legs, and still possesses the first leg issued to him in 1865."

He has three legs?!? That's not possib—ohhh. They must mean PROSTHETIC *legs. Very good. And he's smart to take the cash instead of the new leg if he doesn't need it. No need to stockpile them.*

"A great admirer of Abe Lincoln, the veteran soldier proudly remembers an occasion in Wash. D.C. when the President of the United States at that time shook his hand. Pictures of Lincoln adorn the walls of Danbert's home and he frequently refers to the hand-shaking episode."

He shook Lincoln's hand! This may be the coolest person who ever lived. I'm going to name my next child after him!!

"Mr. Danbert's wife Barbara died five months ago at the age of eighty-five years. He has two daughters and a son—Charlotte, Tillie and Edward, all of Chippawa, and six grandchildren."

... Umm. Barbara? Tillie?! Who are these people?? Where is Clara? What happened to his son, John?! What in the name of George McClellan is going on here?!?

As it turns out, there is a very good reason our ancestors did not shout John Danbert's name from the rooftops and hang his portrait above the mantle. In fact, it appears that John's wife and children did everything they could to forget him. According to family records and interviews, John chased around after women, fathered a child with one of his mistresses, and then left town with her, leaving Clara Sussanna to raise six children on her own.[7] He remarried in upstate New York and then settled in Niagara Falls, Canada, where he lived for the next 35 years with his new family. Now in a foreign country, he never acknowledged his first six children or provided for them in any way. He lived to be 91.

---

7 Summaries of the aforementioned family records and interviews are maintained electronically in The Hahn Library,
available at http://www.hahnlibrary.net/genealogy/Hahn-Claus/index.html.

And what of Grandma Clara? She became sole provider for the children and died young, at age 46. According to one family interview, Clara "died of a broken heart." Not technically a medical diagnosis, but there may be something to it. John Joseph Danbert, the eldest of John's children, would later tell his own children, "You don't have a grandpa."

To say that John Danbert's legacy is complicated understates the situation. Nobody is perfect—I get that—but *not* abandoning your wife and six children in the dead of night and *not* subsequently refusing to acknowledge their existence seem like basic prerequisites for being a "good guy."

On the other hand, any man willing to sacrifice his life for a cause so noble should be honored. We took a family pilgrimage to Gettysburg battlefield one summer. We walked the route of Pickett's Charge, climbed to the peak of Little Round Top, and gazed across Seminary Ridge. It's a humbling experience to stand where so many fell. But John Danbert was there—*actually* there—at Gettysburg perhaps, and certainly at Laurel Hill and Hatcher's Run. He stood across the field from thousands of men who meant to kill him. He stood amidst the storm of bullets and cannon blasts and watched his comrades die, one after the other, resolved to hold the line. He lost his leg, and nearly his life, for the cause.

There is a statue at Gettysburg—loads of them, actually—the place is crawling with statues. But the one I reference is a monument to the 24th Michigan infantry regiment. On top of a tall pedestal stands a soldier loading his rifle and wearing the distinctive hat of the Iron Brigade. He has a handlebar moustache and focused, slightly sunken eyes. If you compare the statue to a lone photograph we have of John Danbert, the resemblance is more than striking. They are *identical*. You couldn't sculpt a better likeness.

To be fair, there are only a handful of generic "models" one can use for a Civil War statue. There's your handlebar mustache guy. Your bushy beard guy. Strangely clean-shaven guy. Big ol' muttonchops guy. Drummer boy. That's about it. So, is it *really* a statue of John Danbert? If you can produce some concrete evidence that it's not, I'll believe you. Until then, I'm telling everyone that they built a statue for our family at Gettysburg.

He can remain there on the battlefield, his finest hour, loading his rifle for all eternity. In a book of war stories, John Danbert is very much a hero. But this is a book of *family* stories. The man deserted his family—our family. In this book, it pains me to admit, John Danbert is no hero.

We now turn to his son, my great-great grandpa John Joseph Danbert. A John Danbert who, as we will see, is even more mysterious than his forgotten father.

Theory 4: Bear got 'im.

4
The Missing Danbert

In seventh grade I wrote an essay about my great-great grandfather, John Joseph Danbert, for a unit on "Family Stories." In a way, you might consider it the very first draft of this book. However, the writing is a disaster. There are several factual errors, misplaced commas throughout, and—worst of all—I labeled the short *epilogue* at the conclusion, a "*prologue*." Ever hear of proofreading, kid? Blunders like that are why teachers invented dunce caps. Now, some twenty-five years later, I get another crack at it.

John Joseph Danbert was born November 15, 1866.

Stop the tape.

There are certain Truths—capital T—in life. Man will sin. Prices will rise. A Pomeranian dog will incessantly yap at every innocent stranger that strolls by. Troubling, yes. Bothersome, of course. But denying the infallibility of these Truths does us no good. Rather than fight the natural order of things, we're better off figuring out how to live with these problems and address them. Using the foregoing examples, we could: go to church; invest in a fund with compound interest that outpaces inflation, and; muzzle the dog.

I have learned that the same is true of historical records. Records, particularly records pertaining to Danberts, are going to conflict. They just can't help themselves. One record will state with great certainty that a Danbert was born in 1866. The very next record in the stack will swear that the year was 1865. It used to drive me crazy. After all, how difficult can it be to pinpoint a man's birthyear? But I've grown to accept these little frustrations. We make our best guess and move on. The serenity to accept what we cannot change, and all that.

As to the question of John Joseph Danbert's birthday, November 1865 was exactly nine months after his father got his leg blown off at the Battle of Hatcher's Run in Virginia. Senior then recuperated in the hospital for three months. Based on my understanding of mid-19th century transportation capabilities and the human gestation period, it is highly unlikely that John Joseph Danbert was born in 1865. So, we'll go with 1866. If I'm wrong, so be it! It doesn't affect the story.

Roll tape.

To recap, at the war's end, John Danbert returned to Michigan on one leg and married Clara Sussanna Karrer. John Joseph Danbert was born on November 15, 1866. By the year 1890, but perhaps as early as 1876, the elder John Danbert had abandoned his wife and children and married his mistress. Government pension records peg the earliest of that date range, though it seems unlikely because John and Clara's youngest son was born two years later in 1878. ... It doesn't matter though! We can't let these minor discrepancies in the records derail us. Now please permit your author a moment for his breathing exercises. It helps with the blinding rage. It does ... Not ... Matter ...

What *does* matter is where John's misdeeds left John Joseph. Somewhere between age 10 and 24 he was the new patriarch of the family. He probably comforted his heartbroken mother, helped look after his siblings, and brought in money when he could. Eventually he found steady work as a painter. He married Bertha Fleming in 1889 and they had seven children of their own—the fourth a daughter named Louise. John Joseph resented his father until the day he died.

Speaking of the day he died, and not to skip right past the poor guy's entire adult life, but John's death and the unresolved circumstances surrounding it remain the subject of spirited debate to this day. The first John Danbert vanished and later resurfaced in Canada with a new family. John Joseph Danbert also vanished—but unlike his father, never resurfaced, dead or alive.

This much we know:

On Tuesday evening, July 23, 1940, 74-year-old John J. Danbert left his home near Rogers City, Michigan, bound for the house of a Mrs. Josephine Pauquette, where he stayed the night. Shortly before noon the next morning, John left the Paquette home to pick berries at Hoeft State Park. Several hours later he was spotted near a cottage at Sacred Rock, a local landmark on the shores of Lake Huron near the State Park. He was never seen again. On Friday morning, Mr. Edward Pauquette reported the disappearance.[1]

A desperate search party was led by the County Treasurer, John's son-in-law, William R. Claus. The newspaper account describes "continuous lines of men, close together, that swept back and forth over the area in which it was thought Danbert might be, but no traces of the man were found." According to Treasurer Claus (husband of Louise Danbert and my great-grandfather), "the entire section from the lake on the north to the swamps on the south, between the Ocqueoc River and the Park, have been thoroughly covered." They never found so much as a footprint. John was declared dead.

Family accounts recorded over the years offer inconsistent particulars concerning John's disappearance.[2] Recollections differ and, in some instances, defy logic. There are four prevailing theories, each compelling in its own way, but with irreconcilable flaws.

Theory 1: *Heat Exhaustion*

One point on which everyone agrees is that John did not simply get lost while out for a leisurely berry pick. True, the region is rural, and one tree looks exactly like a thousand others you just passed, but he would have known the roads and trails from decades of navigating the area. That is, unless he was disoriented and confused for some reason. The theory in the

---

[1] *Wide Search Made for Rogers City Citizen*, Presque Isle Advance (Aug. 1, 1940).

2 As in the previous chapter, summaries of numerous family records and interviews, painstakingly cited, are maintained electronically in The Hahn Library, *available at* http://www.hahnlibrary.net/genealogy/Hahn-Claus/index.html.

newspaper at the time of John's disappearance was that he suffered from heat exhaustion. As described in the *Presque Isle Advance:*

> John Danbert, age 74, well known Rogers City painter, disappeared in the vicinity of Hoeft State Park ... Wednesday was a terrifically hot day and it is generally thought that he must have succumbed to the heat and perhaps in a dazed condition wandered off through the woods and died.

To that I say ... *meh.*

Oh, it's a fine theory. A clean theory. A theory that requires no wild conjecture. A theory that comfortably satisfies Occam's Razor.[3] It suffers from a major weakness, however. It fails to account for John's bizarre behavior around the time of his death.

For example, John supposedly made a large withdrawal from his bank account just a few days before his disappearance. And, according to one rather perplexing family report, two weeks before John's death he was painting the church with one of his sons, when he suddenly announced that his children wouldn't have to worry about burying him when he died. One wonders how that conversation played out.

> John: Alright, the basecoat is dry. Son, why don't you work on the ceiling and I'll get started on this wall?
>
> Son: Sounds good. I'll grab the ladder.
>
> John: I may go into town later for some new paint brushes. There's a shop over by the cemetery. Speaking of cemeteries, you children won't have to worry about burying me when I die.

---

3 The principle that the simplest explanation is often the best. You use the "razor" to shave away unlikely assumptions and are left with the most logical solution. But who Occam is and why he would know anything about John Danbert's disappearance, I couldn't tell you.

42

Son: . . . Uh, how's that now?

John: Nope. When I go, my body *will never* be found. Looks like you missed a spot under the eaves there.

And can you believe it? He called his shot! By a complete fluke he died of heat exhaustion after getting himself so lost that his body was never found—just as he had predicted two weeks earlier!

Seems a little far-fetched, doesn't it? Occam's razor is looking more like Occam's laser—a laser being a much more complex invention than a razor. (A logician can tell me if I've got that analogy right.) Other possibilities must be considered.

Theory 2: *The Jealous Husband*

Nothing is hotter than True Crime these days. If you're among the millions of amateur detectives who crave nothing more than cozying up with a bloody tale of unsolved murder, your eyebrows may have raised at the mention of Mrs. Josephine Pauquette. As a reminder, John stayed at Mrs. Pauquette's house the night before he went missing. Although John had been a widower for over a decade, there is nothing to suggest that Lady Pauquette's status as a Mrs. was in question. Perhaps Mr. Paquette was surprised to discover a slumbering (or worse) John Danbert under his roof. Having exposed the misdeed, he may have exacted his revenge, then disposed of the body. The eyebrows raise again at the newspaper's description of John Danbert as a "*well known* Rogers City painter"—just *why* was he so well known? Maybe Mrs. Pauquette was but one name in his little black book.

The jealous husband is a common hypothesis among the Clauses. Indeed, it is what I settled on in my typo-riddled essay in the seventh grade. I'm not so sure now.

This is just a hunch, but I suspect some accounts told over the years blended the fates of the two John Danberts. Someone remembered that "John Danbert" had a mistress; someone else remembered that "John Danbert" disappeared while berry picking—and the story evolved that the two things were related. Eventually, the second John Danbert's death was explained by the actions of the first John Danbert. It is certainly possible that John Joseph was a regular rake just like his father. But let's face it—the man was 74-years old. Did he really have the energy to chase skirts all over the backwoods of northern Michigan? Besides, none of the most reliable sources—the articles, interview notes, letters, etc.—ever suggest that John was romantically involved with Mrs. Pauquette, and I, for one, am not going to besmirch a lady's name without some hard evidence.

As enticing as the jealous husband theory is, there is a perfectly logical explanation for John's slumber party at the Pauquette house on July 23, 1940. Other than downtown Rogers City, much of the region is either farmland or woods. Some homes are miles apart, and I have seen nothing suggesting that John owned a car. If a home took more than a day to paint, it would make sense to stay there overnight and save himself multiple long hikes back and forth. In other words, he spent his last night alive sleeping on the floor, snoring innocently among the buckets and brushes.

Theory 3: *Gambling Debts*

This popular theory suggests that John was killed for money by some associates—possibly gangsters—who then dumped his body under Highway 27, which at the time was under construction. Little direct evidence supports it. Rather, the case is circumstantial, premised on hearsay and a complicated chain of inferences. But it should not be dismissed outright. More than the others, this theory attempts to reconcile and explain John's decidedly strange behavior in the days before his death.

Theory 3 is not for amateurs—it's a Professional-Strength detective job. Luckily, I am a Professional-Strength detective, or at least I aspire to be one. As I considered the more perplexing records, I liked to imagine myself as a grizzled private investigator. I'm in a dimly lit file room, a cardboard box crammed with scraps of paper and notes placed on the table before me. My tie loosed, a smoldering cigarette in the ashtray, I hunch over the box and continue the quest for that elusive key piece of evidence. (In reality, I was at my computer in my pajamas and my wife wouldn't let me smoke in the house—even though, as I tried to explain, the cigarette was *the* key element to establish that *noir* atmosphere. She would not be moved.) I can picture the headlines when I inevitably crack the case:

GREAT-GREAT-GRANDSON SOLVES EIGHTY YEAR COLD CASE.
SOLUTION UNDER OUR NOSES WHOLE TIME.
HUMBLE AUTHOR HAILED AS GENIUS.

The investigator gets to work.

The first record states that a family member reported that John "made a large withdrawal from his bank account, then went out with a lantern for some late-night berry picking." Suspicious behavior. *But,* the investigator asks himself, is the story reliable? I mean, really. The full checklist of supplies needed for "late night berry picking" is as follows:

1. Pail.
2. Lantern.

If there's one thing you *don't* need for berry picking, be it late night or at high noon, it's a large wad of cash. The berries are free—that's the whole point of the exercise. The investigator sets it aside.

The next sheet of paper. Someone claims they observed John walking down the road, when suddenly a group of men came driving up in a truck, forced him in, and sped off. A powerful development. The sinister work of gangsters, perhaps? *But,* thinks the investigator with jaded skepticism, surely the original newspaper article or police reports would have included this information if they had thought it credible. When analyzing a man's disappearance, one does not simply overlook same man being stuffed into a truck. It would be like the Warren Commission omitting mention of shots heard from the nearby Book Depository.

Next. "In the early 1990s, human remains were discovered under Highway 27." Well, that seems promising. *But,* the investigator observes with growing consternation, the State did not care to run any analysis to identify the remains.

The investigator sighs. It's all rumors and hazy memories. Nothing solid to build his case. He sits back in his chair and stares at the ceiling fan. Just then, a previously unseen scrap of paper flutters from the lid of the box. The amateur sleuth snatches it with a trembling hand. He can scarcely believe it:

A family member who was interviewed thinks that John once owned a beer garden ... but lost it betting on cockfights.

Now we're getting somewhere!

Lost his beer garden betting on cockfights, eh?

To be clear, no article or report even remotely corroborates this. No other interview summary, nor handwritten account, nor hastily jotted remembrance mentions an alleged cockfighting addiction, or for that matter, a beer garden. It's just one line from one note from an unknown author with no further details. *And yet,* thinks this shrewd Sherlock, it can't be made up. It is *too* specific, *too* strange to misremember.

But how does it fit with the big bank withdrawal and the truck-stuffing and the prediction that his body would never be found? *Okay,* thinks the investigator, let me work this out.

Wheels turning, wheels turning, wheels turning—got it!

John Joseph Danbert was badly in debt and saw cockfighting as his salvation ... so he chose his best Rhode Island Red and trained it to spar and had some early success against a couple palookas and soon earned a title shot against the champ (a real monster named Foghorn Legbreak) and so desperate for victory was John that he started cutting corners—added some steroids to the chicken feed here, a razor blade to a talon there—he knew it was wrong but the guy was in over his head, and when his deceit was discovered he offered up his life savings as a way to make amends, but that wasn't enough, so he gloomily handed over the deed to his secret beer garden ... but this was the Northwoods German Mafia we're talking about and they do not tolerate being cheated, so when they spotted him walking down the road they drove up and threw him into their truck and did their horrible deed—now all that was left was the body—they knew the road was being paved so they dug a shallow grave and tossed him in and the next morning the road crew paved right over poor great-great grandpa.

Elementary.

With smug satisfaction, the investigator types up his findings and sends copies to *The New York Times, The Wall Street Journal,* and the *Presque Isle Advance,* carbon copy to the Federal Bureau of Investigation. He has not yet heard back.

Yes, it requires a few assumptions—I'm not even sure if there is a Northwoods German Mafia—but if this were so easy, they would have solved it back in 1940. Chalk this theory up as: plausible, but unverified.

Theory 4: *Bear got 'im.*

This theory addresses the problem of John Joseph's missing body. If he had indeed become lost in the woods and perished, it should have been a relatively simple task to find the body, especially with a large search party of experienced hunters and trackers. So, maybe ... a bear got 'im?

That's it. That's the theory. Now, bears aren't known as delicate eaters, so I'm not sure how that explains why no trace of him was found. You'd think there would be a pile of bones or a fragment of the man's overalls—something. Maybe this bear heeded the posted signs and left the campsite cleaner than he had found it.

EPILOGUE[4]

John Joseph Danbert's body was never found. Perhaps those remains unearthed from Highway 27 were stashed away somewhere, their secrets waiting to be unlocked by some futuristic technology. Until then, the tragedy of the Missing Danbert remains a sad and unexplained chapter in family history.

John's wife, Bertha, is buried in Memorial Park Cemetery in Rogers City. Next to her, in what was supposed to be the plot for John Joseph Danbert, is the body of ... John Danbert. Seriously! This *third* John Danbert is John A. Danbert, son of John Joseph and Bertha. John A. Danbert is not a direct ancestor, and it's a very good thing he's not, because I'm not sure I can handle another John Danbert mystery. Studying family history is a lot of fun, but I have my limits, and my limits end at exactly two John Danberts.

---

[4] Nailed it!

Tougher than a Pomeranian in a box full of razor blades.

5

Some People Called Us Klaus

Pomeranians have it tough. Not the fluffy little dogs—those Pomeranians are notoriously pampered. Queen Victoria owned one! It slept in the Royal Bed and ate at the dining room table. No, when I say that Pomeranians have it tough, I refer to their lesser-known human counterparts—the people of the region of Pomerania.

Pomerania sits between modern-day eastern Germany and northern Poland, partially spanning the current borders of both countries. With mostly flat land and the strategically important Baltic Sea to the north, the region is, historically speaking, prime invading territory. At various times Pomerania has been under Swedish control, Polish control, Prussian control, Soviet control, and German control. If any European dictator has designs on world domination, all roads lead through Pomerania.

Consequently, Pomeranians have always been a tough breed (still talking about the human variety). Where do you think the expression that someone is "tougher than a Pomeranian in a box full of razor blades" comes from? It comes from my own head, of course—I just made it up. But it very well could have been in *Bartlett's* if anyone as clever as Mike Claus had bothered to think of it.

The Klauses hail from Pomerania (they probably would have considered themselves Prussian) and, by all indications, our ancestors were as tough as they come. Forged from iron. Nothing soft about this family. For example, they left Pomerania for a vast, blank slate of a continent. They could have settled anywhere. Bustling New York City. The resource-rich hills of Pennsylvania. Maybe give the new state of California a try. They passed on all those appealing settings. Instead, the Klauses chose the coldest, most desolate location on the map—the frozen woods of northern Michigan. Presque Isle County to be precise, a place surveyors contracted by the State had deemed worthless and uninhabitable. The Klauses inhabited the uninhabitable because they weren't just tough. They were Pomeranian Tough.

My Great-Great-Great-Great-Grandfather Johann Klaus was born in Pomerania in 1777 and worked as a schoolmaster.[1] Johann died at age 58 of cachexia, a "wasting" disorder that results in extreme weight loss. A polite way to say that he starved to death. Such were the conditions the Klauses faced in Pomerania. It is no surprise then that his son, Ferdinand Klaus, figured he might fare better in America, even in uninhabitable Presque Isle County. In the winter of 1873, Ferdinand, along with his wife Friedericka and their two youngest daughters, left Pomerania and headed west to Hamburg, where they boarded a ship that took them to Liverpool. They waited there for two weeks, then boarded the *City of London* for passage across the Atlantic. The average age of immigrants at the time was 35.[2] Ferdinand was 60.

The *City of London* was a three-mast steamer with a single smokestack protruding from the middle. It boasted amenities such as ladies' sitting rooms, gentlemen's smoking rooms, pianos, a library, private bathrooms, a barber shop, and a lavishly furnished saloon. These luxuries, however, were reserved for "cabin" passengers. Nine out of ten passengers aboard the *City of London* were "steerage" passengers—immigrants. Of steerage passengers, the ship's advertisement proudly declared, "they are carried on the same deck as the cabin passengers, the sleeping rooms being enclosed, containing a limited number in each, are well lighted, warmed, and

---

[1] You know the drill. Summaries of numerous family records and interviews are maintained electronically in The Hahn Library, *available at*
http://www.hahnlibrary.net/genealogy/Hahn-Claus/index.html.
Other details are gathered from observations posted on the Claus/Klaus Family Facebook page. Assume that all information pertaining to specific relatives comes from those sources unless otherwise noted.

2 Age Distribution of Immigrants to U.S., 1870-Present, *available at*
https://www.migrationpolicy.org/programs/data-hub/charts/age-profile-immigrants-over-time.

thoroughly ventilated throughout. Ample space is provided for the partaking of meals and promenading."[3]

Here's a little travel tip: If one of the main selling points of a cruise ship is that the sleeping rooms are "enclosed," you probably should lower your expectations. In reality, steerage passengers like Ferdinand and Friedericka crammed into tiny bunks alongside hundreds of others, many of whom spoke a different language. Those on the bottom bunk prayed the person above didn't get seasick. Meals were meager and the deck was far too crowded for the advertised promenading. Even so, tickets were not cheap. The fare for an adult in steerage was $24—about $600 in today's money. Round-trip rates were available for cabin passengers. No one traveling in steerage would require a round-trip ticket.

The journey would take about two weeks. Late nineteenth century steamers were much safer than the old sailing ships and most crossed without incident, though it could be perilous. Ten years after Ferdinand and Friedericka enjoyed the fine enclosed sleeping rooms aboard the *City of London,* 41 people perished when the ship was lost at sea. Our Klauses, however, arrived safely in New York Harbor on December 3, 1873. Their first stop would be Castle Garden at the tip of Manhattan—America's first immigration center. From New York, they made their way west and crossed Lake Huron to Alpena, Michigan.

They were genuine pioneers. Legend has it that they traveled on foot from Alpena, in the middle of winter, through the woods and marshes, carrying all they owned. They slept under umbrellas until better shelters could be constructed. They eventually settled in the tiny community of Hawks, near Rogers City. Six of Ferdinand's and Friedericka's seven children arrived in Michigan around the same time, including Johann Klaus and his wife Caroline, my great-great-grandparents.

Several new laws of the day, "Homestead Acts," gave Americans the opportunity to acquire public land at bargain prices in exchange for the promise to live on the land and improve it. It made land ownership possible for poor immigrants on a scale that would have been unthinkable in

---

3 The Inman Line, *available at* http://www.norwayheritage.com/p_shiplist.asp?so=tonn&co=inman.

Europe. Of course, some plots of land were preferable to others. In Presque Isle County, the pioneers would climb the tallest hills and then scale the tallest trees to scope things out. Farmland was good; a supply of hardwood was better.

In 1882, Ferdinand bought 80 acres of land from the State of Michigan. The plot was classified as "settlers' swampland." The entire purchase price: $1. Son Johann purchased a nearby plot and built his own farmhouse. Theirs were the backbreaking lives of subsistence farmers. They spent their days chopping wood, working their fields, caring for animals, mending fences, hunting and fishing for their dinner, picking berries, baking bread, handwashing dishes, stitching up clothing, and clearing heavy snow off the roof.

Ferdinand died in 1892, having lived two decades in America. Friedericka, a hearty gal, lived to age 90. Their deaths were apparently less eventful than their son's. Indeed, Johann (by then known as John) indisputably holds the title for Most Ridiculously Arduous Funeral Procession in family history. It was February 1926. By then, the ailing Johann was living with his daughter Bertha's family in Royal Oak, just outside of Detroit. When Johann expired, they loaded the body onto the Michigan Central Railroad and rode with it to his hometown of Hawks, where they were greeted by the rest of the family. February in northern Michigan always makes for difficult travel—especially when one among the traveling party is a corpse. Snow was so deep that the roads were invisible. They navigated the trail by following the tops of fence posts that stuck up through the drifts. The entire party traveled via *sleigh*. Not your "oh-what-fun, one-horse open" kind, but sleighs pulled by teams of horses acting as snowplows. At one point the casket toppled over and fell off the rig and into a snowdrift. To everyone's relief it did not pop open, but getting the box back up in five feet of snow must have taken a real Pomeranian effort.

Another legacy of Johann's: the family name. Perhaps as early as 1880, he changed his name from Klaus to Claus. The generally accepted explanation is that he made the switch due to anti-German sentiment in America. That, however, has always struck me as silly. It's just one letter after all. Were the Anglo-Americans really that dense? Picture two old German-hating Englishmen sitting at a pub, enjoying one of their famed room-temperature English ales (and picture Yours Truly reciting this bit in my best cockney accent).

"Blimey! I could never trust a Klaus. Much too German for me. But swap that K for a C, and I'll invite the chap over for tea and crumpets, I will. Why, a Claus is as pure of heart as old Queen Victoria 'erself!"

"Hear hear! God save the Queen! Cheers to her, and her li'l Pomeranian too."

"Oy?!? ... You would toast the health of those Pomeranian blighters?!"

"Her dog, mate. I'm talkin' about her dog."

Anyway, we're Clauses now and that's fine by me. If anything, the name is a source of endless amusement for store clerks and bank tellers come Christmastime. And, interestingly, there are still some Klauses out there. Ferdinand Klaus came to America with six children, but one son, also named Ferdinand, remained behind because his wife was too nervous to make the ocean crossing. Ferdinand Jr. was less concerned about the anti-German sentiments of his neighbors (it probably helped that he lived in Germany), so retained the name Klaus. He had ten children of his own, so now there is a whole mess of distant Klaus cousins living in Europe.[4]

But I digress. Back on the topic of old-fashioned prejudices. Presque Isle County was largely settled by two groups: German (and Polish) Lutherans, and German (and Polish) Catholics. They did not like each other. It was a smaller version of the conflict back in Germany, where the Lutherans and Catholics also did not like each other. The dispute in Europe was as much a political power struggle as it was a religious debate. The Roman Catholic Church led by Pope Pius IX was a powerful secular political force in those days. The Church chose the wrong side in the Franco-Prussian war in 1870 and the victorious Prussians, led by Otto Van Bismarck, did not forget it. Meanwhile, a number of German states unified in 1871 and formed a mighty empire that now included German-speaking Prussia, which in turn included German-speaking Pomerania. The new German empire was home to 25 million Protestants and 15 million

---

[4] Not in the Pomeranian homeland, regrettably. After World War II, most of the German population was expelled from Pomerania and the region was resettled with ethnically Polish peoples.

Catholics.[5] The aforementioned O. Van B. waged a kind of culture war *(Kulturkampf)* against the Catholics in an effort to stamp out Rome's influence and sever church from state.[6] Meanwhile, during this upheaval, millions of Germans—both Protestant and Catholic—emigrated to the United States, bringing their mutual disdain with them.

Up in Presque Ilse County, Catholics in Posen (current population 205) and Protestants in Hawks (current population 767) formed mobs and actually marched on each other. Shots were fired, but things eventually simmered down without casualty.

I don't know whether any Clauses were involved in the Hawks-Posen shootout, but it is clear they were not progressive on the issue of religious co-mingling. According to family sources, Great-Great-Grandpa Johann's offspring were forbidden from associating with "the Pope's children." Marriages between Lutherans and Catholics were shameful and considered to be, in the words of the family records, "dog marriages." The rule could not have been clearer if it were posted on a sign in the front lawn: No Dogs Allowed.

The prohibition hasn't been all that effective. It was inevitable, really. Those Catholic girls often fall for the bad boys and, as we have established, Pomeranians are the baddest boys of them all. I am a Pomeranian Lutheran who met a Catholic girl that could not resist my charms. So, my own marriage is a dog. My brother Dan and his wife, Mary, are dogs. My parents are very good dogs. Most startling of all, one of Johann's own children apparently had a dog marriage. And at this juncture I beg the reader's pardon, but duty requires that we reintroduce the Danberts back into the proceedings.

Johann had seven children, one of whom was William R. Claus—you may remember his brief cameo in the previous chapter when he led the unsuccessful search for his missing father-in-law. William lived in Detroit for a time, working in a bank, but eventually returned home to Rogers City where he was elected County Treasurer. He married Louise Danbert. Louise's father was John Joseph Danbert, aka "The Missing Danbert."

---

5 *See* https://en.wikipedia.org/wiki/Kulturkampf

6 *See generally*, Catholic Encyclopedia, Kulturkampf, *available at* https://www.newadvent.org/cathen/08703b.htm

John Joseph's Certificate of Baptism indicates that he was baptized at St. Joseph Catholic Church in Detroit. So, the Danberts were Catholics—another dog marriage in the family! This revelation was a surprise. But not as surprising as the paternal name listed on the Certificate of Baptism. In 1866, John Joseph's father, aka "The Forgotten Danbert," aka the one-legged Civil War scoundrel, presented himself in the House of God for his son's Baptism not as John Danbert, but as John Tampuret.

Tampuret. Why on earth was John Danbert going by Tampuret?! There *is* some scant evidence that his name might have been Tampuret before he came to America—but he was a Danbert by the time he joined the Union Army. He was a Danbert when he collected his pension. He was a Danbert when he was buried in Ontario. His children were all Danberts. What possible reason would he have to revert to his old name for this blessed event—if indeed he was a Tampuret in the first place. Did he lie to the priests? Was he on the run from the law? Setting up another of his famous long cons? Tampuret doesn't even sound like a real name! *Why would he—*

Sigh. There I go again. Right back in with the Danbert mysteries. Whenever you think you've got things worked out, a Danbert pops up with a different name or a second family or rumors of a cockfighting addiction and the train goes right back off the rails. Going forward, let's just agree that nothing makes sense when we're talking about the Danberts and get back to the matter at H.

Resetting. What we know of the old Klauses:

1. Johann the schoolmaster lived in Pomerania his whole life.
2. Johann's son, Ferdinand, and Ferdinand's son, Johann, both emigrated to America in the 1870s.
3. Klaus became Claus, except for Ferdinand's son, Ferdinand Jr., who stayed in Pomerania and remained Klaus.
4. Johann's son, William, had a dog marriage with Louise Danbert.

That gets us current up through my great-grandparents. A look at my paternal grandparents is next, but let's pause to consider the group. On the whole, the Clauses and their kin are a sturdy, down-to-earth, unpretentious lot. Many of Ferdinand's offspring still live in "uninhabitable" Presque Isle County. Some old family farms are still there, long grown over after sitting dormant for decades. There is even a Claus Road—dirt, of course. We wouldn't have it any other way.

My mom's side were mostly city dwellers. My in-laws, too. There's a different mindset in the city. I think they secretly view the Clauses as a fascinating curiosity. A sort of novelty act from the backwoods—like an attraction of exotic cultures at the World's Fair.

There may be some truth to it. Consider a recent episode involving Clauses from the year 2022—150 years after Ferdinand and his Pomeranian family arrived in America and set their compass due North. There is a county park that borders my parents' house in Clarkston, Michigan. The large, wooded area is home to, among other wild and scary things, whitetail deer. One of these beautiful, dumb creatures managed to hop over the fence that separates the park from the busy road outside, and was trying, quite unsuccessfully, to get itself back over the fence to safety. A very dangerous situation. If the deer wandered just a few feet too far it would find itself in the road and the results would be catastrophic for deer and human alike.

From inside my parents' house, someone spotted the deer hopelessly running headfirst into the fence, trying to break through. Again and again, it backed up, took a running start, and smashed its skull into the chain link barrier. There was blood. There was fur. There were the haunting screams of a terrified deer. And there were cars whizzing past at sixty miles per hour.

My brothers, Dan and Chas, and my brother-in-law Don (a Pomeranian by marriage and in temperament) are men of action. They ran out to the scene and began to try to guide the deer further down the road where there might be a break in the fence. No luck. The poor thing continued its routine of smashing into fence, backing up, and smashing into fence again. One of its eyes appeared to be partially dislodged from its socket. This was no baby deer either. It was a teenager[7] at least—very wounded and very afraid.

Lesser men would have hesitated. I must admit that I, being one of the softer Clauses, probably would have advocated for keeping a safe distance.

---

[7] Dan assures me that the correct word is "yearling." Shows how much he knows.

I'm quite certain a few of my in-laws would have been hiding under the bed at this point. But with that Pomeranian blood coursing through their veins, these Clauses met the trial with resolve.

"Well," announced my brother Dan solemnly. "There's only one thing left to do."

In a flash, he took off on a dead sprint towards that deranged, screaming, bloody, one-eyed beast. About two feet away, he launched into a perfect form tackle that would have made Dick Butkus proud and took it to the ground. Chas and Don arrived a half-second later and each secured a limb (of the deer, I mean). Together, the three of them carried the thrashing animal nearly a mile until they found a spot where the fence was bent and tossed it over, back into the park. The deer paused, respectfully bowed its head to them, and returned to the safety of the wood.

I tell this story now for three reasons. First, it's a good story and I didn't have a better place to put it. Second, because it demonstrates the difference between my mom's side of the family (they will be astonished when they read it) and my dad's side of the family (they won't read it because they are out chopping wood). And third, to take another run at *Bartlett's*. If he won't have my gem about the Pomeranian and the razor blades, perhaps this will be deemed worthy of his *Familiar Quotations*. Something as insane as football tackling a bloody deer and tossing it over a fence just goes to show, *ahem*... "You can take the Claus out of Pomerania, but you can't take the Pomeranian out of the Claus."

We walked just a couple of blocks down Broadway and hung a right on 34th Street. There it was.

6
Miracles on 34th Street

She was born Ruth Marie Wahrow. She would later become Ruth Claus and then Ruth Kresge. For many of us, she will always be called Granny.

My grandmother was a woman of almost impossible sweetness. One of those rare people for whom ordinary English adjectives fail in their mission. So warm was her demeanor, so generous was her nature, so patient was her temperament, that she could have come from a different, more pleasant species. It was as if a scientist emptied his entire stockpiles of sugar, spice, and everything nice; feverishly mixed them all together, and out from the beaker stepped Granny.

She was relentlessly cheerful. The human embodiment of goodness. Always indulgent toward us kids and never raising her voice even when a raised voice was long overdue. She was often the target of silly jokes and would laugh harder than anyone—so much that she frequently would sprint to the bathroom to avoid peeing her pants. She was the star attraction of every party even without trying to be. If the spirit moved her, she would break into a highly animated rendition of Shirley Temple's *On the Good Ship Lollipop*, complete with leg kicks, hair twirls, and, as a finale, a playful sucking of her thumb, all of which was as hilarious as it was disgusting.

I knew Granny as a vibrant, gracefully aging grandmother. Her children would probably nod in agreement at the above observations of their mother, though might object that she never raised her voice. Her parents, if we could chat with them, would have their own, fascinating recollections of a young Ruth. Hers is, in this book, the first childhood about which we have any meaningful detail. It can be strange, even surreal, to imagine a beloved grandparent as a whining, mischievous, or even annoying kid. All kids are those things to some extent, so Ruth must have been too, but, as I say, it is difficult to imagine. Did she make faces behind her father's back? Did she smack her sister? Did she stay out past curfew? *Did she swear?* The answers to those questions, speaking as her grandson and giving my best guesses, are: Once; Rarely; Often, and; My Granny?! Never!! Her parents, William and Julia, might give different answers.

Her life began in New York City and ended ninety years later in Clarkston, Michigan. Perhaps it is fitting that the story of my time with Granny begins in Clarkston and ends in New York City. The end was a sunny morning in 2015, just a moment really, that is difficult to describe—another instance of the English language being not quite equal to the job. It was fleeting but epic, laden with emotions and contradictions. A moment of great joy and deep melancholy. Sadness overflowing with excitement. The mental images of a laughing child and a dying old woman, and maybe a glint of my own children mixed in there somewhere, though they did not yet exist. "Overwhelming" is the best I can come up with to describe it. The French probably have a better word for it. A *coup de sentimént,* or something like that.

But that's the end of the story. The "Rosebud" foreshadow, if you will. If any of the gibberish in the preceding paragraph is to have any impact (and I make no representations on that), we must return to the beginning.

Ruth Wahrow was born June 2, 1925. The family of four lived in a walkup apartment at the memorable address of 3232 34th Street in New York City, in the heart of Queens. The building is still there with its faded light brown bricks and stone accents. A nearly identical structure stands about 100 yards away on the opposite side of the street. At five stories tall, the buildings rise above the two-flat apartments and single-family homes that line the rest of the block.

Granny never expressed to me any fondness for New York generally, but she did tell me once that she loved life in the apartment. With crowded families stacked atop each other, the sounds of floorboards creaking, babies crying, and radios playing would have echoed through the thin walls and ceilings. Neighbors became like family, with moms trading babysitting duties, dads swapping gripes about work, and children sharing lunches. Living on the third floor of five, the Wahrows were at the center of the action.

A black-and-white studio photograph, probably taken around 1930, shows that Ruth was an adorable kid with bright eyes and beaming smile. She was such a cutie that the picture was prominently displayed in a shop window to promote the photographer's services. A film producer noticed the photo and tracked the family down, telling them he wanted to feature young Ruth in an advertisement in which a mother brushed her daughter's curls. The key to the bit was Ruth's long, beautiful hair. Her dad saw dollar signs in his future and was delighted. Her mother saw a spoiled brat in her future and was not. She politely declined the producer's offer and promptly gave Ruth a haircut.

Thanksgiving at the apartment on 34th Street was particularly memorable. Not much has changed since then—they had everything you might expect. The big family gathering. The bird. The cranberry sauce. The parade. The children dressing up like gypsies and taking to the streets to beg for coins.

Granny was adamant about that last part as she relayed it to us some seventy years later. We quizzed her and politely suggested that she was thinking of Halloween and that it wasn't coins she collected, but candy. But she persisted in her story. It was Thanksgiving, she said. They wore costumes, she said. They begged for coins and carried them in socks, she said. They played tricks on the people who didn't hand over any coins, she said. And when the kids returned home, they chased through the halls of the apartment building trying to bludgeon each other using the loaded socks as weapons, she said. She would not be moved, so we smiled and winked, certain that Granny was having a "senior moment."

To our surprise, subsequent research fully and absolutely vindicated her memory. Decades before trick-or-treating became a Halloween staple, New York City children celebrated "Ragamuffin Day." It was *just* as Granny described it—a day for children dressed in tattered and oversized clothes to wander the streets, stopping any adult in their path to ask, "Anything for Thanksgiving?"[1]

---

[1] Carmen Nigro, Thanksgiving Ragamuffin Parade, New York Public Library, *available at* https://www.nypl.org/blog/2010/11/23/thanksgiving-ragamuffin-parade

A bulletin from the Hearst News Service in 1908 described the bewildering spectacle for the benefit of non-New Yorkers.[2]

New York, November 24. – Day after tomorrow will be "Ragamuffin Day" in the metropolis. Umpty thousand little children are preparing to band themselves into a fantastically arrayed army of beggars and celebrate Thanksgiving by asking alms from adult pedestrians. The man who fails to provide himself with a plentiful supply of pennies and nickels with which to placate the beggars before venturing on the streets is likely to fare ill at the hands of the little angels.

Zow! A stocking full of flour whacks you over the head.

Zoom! A fish horn disrupts your eardrums.

But what's the use of getting mad? It's only a bunch of Thanksgiving Day "Ragamuffins," out for their carnival. Give them a nickel and they'll let you alone.

There are thousands of them all over New York on Thanksgiving Day. Kids of all shapes, sorts and sizes, arrayed in the funniest, weirdest motley you can imagine. They make the day hideous, and raise the deuce generally.

But where on earth did the custom originate? People from out of town who visit New York on Thanksgiving Day look in astonishment at the ragamuffins parading the street and say, "What a strange custom. We don't have this at home." No more they do. The Thanksgiving Ragamuffin is New York, all through.

Some adults had their own tricks, such as heating the pennies on the stove and then dropping them out of apartment windows—glowing hot—down to the greedy and soon-to-be howling youngsters below.[3] The whole thing was madness. Children overtaking the streets. Children smacking adults. Smacking each other. Red hot coins raining fire from the sky.

---

2 *Available at* https://www.hhhistory.com/2019/11/ragamuffin-day.html
3 *See* https://preservehalloween.com/2018/11/22/ragamuffin-day/

The Great Depression, the growing popularity of the Macy's Thanksgiving Parade, and boring adults all contributed to the decline of Ragamuffin Day. The Superintendent of the New York City school system, who was a real drag, told *The New York Times* in 1930 that, "modernity is incompatible with the custom of children to masquerade and annoy adults on Thanksgiving Day."[4]

To which I say: modernity isn't all it's cracked up to be. Nevertheless, the dullards got their way and the tradition completely disappeared by the 1950s.

As she grew from ragamuffin to young woman, Ruth was radiant and charming and her fellow students at William Cullen Bryant High School voted her "the All-American Girl." After graduation, she took a job across the river in Manhattan at the original Macy's Department Store (which famously also sits on 34th Street). Her supervisors were no doubt pleased by her friendly demeanor with customers.

By contrast, Ruth's older sister, Lillian, was an introvert. One gets the impression that Ruth had an assembly of pals and social engagements, while the more serious Lillian was quiet and reserved. Ruth enjoyed reading, but Lillian poured her life into books. She went on to earn a master's degree from Columbia University and spent her career as a medical librarian in New York City. She never married. Despite their differing personalities, frequent letters, phone calls, and visits kept Lily and Ruth close throughout their lives.

At a family party Granny once let slip—to the delight of those present—that as a teenager she had no shortage of dating opportunities. In particular, the sailors docked in port were always fond of her and would vie for her companionship. Yet, it was a man in a different sort of uniform who she noticed immediately. Less than a half-mile away from the Wahrow's apartment was the family church—Trinity Lutheran. It was at Trinity Lutheran that Ruth met a young vicar named Ralph Claus. (A vicar is, essentially, an intern on his way to becoming a pastor).

Vicars, being Holy Men in training, are subject to all sorts of rules, but one unique to Trinity appeared to foreclose any potential romance

---

4 *See* Nigro.

between Ruth and Ralph. By order of the pastor, Trinity vicars could not date parishioners. It seems that a previous vicar had seriously courted a young lady of the flock, got the gal's hopes up, but had not returned to marry her. So, the pastor ended the practice. Those seminary students lucky enough to vicar in New York City were forbidden from testing the waters of its large dating pool.

Ruth took a selective approach to rules. She appreciated rules and would never willfully break one. However, if there was a rule she didn't feel like following, she would simply pretend it didn't exist. A lawyer might argue that her approach was a distinction without a difference, but she must have convinced the straightlaced Vicar Ralph of the wisdom of it.

"Oh, that is just for the *immature* vicars," she may have told him. "Of course, *we* can date."

By late 1944, Ralph and Ruth were engaged. She was 19. And I am pleased to report that Grandpa Claus was a man of his word. After spending a final year at seminary in Missouri, he returned for her as promised.

What a time for an engagement! In May 1945, amid wedding planning and bridal showers, the entire country rejoiced at the surrender of the Nazis and the end of World War II in Europe. Still, the war raged on in the Pacific, with hundreds of thousands of American troops in harm's way and Japan vowing to fight on. Then, on August 7, 1945, *four days* before Ruth and Ralph were to be married, President Truman issued a momentous radio address to the nation. The couple probably listened together, and if not, they certainly would have read the text of the message in the evening editions of the newspapers. The President announced:

> Sixteen hours ago an American airplane dropped one bomb on Hiroshima. ... It is an atomic bomb. It is a harnessing of the basic power of the universe. ... We are now prepared to obliterate more rapidly and completely every productive enterprise the Japanese have above ground in any city. ... If they do not now accept our terms they may expect a rain of ruin from the air, the like of which has never been seen on this earth. ...

It may cause some folks to shift uncomfortably in their chairs today, but most Americans at the time welcomed the announcement with a mixture of joy and relief. It meant a quick and decisive end to the war that had for four years separated parents from their children and claimed the lives of more than 400,000 American soldiers. Sweethearts, relatives, and friends would be coming home. Families would be reunited. Young men would have a chance to grow up.

The United States dropped a second atomic bomb on Thursday, August 9. And that Saturday, August 11, 1945, with these truly historic events as backdrop, Ruth and Ralph were married at Trinity Church.

When Japan gave its unconditional surrender on August 14, folks poured into the city streets to celebrate. In Times Square, a photographer snapped the iconic picture of a Navy sailor kissing a woman in a white dress. In a room somewhere above the tumult, the young couple heard the cheering in the streets.

"What's going on?" asked Ralph. Ruth looked out the window.

"The war is over!"

"Oh?" said Ralph with his typical dry wit, looking at his bride of just three days. *"Mine* is just beginning."

Keeping a sense of humor was essential, as the life awaiting the newlyweds would not be easy. They had neither time nor money for a honeymoon. (Ralph's salary as a vicar had been $90 a month). Instead, they packed up their possessions, said goodbye to their family and friends, and drove 3,000 miles to the exact opposite end of the country, Encinitas, California, where the newly minted Reverend Claus would lead his first church.

Encinitas is a beach town on the Pacific Ocean, just north of San Diego, and quite a change of scenery from Queens. Everything was new. A new marriage. A new church. New friends. New stresses and anxieties. And new jobs. A pastor's wife is really the First Lady of the congregation, and Ruth would have gotten right down to the business of teaching Sunday School, heading the women's group, and organizing potluck meals. Not long after, Ruth also became a mother when daughter, Julie, was born. (The young Claus family stayed in Encinitas only a few years, but as an adult Julie would make the return journey to live in sunny California.)

If life among the palm trees and ocean breezes was a culture shock for Ruth, at least the shock was warm. The Claus' next destination was an entirely different challenge. In January 1949, Ralph agreed to become pastor of a church in Gaylord, Michigan. Ruth and Ralph, now with Julie in tow, once again packed up their things and drove from their modest home near the beaches of southern California to an even more modest home in the icy woods of northern Michigan.

Actually, to call their Gaylord home "modest" overstates things. The parsonage (a home for the pastor owned by the church) was a run-down log cabin that sat next to the church. The Gaylord parsonage technically had a roof and four sides, but the gaping holes between the logs tended to compromise the protective elements of the structure. Wind and rain blew in through the walls. Part of Ruth's morning routine in the winter months was to brush away the snow that had accumulated on their bed and baby Julie's crib overnight.

From a third-floor apartment in the nation's largest city to a log cabin in the woods. It must have felt like a foreign country. When Ruth left home in 1945, the population of New York City was 7.5 million. Well over a million people lived in Queens alone. When Ruth arrived in 1949, Gaylord's population was about 2,000, and not a single Macy's to be found. The Clauses did their part to close the population gap with the Metropolis, adding one more to Gaylord's tally when a second daughter, Laurie, was born.

Ruth endured four winters in the log cabin. The next move was to St. Trinity Lutheran Church in Pontiac, Michigan, in 1952. While Pontiac would never be confused with New York, it was, at the time, a growing city of more than 70,000. Busy intersections and department stores were back in her life, even if skyscrapers were not. Ruth remained a member of St. Trinity for the next 63 years.

Two more sons born in Pontiac made it a family of six. A letter from Ruth to her parents written in 1958 shows a loving mother in the midst of the day-to-day routines of parenthood. She wrote:

Mike is telling himself a story in the play-pen. He walks around now holding onto things. He's slow and very wobbly but he does it. He coughs when we do and claps hands when we do and when we're sitting at the table and laughing he looks very wide-eyed from one to the other and then laughs too. He's a big boy and chubby and active like Julie used to be. He's very strong and it's a fight to get his diaper on him. The children are crazy about him and they lug him around and play with him and argue over who's turn it is to sit next to him at the table. Ralph says Mike thinks Julie is his mother.

Julie is really growing up. She loves clothes and wears a little bit of lipstick every chance she gets and wants to know when she can have nylons! ...

Laurie is still sailing through life. She's a real cut-up and has a marvelous sense of humor. ...

And as for Chuck, he is definitely all boy. He loves to fight, play ball, fight, ride the bike, fight, play cowboy, fight, and so on. ...

(For the sake of keeping the reader up to date, I can confirm that Aunt Laurie is still considered a real cut-up, and that Dad continues to be "definitely all boy." I have not asked whether Aunt Julie ever got those nylons.)

When they grew a little older, in the category of Things That Would *Never* Happen Today, Ruth and Ralph would occasionally send the kids off—alone—on a train to New York, where they would be greeted in Grand Central Station by their grandparents and stay at the 34th Street apartment.

I have mentioned her boundless positivity as a grandmother, but this was not an inevitable outcome. Ruth's life story is assuredly a happy one—but flecked with events of inexpressible heartbreak. On November 11, 1974, her youngest son, Michael, drowned in an accident on Whipple Lake. Mike was a junior in high school, a popular and attractive teenager, as his mother had been. He had been duck hunting on this cold, wintry morning and fell out of the boat, his heavy hunting clothes weighing him down. No one was able to rescue him. No doubt this was the singular cataclysmic event in her life. To lose a child, in the most staggering fashion, would shake anyone. And shake her it did. But even in the face of this horror, Ruth never lost her faith.

Another event very nearly killed her. In 1978, she was driving on I-75 to visit her mother Julia, who was now living in a nursing home in Frankenmuth, Michigan. Out of the corner of her eye, she noticed that a car next to her was keeping a consistent speed with hers. If she slightly accelerated, he would keep up. When she slowed down, he would do the same. Eventually she glanced over and made eye contact with the man. Abruptly, he turned his wheel, slamming his car straight into hers and sending it spinning in a circle, and then colliding with another, and finally smashing into a concrete overpass.

Granny survived, but spent weeks in the hospital and would never fully recover physically. As for the madman who tried to kill her, he got out of his vehicle, climbed up the overpass, and hurled himself off into the path of a passing pickup truck. The man had been recently laid off from his job as a counselor at a local college. He was deranged, out to kill himself and take the life of a random stranger with him. By unlucky chance, that stranger happened to be Granny.

Later at the hospital, Ruth's children tried to explain all they knew from the police and news reports. Though in horrible pain and likely still in shock, Granny's reaction was not of anger, but sympathy for her would-be killer's family. The first thing she asked was whether the man was married. The newspaper article confirmed that he was. Granny's response, laying in her hospital bed:

"Oh, his poor wife."

The grief in Ruth's life persisted. Ralph suffered numerous health problems throughout the decade and died in 1979, at age 58. Ruth lovingly cared for him until the end. She was lifted by her children and the endlessly supportive church congregation, but she was heartbroken.

Now, here is where the story gets happier again.

Ralph's best friend was a man named Walt Kresge. Back in 1959, Ralph and Ruth invited Walt to stay with them for a while following Walt's divorce. When St. Trinity moved relocated out of Pontiac, Walt bought a house on Whipple Lake in Clarkston and, returning the favor, invited the Claus family to stay with him. (This is all rather complicated and will be covered in far greater detail in later chapters. For now, just understand that the Clauses and Walt were dear friends and lived together for decades.) To Ralph and Ruth's children, he was "Uncle Walt."

Walt remained living in the basement at the lake house after Ralph died. Ruth and Walt were not naïve. There would be gossip about the pastor's widow living with his best friend. Walt floated the idea of moving out, but Ruth and her children talked him out of it. They were adults, Walt had been invited to live with the family, and their living arrangements were nobody's business. Walt stayed. But much to everyone's surprise—Ruth among them—the two would soon fall in love.

Granny hosted hundreds of picnics at the lake over the years, but nothing in the recorded annals of picnics-past quite touches this one. It was the summer of 1980, or thereabouts. My parents were there, my Aunt Laurie and Uncle Mark were there, perhaps some others were too. Discussion may well have centered on the Republican National Convention, held in Detroit that July, giving candidate Ronald Reagan the party's nomination for the presidency. The picnic table was set. Dishes were passed. The whirring of pontoon motors filled the air.

All seemed normal until Walt, looking rather discombobulated, called for the group's attention and began a rambling sort-of speech. Walt was never one to seek the spotlight, so this was *highly* unusual.

There is some debate concerning his exact remarks, but it is undisputed that the words "in front of family" and "in the eyes of God" were uttered. He praised Ruth's character and disposition, and said, in so many words, that she would be an idyllic partner. In a roundabout way, Walt seemed to be proposing!

Now, as far as anyone is aware, Ruth and Walt were not dating, and until that moment neither had even mentioned the possibility of a romance, much less marriage. Some of those present were stunned. The rest were simply confused.

Was he? No, he couldn't have been. Well then, what was that??

As for Ruth, she clearly understood the speech as a proposal and was ... *flabbergasted*. She was rendered completely speechless. Eventually she squeaked out that she would need to think it over. Two weeks later, at another unusually dramatic family picnic, she accepted. And so, it was set. After a total of zero days dating, Ruth and Walt were engaged.

One must concede that, for readers unfamiliar with the story, this arrangement may appear awkward. On the one hand, there is a soap opera element to marrying the best friend's widow—a hint of scandal completely out of place with Ruth's life and character. And as supportive as everyone was, it must have been at least *strange* for their children and friends. But any uneasiness soon vanished with the appreciation that the match, while unconventional, was sincere. It worked. Ruth and Walt married in 1981 at St. Trinity in Clarkston and remained completely devoted to each other for the rest of their lives.

Granny had lost her youngest child Mike, her beloved husband Ralph, and had barely survived a random act of attempted murder by the time I came along in 1984. She would have been justified spending her remaining years bitter and resentful. What a gift for her children and grandchildren that she did not.

When I think of my grandmother, I usually start with Christmas.

Charles Dickens wrote of the transformed Ebenezer Scrooge, "it was always said of him, that he knew how to keep Christmas well, if any man alive possessed the knowledge." With all due respect to Mr. Dickens, he never met Granny.

For Granny, Christmas was not just a day, it was a month-long bonanza. Decking the halls took weeks. It started with Christmas tree shopping. We escorted her to the local nursery to carefully select her tree, as well as two more for our own house, with hours of decorating to follow. Trips to Canterbury Village and Frankenmuth with their world-famous Christmas stores were scheduled. She made it an annual tradition to give the kids ornaments and books, which were typically delivered to us with much fanfare, on separate nights, about a week before Christmas Eve.

On Christmas day, after Santa did his thing and Mom and Dad had their naps, we made the ten-minute drive to the lake where we would join Granny and Walt and aunts and uncles for The Main Event. Festive packages were stacked several feet high, literally taking up half of the living room. Gift opening commenced around 2:00 in the afternoon and the final bow would not be ripped until hours after the sun set. Dressing in layers was critical, as Granny and Walt kept their thermostat at about 85-degrees, creating a holly jolly sweatbox. We eventually built in an intermission—a precious respite to hydrate, grab a breath of fresh air, and collect ourselves.

The challenge of the length of the proceedings was compounded because Granny took longer than anyone I have ever met to open a present. She performed a little ritual with each gift. Without fail, she carefully unfastened each individual piece of tape, pausing to comment on the loveliness of the wrapping paper and overall presentation of the package. Careful not to rip anything, the wrapping paper was delicately removed. Then, without yet glancing down at the present inside, she would painstakingly fold the wrapping paper into a compact rectangle, apparently with the idea that she might reuse it the next year. Only when the wrapping paper was safely set aside would she address the contents of the box. Slowly ... slowwwly she would lift the lid and peek. Then she would go wide-eyed and mouth agape, simply *stunned* at what she saw, be it dish towels or a scarf or whatever. Finally, she would deliver at least five minutes of gushing praise to the item, along with the thoughtfulness of the individual who had gifted it. I once gave her a bag of birdseed and she reacted like I had paid off her mortgage.

Granny took hours to open presents, but she spent the full *year* searching for items to give. If she ever got a whiff that you were interested in something—literally anything—she would use Christmas as an excuse to start a "collection" for you. You like apples? This Christmas you now have an apple collection. You would get apples made of wood. Apples made of glass. Apples made of yarn. Paintings of apples. Apples that look like American flags. Apples that look like Canadian flags. Decorative plates shaped like apples. Apples wearing baseball uniforms. Apple puzzles. Books about apples. And so on.

Alas, my apple collection is long gone, but I kept a different one. When shopping with Granny one year, I stopped and admired some displays of ceramic Christmas villages. There were various kinds—*Christmas in the City*, *North Pole*, *Alpine Village*, etc. But the one I liked best was in the Charles Dickens, 19th-century London style. Of course, she gave me two or three pieces to get my collection started that Christmas, and many, many more in the years that followed. To this day, I still set up my *Dickens Village*, courtesy of Granny, which now requires several large tables to display. The whole process takes careful planning and multiple days of work. But all that work pays off on Christmas Eve when friends and family gaze for *seconds on end* at my handiwork.

"Oh, wow Mike, this looks great. Someone is in the bathroom. Could I use the one upstairs?"

And that makes it all worth it.

By the early 2000s, Walt was growing progressively unhealthier, so the two reluctantly moved into an elder care facility, where he lived only a few days. Granny would stay there another decade. She became a favorite of the staff (a staff that included my sister-in-law, Mary.) Every nurse, housecleaner, and caretaker of any variety was greeted with a "bless you, sweetheart" or "thank you, darling."

The only caretaker who ever saw a hint of frustration from Granny was my father. He means well, but Dad is not exactly Florence Nightingale with his bedside manner and would sometimes bark orders about how she needed to take her medicine or be more careful moving around. When he got too bossy, Granny would lower her voice and reply in a thick German accent, *"Jawohl, mein Führer!"* That usually softened him up.

Her health continued to decline but her great faith in the face of suffering did not. After falling and shattering a bone, she told me that she tried to view her pain as a blessing, because no matter how badly she felt, she knew that the pain and anguish of Jesus was far worse.

In the spring of 2015, I visited my girlfriend Cortney who was living in New York City at the time. It was an important visit. We knew that if things went well, it would be time to seriously discuss an engagement. We had a jampacked itinerary of sightseeing, brunches with friends, and bar hopping, but I told Cortney we needed to reserve time for an extra daytrip.

"Cortney." I announced. "While I'm here, I need to go on a spiritual journey."

"Hmm... Okay?"

I explained that Granny did not have long to live and I wanted to visit her childhood home as a tribute to her. Cortney's puzzlement quickly turned to enthusiasm. She was all in. We rode the subway from her apartment in lower Manhattan, across the East River, and into Queens. Off the train, we walked just a couple of blocks down Broadway and hung a right on 34th Street.

There it was. The old five-story brick apartment building, looking the same as it did in the grainy photographs I had seen. Stone steps led to the entrance in the middle of two towers. Rusty fire escape staircases ran from the second floor to the fifth. Painted signs reading "POSITIVELY No Ball Playing Allowed" flanked the entrance.

I imagined young Ruth Wahrow running down those same stone steps eighty years ago. Perhaps meeting friends for a day trip to Coney Island or to see her first movie in a theatre (it was *King Kong*). She may have dragged her reluctant older sister along with her. She played stickball in the street, right where I was standing. And hopscotch, and jump rope, and hide-and-seek. A few years later, boys would have walked her to that door after dates. In the apartment above, she would have opened the windows to catch a breeze on a hot summer day. She read books, danced to records, and finished her homework there. She listened to her sister tell bedtime stories and decorated the Christmas tree. She chased her friends down the hallway with a sock full of coins on Thanksgiving. She told her astonished mother about her blossoming relationship with the church vicar. She had her whole life in front of her.

We took some cellphone photographs in front of the building and I sent them to my family. By great providence, Dad happened to be with Granny at the retirement home and showed them to her. She slowly realized what she was seeing.

"That's my apartment! ... And that's Mike! Is he in New York? He's at my apartment! Oh! ... *Oh, I am so excited I could jump out of my skin!*"

A dubious claim—it probably had been thirty years since she had jumped anywhere—but the point is that she was thrilled and declared the whole thing to be "wonderful." It was.

We took some more pictures, then trekked back to Manhattan to continue our sightseeing. The "spiritual journey" probably only took 15 minutes, but it was one of the best moments of my life and I am grateful that Cortney was willing to share it with me. A few weeks later I introduced Cortney to Granny. We laughed and talked about New York and said goodbye.

Granny died that year on Thanksgiving night. As we sat around the kitchen table trading stories and gathering photographs for the funeral home, my Aunt Laurie sighed and said to no one in particular,

"Wow. What a woman."

That sums it up. What a woman, indeed.

"Yea, though I walk through the valley of the shadow of death, I will fear no evil; for thou art with me; thy rod and thy staff they comfort me."

7

The Shepherd

It was a somber Sunday morning at St. Trinity Lutheran Church. Many who entered carried tissues or handkerchiefs. Supportive embraces and pats on the shoulder were exchanged at the door. Voices were muted. It was not a funeral, yet a profound grief hung over the assembly. The pews were packed, many of the worshippers dabbing their eyes. The church's beloved pastor of the past 27 years had died that Friday, and while his passing was not completely unforeseen, it nevertheless rocked the congregation to its core. The reverend's widow was there, of course, receiving hugs and words of comfort with grace and solemnity. He had been a friend to so many—a mentor, a guide, and a shepherd to them all.

In time, the church would need to seek a new leader. For now, there was no junior pastor to take on his duties, so a lay assistant would deliver the homily. Remarks had been prepared and printed in the bulletin. But when the man stepped forward, he announced that he would not be reading the text as printed. Instead, he would read words from their departed preacher. Days before his death, the pastor found one of his old sermons, written more than twenty years earlier. It appropriately examined themes of grief, fear, suffering, and hope. He gave it to the church staff, knowing he would not be delivering the message himself.

The man began, and with his words, the spirit of their pastor filled the sanctuary.

Our text this morning is Psalm 23, verse 4: "Yea, though I walk through the valley of the shadow of death, I will fear no evil; for thou art with me; thy rod and thy staff they comfort me." Perhaps the most popular verse of Holy Scripture, next to the Lord's Prayer, is the 23rd Psalm. It has been a comfort and consolation to God's people since the day King David was moved by the Holy Spirit to write it. ...

Ralph Charles Claus was born in Hawks, Michigan, on July 17, 1921, the fourth child of William and Louise. He and his four siblings (Earl, Viola, John, and Arnold) grew up in a cozy, two-story house in Rogers City near the shores of Lake Huron. Once again, I pause here to mention that this area of northern Michigan can be very cold in the winter. I don't mean to beat the reader over the head with these little reminders, but coping with extreme elements has a way of shaping people. A good deal of their time was spent trying to figure out ways to stay warm. A wood burning stove in the living room provided the central heating for the home. Upstairs, they drilled small holes in the floor to help heat flow up to the second-floor bedroom. And, if they constructed extra-long sipping straws and ran them through the holes in the floor, the children upstairs could drink a bowl of hot soup from the kitchen table without ever leaving their beds. (No one ever did this. I'm just saying they *could* have if they wanted to).

What makes a man eschew his casualwear to don the robe and stole? Sometimes people join the clergy in response to some great life event. Martin Luther was a 21-year-old law student when he was knocked from his horse by a bolt of lightning and pledged to join a monastery. For John Newton, the Anglican priest who wrote the hymn *Amazing Grace,* it was a late-in-life conversion after working as a captain of slave ships for many years. Then there are people like Mother Teresa who reportedly resolved to become a missionary at age 12. Ralph Claus was one of those for whom the matter was settled before he had started shaving. He did not follow his older siblings to the local high school in Rogers City. Instead, *at age 13,* he traveled 170 miles south, where he enrolled and lived at Michigan Lutheran Seminary High School in Saginaw. There he studied the usual writing, mathematics, and rhetoric curriculum, but with a heavy emphasis on preparing to enter the ministry.

The tricky thing about writing these biographical sketches is choosing the right bits to highlight. Some details may be of critical importance in the subject's life but not of general interest to a wider audience. Other facts might be crowd pleasers—the kind of thing you might mention while sitting around a campfire with friends—but practically insignificant to the subject of the bio. I know that if Grandpa Claus were reading over my shoulder while I type, he would be asking,

"Why haven't you brought up Pastor Linn?"

"When are you going to mention Pastor Linn?"

"You really ought to have discussed Pastor Linn by now."

He's right, of course. The fair and thorough biographer would have mentioned Pastor Linn pages ago. Linn was Ralph's mentor—a monumental influence in his life, including his decision to attend Saginaw Lutheran Seminary. But do the life and times of the Rev. Louis Linn appeal to the average reader? People are here for the Clauses after all. Give them too much Linn and their eyes will gloss over.

Meanwhile, consider the topic of basketball. *Everyone* wants to read stories about basketball. So, if there's a good basketball story, I'm going to tell it. Even if, as is the case here, Ralph couldn't have cared less about basketball.

First, in accordance with what I believe Grandpa's wishes would be: a very brief word on Pastor Linn. Born in Poland, the Reverend Louis Linn arrived in Rogers City in 1930 after stops at churches in Massachusetts, Saginaw, and New York City. He preached in three different languages: English, German, and Polish, and was a founder of Valparaiso University as a Lutheran institution. Pastor Linn naturally took an interest in an uncommonly devout and mature young student in the congregation named Ralph Claus. Having lived in Saginaw for a while, Linn was familiar with the seminary prep school there and thought Ralph would be a good fit. He encouraged Ralph to consider it, and just as importantly, encouraged William and Louise to allow it.

Ralph excelled at Lutheran Seminary, which should come as no surprise, even if certain of his extracurricular activities are surprising. He was an honor student (not surprising), a member of the choir (naturally), president of his class (ho-hum), and ... captain of the basketball team—*record scratch!*

My record is scratching because, as previously stated, Ralph was not a basketball fan. He never once shot hoops with his children or, as far as we are aware, regaled his wife with tales of his high school playing days. No one recalls him ever mentioning the sport. The only reason we know he played basketball is that someone saved some press clippings and stuffed them in a file. This isn't quite *John-Danbert-has-a-second-family* stuff here, but it is nevertheless a shocking revelation.

Nor is it the case that Ralph was "captain" of the basketball team in name only—a charity title for the nerdy kid who can't dribble but tries his heart out. He apparently had some game. One clipping notes that "high-scoring captain Ralph Claus made 12 points" in a 25-18 victory over Standish. And, as a junior the previous year, Ralph was a member of the most successful team in Lutheran Seminary history. In 1938, the mighty Seminarians made their first, and only, State Finals appearance in school history.

The game has changed considerably since Ralph's high-scoring captaining days. Dunking was prohibited. There was no three-point line or shot clock. Their shorts were *very* short (practically "bun huggers" as my sister used to say of the volleyball shorts her team wore). A personal foul automatically resulted in a free throw attempt, regardless of how many fouls the team had committed. They were still figuring things out. And when it came to determining the winner of a tie game, things were downright ridiculous.

It seems straightforward, right? If the game ends in a tie, simply play overtime periods until someone wins. Well, back in Ralph's day, the Michigan High School Athletic Association's system was a *bit* more elaborate. It was all spelled out in the program for the State Tournament:

> One three-minute overtime period is to be played in case of tie games. If, at the expiration of the overtime period, the score of the game is tied, the winning team is to be declared the one which has the greater total of the following points:

1. Five points are to be awarded to the team which made the greater number of field goals.

2. Four points are to be awarded to the team which made the lesser number of personal fouls.

3. Three points are to be awarded to the team which made the greater percentage of its attempted free throws.

In the event that both teams made the same number or percentage of any of the above items, the points for that item are to be divided equally between them. The team having the greater total of the above points is to be declared the winner.

Can you imagine attending a game that ended like this? The fans must have been baffled.

"Ladies and gentlemen, that concludes the overtime period. The score is 34 to 34. Let's give a round of applause to our competitors and please allow fifteen minutes for the team of engineers to retrieve their abacuses and commence the calculations."

And what happens if—after all the summing and multiplying and dividing and remembering to apply the Pythagorean Theorem—the totals are still equal? The Michigan High School Athletic Association was ready for this contingency. The game would then be decided by (I am not making this up) a good old-fashioned free throw shooting contest! I suppose if *that* ended in a tie, they played H-O-R-S-E. All this effort in lieu of simply playing a second overtime period. The mind boggles.

The Championship game was held at the massive Grand Rapids Civic Auditorium. Lutheran Seminary played Brooklyn in the Class D finals—the first of four games held that evening. In attendance was—get this—the legendary James Naismith, *the inventor* of the game of basketball! Dr. Naismith was on a national tour as an ambassador promoting the sport and stopped off in Grand Rapids for the tournament finals. Naismith handed out the trophies and took pictures with the teams after the game. Perhaps he looked over the rules for tie games and offered some friendly suggestions for improvement. That Ralph never told the story of how he met the great James Naismith tells you how low basketball ranked on his list of life priorities.

As for the game itself, there was no need for advanced calculus to determine a winner. It was a decisive 24-14 victory for Brooklyn. Seminary managed a brief one-point lead in the third quarter, but Brooklyn, backed by 9 of 10 free throw shooting, pulled away. Ralph Claus did not register a stat and the school has never returned to the State Championship game.

After high school, Ralph spent two years at Concordia Junior College in Fort Wayne and then four more years at Concordia Theological Seminary in St. Louis. His workload included classes in Hebrew Grammar, Homiletics, Liturgics, Symbolics, Dogmatics, Latin, and the German Bible. His top grade was in Isagogics—a word I had to look up and still don't understand. His lowest grade was in Sermon: Class, though he did receive an A- in Sermon: Chapel.[1] Along with his studies, Ralph organized new missions in both Fort Wayne and St. Louis. He also vicared at Trinity Lutheran Church in New York City, but of course, you already knew that.

When Ralph met the lovely, 18-year-old Ruth of the congregation in Queens, he was captivated from the get-go. However, if his account is to be believed, he first had to analyze the situation empirically. In December 1944, he wrote a letter to his brother, John—replete with his customary dryness—and announced his engagement. He wrote:

---

[1] I feel badly about mentioning his worst grade. In the spirit of fairness and disclosure, my worst grade in college was in Statistics and my best grade was in Volleyball.

Since [my last letter], things have been pretty much the same—referring to the work; however, there is one thing that makes it all most beautiful. I finally found the one who beyond a doubt fills all the stiff requirements I had set up for my wife. I met her when I first got to Trinity and from then on did a good bit of observing. I looked upon her with the eyes of an observer, with the eyes of a critic, with the eyes of a philosopher, and now I look upon her with the eyes of a lover. I analyzed my feelings syllogistically, platonically, emotionally, and spiritually. Then as a true master I carefully took the results of my diverse observations, compared them and most critically weighed them with respect to the results of the four analyses of my own feelings, and the outcome could not but result in a proposal. Her answer was in the affirmative. So according to my own terminology and feelings I am a married man, except that I am waiting to take up the privileges, responsibilities, and duties of one. Ruth has more than her share of beauty—and a personality and character that are perfect. It is those factors which to me are the most beautiful. I'm sure that when we can get together, we are going to be a most happy couple.

His prediction was right on the money. The Most-Happy-Couple's first stop after the wedding was St. Mark's—a brand new mission church in Encinitas, California. The salary was a mere $145 per month but included housing and $20 for gasoline. Two years later, he was installed as full-time pastor.

Ralph and Ruth loved Encinitas. The work was fulfilling and the young couple made dear friends. Meanwhile, back home, it seems that Ralph's father, William, and Pastor Linn had another path in mind and were busy pulling strings. In 1946, Ralph received a call to lead a church in Cheboygan, Michigan, which happened to be just 40 miles from Rogers City. (A "call" in Lutheran-speak is essentially a job offer from another church. The call is a Divine one.) Ralph was torn between carrying on his work at the burgeoning church in Encinitas and moving to a congregation closer to his family. The folks in Encinitas begged him to stay. Though the decision is supposed to be guided by the Holy Spirit, his father William had his own views on the matter. Hearing that Ralph was leaning towards staying in California, William fired off a curt letter, sounding rather like a lecturing father:

I am writing this letter early this morning since I hope it will reach you before you make your decision. ... We expected that the congregation at Encinitas would give you a battle and reasons not to accept the call to Cheboygan, but that in itself should not be reason not to accept; there is no doubt the Lord will supply the congregation in Encinitas possibly with the man that can do greater work in that vicinity than you can, and the Lord only knows what he has in store for you in offering you the call to Cheboygan and vicinity. ... I will close with Love and God's blessing that the Lord will guide you to accepting the call to Cheboygan, which will bring you nearer to your relatives and we could get together real often and discuss things. There is plenty of work to be done in Cheboygan. Love-Dad

Against his father's wishes, Ralph declined the call to Cheboygan. It was a decision that, given what we know of his commitment to family, must have been painful. But William got his way eventually. Just a year later, Ralph received another call to a different church near Rogers City, in Gaylord. The offer letter from the church noted that "we feel that Rev. Claus, being a native of these parts *and being acquainted with the weather* and ways here, would be best suited to carry on the work here." Quite the sales pitch. In spite of the ominous reference to the weather, Ralph accepted the call, bid farewell to the congregation he loved, and moved his family from southern California to northern Michigan.

The transcontinental journey from Encinitas to Gaylord was part Tolkien, part Homer, with a heavy helping of Moe, Larry, and Curly. It was so memorable that Ralph handwrote a 14-page letter to friends back in California describing the misadventure. I am tempted to just reprint the whole thing because it really is an incredible story. Hopefully an abridged version will convey the general picture—full copies are available upon request.

To set the scene: our heroes left San Diego County in January 1949 via beautiful highway 101, pulling a small, rickety, *single-wheel* trailer behind them. In the trailer was every possession they could cram in, covered by a tarp. (Looking at some pictures, I can't imagine those single wheel trailers were designed for 3,000-mile journeys. It would be like racing the Tour de France on a unicycle.) Up front in the car were Ralph, Ruth, and

84

two-year-old Julie. What followed was the most exhausting and stressful journey this side of Mordor.

Their progress was excruciatingly slow, mostly due to car troubles. People sometimes say, "they don't make things like they used to." Well, in the case of cars, we should all be grateful for it. Every morning the car refused to start, so every morning the car had to be jumped or towed. By the time they reached Fort Worth, the tires were bald and needed to be replaced. Through Texas they also replaced several spark plugs, the starter, and, in Ralph's words, "the gas thing-a-ma-jig." These were not simple repairs. More than once the family sat in a garage in the middle of the night waiting for a mechanic to arrive.

Finally, with new tires, new spark plugs, new starter, and new gas thing-a-ma-jig, their pace began to quicken. Ralph felt optimistic as they left Texas and entered Arkansas. Unfortunately, things were about to get much, much grimmer. Remember that single-wheel trailer? Ralph wrote:

> Ah, it was a beautiful night as we were headed into Arkadelphia, Arkansas. Then, BOOM! We said goodbye to the trailer tire. But yet I actually whistled as I jacked up the trailer, for I knew there in the trunk was another tire to fit. But my whistle turned to moans when I saw that the spare wheel was also suffering from a hunk out of the rim. Nothing to do but get another wheel—that one was broken—couldn't get worse. So we hobbled slowly to the nearest station—it was closed. So I unhitched the trailer and went about 15 miles to Arkadelphia for a wheel. Most of the places were closed, but I found a station where the fellow assured me that the garage next door had what we needed. So we went back, sweated and pulled and tugged and squirmed and finally got the trailer hooked on to the car. Then we hobbled, clipped and clopped to a nearby motel.

Next morn—early. We decided that since the trailer wheel was broken and we were going to get a new one, we may as well pull the whole shebang to the garage—it was only a couple of miles—nothing more could happen—so away we went—5 miles per hour. But the clippity-clop jarred a nut of the wheel assembly, and the trailer fell to the ground, one mile out of Arkadelphia. We dragged the trailer off the road, unhooked, and let it set—all nicely bundled up like when we left Encinitas.

Into town we went for that wheel from the garage. Turns out it was a *wheelbarrow* wheel—no bearings. Then we searched every store in town. No dice. Then we telephoned stores in large towns—Little Rock—Fort Worth—Dallas—no dice. So, we decided the only thing we could do would be to ship our stuff. I got a guy with a pickup truck to come out to help.

(As a reminder, our heroes had left the trailer on the side of the road when the wheel assembly fell apart.)

Back to the trailer we went—but it was gone!—slick and clean—not a nut or bolt to be seen. Both of us almost gave up completely, and both were in need of a strong shoulder. We headed for the police station to have the cops search out the thugs who had dealt so harshly with us. There on the lawn in the town square, high up on a pile of debris, lay a lump of cloth which Ruth immediately recognized as her night gown. Coyly she tried to pick it up unnoticed by the gaping crowd of yokels.

We later learned that some dopes working for the road commission saw the trailer there and thought someone had lost it—fallen off a car and parked itself on the side of the road without a scratch or mark! Well anyway, we had our stuff back. The men with the pick-up were still with us, so we loaded their truck—shipped the trailer freight—the rest express to Michigan.

Several days later, having at last completed their most incredible journey to Gaylord, Ralph and Ruth opened the door of their new log cabin home only to find it was already occupied. A couple dozen mice had gathered in the living room and were having a very nice dinner party—until it was interrupted by the piercing sound of Ruth shrieking. Back into the car they went, thirty more miles on the road to William and Louise's home in Rogers City, resolving to tackle the rodent problem another day.

It was good to be home, but Ralph had always wished to serve a large congregation and he was not going to find that in Gaylord. In 1952, at age 30, he took a call to St. Trinity Lutheran Church in Pontiac. The church was in a diverse neighborhood with nearly 1,000 members. Pastor Claus would serve St. Trinity for the rest of his life. And, though I admit I am biased, I believe he became the most beloved pastor in St. Trinity's 140-year history.

A pastor has many roles and excels in certain ones over others. Think of the five tools of a baseball player: (1) hitting for contact, (2) hitting for power, (3) fielding, (4) throwing, and (5) running. A "five tool player" who shines in all five aspects of the game is considered elite. It is the same with pastors. Among their responsibilities are: (1) preaching, (2) evangelizing and mission work, (3) organizing, (4) administration of the church, and (5) caring for the flock. From what I hear, Ralph was pretty close to a five-tool pastor, but all who knew him agree that what truly set him apart was the final skill on the list. He cared—*truly cared*—about the wellbeing of his congregation, spiritually and otherwise. In turn, the people of St. Trinity adored him.

If someone had a problem, Ralph made it his mission to help in any way he could. To put it in Biblical terms, as their shepherd, he would readily leave 99 sheep to rescue the one who had wandered.[2] His home office in the parsonage saw a steady stream of parishioners seeking support. He counseled, he guided, and he encouraged. He offered solutions, he offered food, and in the case of a lonely, recently divorced son of a retail mogul, he offered his home.

By far, Ralph's greatest challenge as a shepherd came amid the terrible turmoil in the late 1960s and early 1970s. In major cities across the country, but in Detroit especially, racial tensions turned into riots, then into full blown anarchy. The National Guard was called. The chaos spread to nearby Pontiac and St. Trinity sat in the midst of it.

---

2 Luke 15:3-7.

Author's Note: The next several paragraphs are lifted almost word-for-word from one of my favorite historians: my brother, Chas Claus. His work can be found in *A History of St. Trinity Evangelical Lutheran Church* (2010). Rather than try to put his words into my words, I figured I'd just put his words into my book. As you read his account, imagine the horrifying experience of simply going to Sunday services, and imagine the caring, compassionate, Pastor Claus trying to handle the mayhem and keep his flock safe. Here's Chas:

When Detroit exploded into riots in the summer of 1967, Pontiac exploded with it. Sadly, churches and schools frequently served as targets for thieves and vandals, as they tend to be unguarded during non-business hours. That year, there was a failed attempt to fire-bomb St. Trinity's grade school building when the device bounced off the exterior instead of going through a window. A random passer-by put out the fire.

As the 1970s began, violence in the community continued to escalate. In November 1970, a member who lived across the street from the church was murdered in his home. In January 1971, Pastor Claus and his family vacated the parsonage for safety reasons. Two months later, a drug house across the street from the school was bombed, shattering the school's windows. In June, there were several purse snatchings, which necessitated having ushers escort female parishioners to and from their cars. In taking on this responsibility, several ushers came under gunfire. The chairman of the congregation had a shotgun pointed in his face as he exited his car for the school graduation dinner. The church custodian was robbed in broad daylight as he mowed the lawn.

In the city setting, not all parking was immediately adjacent to the church, which made members' cars frequent targets of theft and vandalism. To counter this, volunteers began guarding the parking lots during services. On August 8, 1971, a sniper stationed in a building near the parking lot began firing shots at arriving parishioners, pinning several down behind trees after parking their cars. This was the final straw. For the safety of the flock, church leadership resolved to abandon the Pontiac site and seek a safer home.

[Mike again.]

There was talk of disbanding the congregation and having members attend other nearby churches. Indeed, this was the recommendation of

District leadership. But the congregation refused. They would stick together, with Pastor Claus as their shepherd, with or without the District's blessing. They temporarily moved to an existing structure in Waterford, then broke ground on a new building in rural Clarkston. A fundraising campaign was initiated and raised over $200,000. Two devout Methodists, Mr. and Mrs. Stanley S. Kresge (the retail mogul) chipped in $50,000—likely in appreciation of the great kindness Ralph and Ruth had showed their son, Walt.

Sadly, Ralph suffered a number of serious health problems around the same time the church relocated to Clarkston, including a major heart attack and a stroke. On November 7, 1979, on doctor's orders, he announced his resignation. In an open letter to the congregation he wrote, "After thirty-four years in the ministry, twenty-seven of them spent with the members of St. Trinity, this is a far from easy step to take. I had hoped to work with you in His Vineyard, as your Pastor, for many more years—but now I must bow my will to His." Two weeks later, on November 23, 1979, Ralph went to Heaven.

I never met Grandpa Claus. I cannot recount the time he scooped me up in his arms or told me his favorite Bible story. Exploring his old files has been fascinating, but it is impossible to capture the nuances of his personality. If I had to guess though, I don't think Ralph would really care if his grandchildren and great-grandchildren knew about his extracurricular activities in high school or even the tale of their journey through Arkadelphia. But he would care, deeply, that they knew of the Grace offered through Jesus. What better memorial then, than to close with Ralph's own words—the same words that gave comfort to his congregation so many years ago.

Our text this morning is Psalm 23, verse 4: 'Yea, though I walk through the valley of the shadow of death, I will fear no evil; for thou art with me; thy rod and thy staff they comfort me.'

Perhaps the most popular verse of Holy Scripture, next to the Lord's Prayer, is the 23rd Psalm. It has been a comfort and consolation to God's people since the day King David was moved by the Holy Spirit to write it.

We too have often found peace in the consolation, the assurance expressed in this Psalm: "The Lord is my shepherd; I shall not want. He maketh me to lie down in green pastures; He leadeth me beside the still waters. He restoreth my soul: he leadeth me in the paths of righteousness for His Name's sake. Yea, though I walk through the valley of the shadow of death, I will fear no evil: for Thou art with me; Thy rod and Thy staff they comfort me ..."

"The Valley of the Shadow of Death" – what is it? As you know, Palestine is a very mountainous country. In Biblical times it was very fertile, but yet it was mountainous. So in leading the flock from one meadow to another it was often necessary to go through a passage in the mountains; through a narrow, rocky valley. The sides of the mountain were very close and jagged and pock-marked with caves. In these valleys wild beasts made their dens and were in an advantageous position to attack those who passed through. So "the Valley of the Shadow of Death" held all kinds of dangers, each one able to wound and hurt, to maim and kill.

How often do we look about ourselves and shudder, and feel ourselves to be "in the Valley of the Shadow of Death." It may be sickness, disappointment in ourselves, in our spouse, in our children – problems in business or work; antagonism of people; loneliness – Oh, there are many problems and worries that form a "Valley of the Shadow" for us to pass through.

...

Very often, when a Christian actually loses his trust and confidence there in The Valley of the Shadow of Death it is because he gets to thinking that his trouble is permanent—a lasting thing. He forgets that he is only **WALKING THROUGH!**

Any sheep that straggled behind and lingered or stayed in the valley certainly would have much to complain about. The place was full of fearful things – lacking in food. It was very likely it would perish there.

Any person who will linger or dwell in this valley will also find it a fearful thing, and the longer he stays there, the weaker will be his trust and confidence in his Good Shepherd, until finally he perishes in faithlessness.

But the Valley of the Shadow of Death is not our dwelling place. We must not think of it as such, nor must we act as if it were! Why in the world would anyone want to think or act like the Valley of the Shadow of Death were his dwelling place? Why should anyone increase his problems by emphasizing them in his mind—and multiplying them by talking about nothing else?

Human nature is a strange thing. Sometimes one finds it gratifying to be miserable and even enjoys being the object of pity. Such a one will linger in the Valley and revel in the fact that so many feel sorry for him. But by doing this he makes his problems bigger by emphasizing them, and more numerous by dwelling on them. Sometimes he may think he'll never get through so he just gives up and quits trying.

But beware! For this is dangerous and foolhardy! We must not dwell in the valley lest we perish! We must WALK THROUGH! and FEAR NOT!

...

It is not necessary for us to challenge and struggle with every problem, and make a big issue of the fact that we are in the Valley of the Shadow of Death. We're not to step off the path into the shadows to see if there isn't a difficulty lurking. We are not called upon to hunt out and defeat every danger and problem and sorrow that lurks in the Valley. We are only called upon to WALK THROUGH! So pass by many of the difficulties and problems. Leave them behind as we move ahead to the "still waters and green pastures."

In walking through the way of sorrows let us remember that it is not a strange and uncharted path to our Good Shepherd. He has gone through before. He walked through this Via Dolorosa—this Way of Sorrows—as our substitute.

...

From fear we will learn to cling closely to our Savior. From suffering we will learn endurance. From disappointment we will learn confidence and hope. From temptations we will develop strength. From hardships we will learn patience. From our inadequacy we will learn trust. From evils done to us we will learn forgiveness, and from the Good Shepherd's tender care and guidance, we will learn love.

Oh, there are so many heavenly virtues that we will need to learn before we will fully enjoy the "quiet waters and green pastures," and the only place we will learn them is in the Valley of the Shadow of Death.

Hesitate not, linger not, fear not. WALK THROUGH THE VALLEY! "*Looking unto Jesus the author and finisher of our faith; who for the joy that was set before Him, endured the cross, despising the shame ...*"

And remember, the Scripture says: "If you abide in Christ, you ought to walk even as He walked."

Amen.

For years, he delighted onlookers by performing barrel rolls and loops over the lake in his Citabria stunt plane.

8

That Was Walt

Grandpa Walt was not related by blood, so readers seeking a definitive history of the Kresge lineage will have to look beyond this little project. Luckily there are several excellent treatises available. For example, one could browse *The S.S. Kresge Story* from the Western Publishing Company, Inc. (1979). A word of warning, though—that particular volume (written by Walt's father, Stanley Kresge) is educational, but is not what one might call "light reading." Those expecting the laugh-a-minute riot they've grown accustomed to in these pages will be disappointed. My suggestion is that you read what I have to say, laugh-cry-repeat, leave your 5-star review on Amazon, buy extra copies, tell all your friends, *and then,* if you're still up for it, move onto the volume from the good folks at the Western Publishing Company.

Blood relation or no, Walt's story cannot be understood without some background of his upbringing. The Claus name, proud of it as we all are, has thus far failed to reach the national consciousness. Kresge, however, is among the best-known names in all of American business. Walt's grandfather was Sebastian Spering ("S. S.") Kresge, an entrepreneur and businessman who opened a single shop in 1899 that would eventually become a department store empire. The first Kresge's on Woodward Avenue in Detroit employed 18 associates and carried 1,500 items, none costing more than a dime. Forty years later, there were 740 Kresge's stores scattered throughout the Midwest and eastern United States.[1]

S. S. Kresge grew famously wealthy, and indeed was one of the richest men in America, but was just as infamously frugal. (Frugal is a polite way

---

[1] Detroit Historical Society, Encyclopedia of Detroit, *S.S. Kresge Company,* https://detroithistorical.org/learn/encyclopedia-of-detroit/ss-kresge-company.

of saying that he was cheap. As it relates to his personal spending, both words are accurate.) As one Kresge family historian puts it, "he bragged that he never spent more than thirty cents on lunch, wore inexpensive, plain suits until they practically fell apart, and lined his shoes with paper after the soles wore out."[2]

That is not to say S.S. was a greedy man. He was historically charitable and rewarded hard working employees. Kresge's was one of the first retailers to offer workers paid sick leave and vacations, profit sharing, and pensions.[3] And in 1924, S.S. created the Kresge Foundation with one stated purpose: to promote human progress. The Foundation gave away millions. To this day, you will find a multitude of theatres, auditoriums, and libraries that bear the Kresge name, including the Kresge Law Library at Notre Dame Law School, where for three years I merrily tangled with torts and wrangled with the rules of evidence in the building named for my grandfather's grandfather.

When Harvard Business School opened the new Kresge Hall in 1953, S.S. was invited to deliver some remarks at the dedication ceremony for his latest namesake. The audience expected to hear some valuable insights on a long life of entrepreneurship and business dealings—and that is exactly what they got. Walt Kresge, then a young man, watched his 85-year-old tycoon of a grandfather step to the podium to make the following speech, reprinted here in its entirety.

"I never made a dime talking."

With that, he sat down. An economical speech entirely appropriate for the multi-millionaire with paper lining the soles of his shoes.[4]

Unfortunately, S.S.'s thriftiness seems to have been at least partially responsible for two divorces. In particular, his second marriage to a beautiful socialite who was thirty years younger didn't work out. She left him for a Persian prince. Turns out that some beautiful young socialites don't want to marry a millionaire only to wind up eating thirty-cent lunches for the rest of their lives. (Note to self: the moment I make my first

---

2 Green, Franklin J. *The Story of a Small Twig* (2018).
3 Reference for Business, *S.S. Kresge*,
https://www.referenceforbusiness.com/businesses/G-L/Kresge-S-S.html.
4 *Id.*

million, take the wife out to a very nice dinner. No menu item is off limits, not even the bottomless shrimp basket.)

S. S.'s son, Stanley Kresge, was the obvious choice to helm the family business when his father retired and had, indeed, been groomed for the position. But S. S. had built his empire and simply could not let go. Stanley went on waiting for his turn, and waiting, and ... waiting. S.S. clung to his title of Chairman of the Board until he was—ready for this?—*99 years old!*[5] When S.S. finally gave his two-weeks' notice, Stanley was already 66, ready to retire himself, and perhaps a little wounded that his father had not tapped him earlier. Control of the business quickly passed to non-family members and in the 1960s Kresge's officially rebranded to Kmart.[6]

Stanley was made of even straighter lace than his father. He and his wife Dorothy were strict Methodists, never drank or smoked, and reportedly gave about $500 *million* to charity.[7] Dorothy objected to Kmart opening on Sundays and later disposed of her company stock when they learned that the chain would begin selling beer and wine.[8]

Walt was the oldest of three sons. While he grew up in a very wealthy household by any possible measure, he was not spoiled or elitist. Like the Kresges before him, he believed in diligence, humility, and charity. Walt appreciated the family business and worked in it for a while, but decided he wanted to do something on his own. In 1954, he started a metal plating company called K-L Industries. The company dealt in "barrel electroplating and phosphating." Not exactly my wheelhouse, but I gather that the general idea was applying some kind of chemical coating to metal gizmos that would then end up in automobiles. It was a modest endeavor by Kresge family standards—there were only about ten employees—but he

---

5 "Executives: The Pinch-Penny Philanthropist," *Time* (October 28, 1966).

6 In 1990, Kmart was the second largest retailer in the United States. As of 2022, there were only three remaining Kmarts in the country. Tyko, K., "Kmart store closings 2022: Just three Kmarts remain after new round of closures," *USA Today*, (April 11, 2022).

7 Saxon, W., "Stanley Sebastian Kresge, 85, Retailer and Philanthropist, *New York Times* (July 3, 1985).

8 "Philanthropist Kresge, Son of Stores' Founder, Dies at 85," *Los Angeles Times* (July 5, 1985).

enjoyed interacting with his customers and the camaraderie in his small plant in Madison Heights, Michigan.

While this backstory (so capably recounted by the author) is fascinating, I never would have known the name Walt Kresge but for one life-changing event. Walt, born and raised Methodist, began attending the Lutheran church in Pontiac. He struck up a close friendship with my grandfather, Pastor Ralph Claus and, by extension, the pastor's family.

I don't know the specifics of how it was determined that Walt would move into the parsonage—obviously, he could afford his own place—but perhaps he was downcast about his recent divorce and just needed friends and guidance. Ralph and Ruth were happy to have him. My dad was less enthusiastic. Oh, he liked Walt, of course. But poor little Chuck couldn't watch his Saturday morning cartoons with "Uncle Walt" crashed on the living room floor. Eventually, Walt moved to a more permanent space, a tiny room in the basement, and Chuck could get back to his beloved *Captain Kangaroo*.

A quick non-sequitur on *Captain Kangaroo*. I had never seen the show and was curious as to what exactly was so captivating about him, so I did a little side research. I assumed that it was a cartoon about a kangaroo who was a military captain. Kind of like G.I. Joe, but for marsupials. Turns out Captain Kangaroo was neither captain nor kangaroo, but just a kindly (creepy?) old man who did comedy routines for kids. The internet provided the following description of one of his most popular bits, which I am quoting verbatim.

> One of the show's long-running gags was the "Ping-Pong Ball Drop," instigated by the telling of a joke (usually a knock-knock joke) by Mr. Moose, in which the punchline included the words "ping-pong balls." At the mention of those three words, a shower of ping-pong balls was released from above on the Captain.[9]

This was the "Golden Age of Television," folks! Is it any wonder why Dad simply could *not wait* to get the TV back?

---

9 https://en.wikipedia.org/wiki/Captain_Kangaroo

Anyway, Ralph and Ruth let Walt stay indefinitely. He lived with the Claus family, became like family, and then he became not "like family"—but actual family. When Ralph's church moved from Pontiac to Clarkston, Walt bought the house on Whipple Lake in 1971 and invited the Clauses to live with *him*. He needed only his small space in the basement (like his grandfather, he embraced the Spartan lifestyle) and was delighted to return the kindness Ralph and Ruth had shown him all those years. Walt had two children from his previous marriage, Walt Jr. and Carol, and they too integrated with the Clauses. Walt Jr. and his wife Joyce are wonderful people who have been a part of our lives for as long as I can remember, and Carol, as a teenager, lived with the Claus family in Pontiac for several years.

Pastor Claus died in 1979, and we have already learned the account of Walt's public proposal to Ruth before bothering to do any private courting. I should add one more detail, however. The surprise proposal also included, of all things ... an *ULTIMATUM!* She had two weeks to decide. Otherwise, the offer was off the table and he would need to move on. What a gambit! But that was Walt. Direct and practical. The match was right—it was plain to him—and he would not waste his time pretending there was any question about it. Two weeks later, the ultimatum paid off.

As serious as he often was, Walt's admiration for Ruth brought out a softer, even cheery side. His excitement practically jumps off the page in a letter to friends and family shortly after their marriage.

> I couldn't wait 'till Christmas to let you all know about a recent earth-shaking event. The old, fat, bald bachelor has been had -- "another good man gone wrong," as a time-honored saying goes!
>
> ON 20 JUNE 1981, RUTH CLAUS AND I WERE MARRIED!

So who the heck is Ruth Claus, you say. Well, Ruth is the widow of my Pastor, who got his transfer to his Heavenly Home in Nov. 1979. Most of you know that I have lived with him and his family since shortly after my divorce in 1959, first at the old parsonage in downtown Pontiac, then for the last 10 years here in Independence Township on a small, pretty lake near Clarkston. Ruth is a lovely, warm, soft, delightful lady – and BEAUTIFUL, too, as you can see from the picture. You can also see rather conclusively from the picture that she sure got the short end of the stick on *this* deal! Joking aside, we've known each other for a million years, and this surely seemed like a fine idea --- so we did it. ...

My best wishes --- OOPS --- *our* best wishes, and may God bless each of you very richly.

Grandpa Walt had a wry sense of humor and a deep, contagious laugh. Most of the time though, Granny was the center of attention, the social butterfly, the "face of the franchise," and Walt was pleased to stay in the background. During family gatherings at the lake he would quietly sit in his desk chair at the living room table and play Solitaire—perhaps for five or six hours at a time. The constant sound of cards *flip-flapping* was part of the soundtrack of our holidays and birthday parties. If something caught his attention, he would lean back in his chair and state his piece—that this man was an idiot, or that woman was a damned communist—and then escape back into his cards.

He had a mechanical mind and a "system" for everything, even something as simple as ordering a cup of coffee. At his favorite restaurant (Big Boy), regular coffee was served in a brown mug, while decaf was served in a white mug. When the servers came round to refill the mugs, they could identify whether the person was drinking regular or decaf by the color of the mug. Walt's order was always the same: "a regular coffee in a decaf cup." Why? He wanted to drink one coffee with caffeine, and then finish his meal with another cup of decaf. Using his system, the servers would know to switch to decaf without him asking. That was Walt. Efficient.

Another of Walt's famed systems was for grocery shopping. He maintained—*meticulously* maintained—dozens of notecards in a small metal box, which he carried with him on trips to the store. Each notecard listed a food item, with very detailed instructions on where to find said item, as well as commentary regarding how many of the item should be always kept on hand at the house. For example, a card might say:

Item 37: Bertolli Spaghetti Noodles.
2 packages to be kept in inventory.
Location: Aisle 7. North side. Fifteen feet from aisle entrance. Approximately chest level.

He would flip through the cards in order as he traveled down the aisles in a precise and carefully planned route, resulting in maximum Grocery Store Efficiency. No wasting time hunting for hot dog buns or backtracking because he had overlooked the sour cream—it was all right there on the cards. It was a great system, but heaven help the store managers if they ever rearranged their inventory.

It should also not surprise you to hear that the man who successfully pulled off the ultra-rare, Pre-dating Surprise Proposal Ultimatum, could be rather blunt. He did not mince words. The members of the church Ladies' Guild learned that lesson the hard way. Granny was head of the Guild and often invited the group over to the house for picnics or coffee. Walt was put in charge of captaining the pontoon boat for a leisurely float around the lake. Granny even forced him to don a sailor's cap, which always drew *oohhs* and *awwws* from the aging female set.

Well, one day the Guild had simply brought too many ladies, and most were gathered near the front of the boat, chattering away. From his captain's position Walt could see the front of the pontoon was riding far too low in the water. He quickly called for the group's attention.

"Listen up! We're too heavy. *Some of you fat ones need to move to the back!!*"

That tactfully delivered warning sent the ladies scattering, and left Granny in damage-control mode.

"*Oh, dear.* Okay girls, maybe we should all find a chair. Bertha, why don't you try this one back here in the shade?"

That was Walt. Straightforward and right to the point.

I wish I could say that Granny and Walt lived out their golden years bobbing along as breezily as a properly balanced pontoon on the lake. But just two years after they were married, a horrifying tragedy struck the family. Walt's adult daughter, Carol, went missing.

Carol Kresge DeArment had been in the middle of a bitter divorce from her husband. In October 1983, she disappeared, her car still in the garage. Initially it was handled as a missing person case, but police subsequently treated it as a murder investigation. Walt had additional telephones installed throughout the house in case someone called asking for ransom money. Her husband was the only suspect, and the case was closed in 1986 when he died of cancer. Carol's body was never found, and the crime remains unsolved.

Returning to sunnier topics. The thing that made Walt happiest, or perhaps a close second behind his marriage to Granny, was flying airplanes. In the 1940s, he joined the U.S. Army Air Corps where he could both tinker with and fly planes—two passions that he embraced for as long as he was physically able. For years, he delighted onlookers by performing barrel rolls and loops over the lake in his Citabria stunt plane. And when my mom was a young mother, Walt would fly her and baby Chas in his Cessna to visit Grandma Murphy for lunch. An express, private, round-trip to Chicago, all in time to be home for supper—and no security lines either!

Walt's other passion—one that did not necessarily make him happy, but it sure occupied a lot of his time—was quarrelling with various government entities. These epic battles took the form of editorials, letter writing campaigns, missives, communiqués, and essays. His artillery was the typewriter; his combat headquarters, the desk in the basement, flanked by bookshelves packed with well-read volumes filled with handwritten notations. His primary objective: destroying communists. A bumper sticker on the wall displayed his rallying cry: "I love my country, but I fear my government."

Today, thanks to that scourge of society, social media, "intellectual" debates are generally a contest to see who can take the most extreme positions and be the biggest jerk online. But that was not Walt. Sure, his positions might be called extreme, and he could *ad hominem* with the best of them, but he could back up any argument with a citation to the Federalist Papers, or Friedman, or John Locke. You were not going to *outthink* Walt in an argument about the Constitution or the benefits of a free market.

In 1970, the City of Madison Heights adopted a city ordinance targeting one specific individual. It seems Walt had ruffled some feathers in City Hall for the unconscionable crime of ... flying the American flag at half-mast. He was appalled by the fate of the tens of thousands American soldiers killed in Vietnam, so he lowered the flag that flew over K-L Industries to half-mast and left it that way 24-hours a day, seven days a week, in memoriam for the fallen and forgotten victims of the war. Uproar ensued. The city council found his display unpatriotic—they said the flag could only be flown at half-mast on a day of national mourning—and, *in an emergency measure,* voted 6 - 1 that any "desecration" of the American flag be punished by a fine and up to 90 days in jail. But Walt knew flag etiquette better than anyone and was the last person who would ever desecrate it. He skillfully—and of course forcefully—explained his position and declared that the flag would stay that way until the treatment of American soldiers in Vietnam improved. That was Walt. A true patriot, willing to fight for his cause.

My favorite fight of Walt's pitted him against the Michigan Department of Labor, more specifically the Board of Safety and Compliance, more specifically the Office of Weenie Bureaucrats Seeking to Justify Their Existence (I am allowed to say that, being a weenie bureaucrat myself). In the 1970s, national, state, and local governments passed a flurry of workplace safety and anti-pollution regulations. These laws were arguably well-intentioned, but, as is often the case, lawmakers failed to consider the unintended consequences of their schemes. The problem was the "one size fits all" approach. Massive factories, which were producing the most pollution and had the most workplace accidents, could absorb the cost of implementing strict safety and anti-pollution measures. The little guy like K-L Industries, who was responsible for a miniscule amount of pollution and had no workplace accidents, could not afford expensive (and ineffectual) overhauls to the facility. Nevertheless, the regulators went right on regulating and eventually drove a lot of small companies like K-L out of business.

Walt's company was forced to make dozens of changes to its operations, each more pointless than the last. In 1973, yet another safety inspector paid K-L a visit and issued a very official looking "Safety Order" that identified various areas that needed IMMEDIATE updating in order for the State of Michigan to consider the plant "safe." The primary issues identified were (1) adding guard rails to the chemical tanks, (2) issuing licenses to any hi-lo (forklift) operators, and (3) moving the location of a fire extinguisher. K-L probably could have made these changes, but Walt was fed up and knew no matter how many times they tweaked things it would never satisfy the bureaucrats. So, he drafted a response letter addressed to the inspector. As usual, Walt made his position crystal clear:

> Item 1 on the Safety Order. We cannot comply with this. Putting guard rails in front of the tanks would make it nearly impossible for the operator to run the tanks.
>
> Item 2. Every man in this plant operates the hi-lo. Also, every man employed here has a license from the state of Michigan to take a hi-powered car out and play in the traffic, and also had an eye examination to obtain that license. In a very large plant, operator permits may be a desirable thing -- in a small plant such as ours (8 men) it is about the most absurd thing I have ever heard of, and I'm not going to comply by issuing permits.
>
> Item 3. The fire extinguisher referred to is hanging within easy reach of any adult. It is mounted where I want it in a very accessible spot. If it was mounted lower, it might be hit by a load on the forks of the hi-lo, so I want it left just where it is.
>
> SUMMARY: I want to operate a safe plant. If anyone can show me anything that is unsafe, I want to, and will, correct it. However, on 5-30-72 we had an inspection from Mr. Gillespie from your department, and he listed twelve items we were to comply with, and we did comply with every item. At that point, I must assume that our plant was in compliance with the safety laws. Since then, nothing has changed, so as far as I'm concerned, we are still in compliance.

That was Walt. Steadfast and unwavering. When K-L Industries shut its doors for the last time, Walt made sure to tell his employees and customers how sorry he was and how much he appreciated their friendship.

Walt detested big government and over-officious regulators, but it was his clash with a good old-fashioned capitalist corporation that was the scene of his most legendary battle. The restaurant chain *Little Caesars* was running a buy-one-pizza, get-one-free promotion. The only caveat—in order to get the second pizza for free, the customer was supposed to say the company's tagline: "Pizza! Pizza!" Not an especially onerous requirement, but also not strictly enforced at most locations.

Walt called the restaurant to place his order and was greeted by an enthusiastic, budding bureaucratic teenager. This young man was bound and determined that every customer who wished to avail himself of the pizza deal recite the magic words. The rule is the rule, and the rule must be followed! But the rule in this case ran contrary to one of Walt's rules, namely, his rule against doing dumb things. And *that* was a rule Walt took very seriously, indeed. If by any chance the phone conversation between these two titans of stubbornness was recorded, it surely is used in *Little Caesars* employee training presentations.

> Pimple-Faced Teenager: Hello, this is Little Caesars. What would you like?
>
> Walt: Two large pepperoni pizzas, please.
>
> PFT: Okay. We actually have a buy-one, get-one-free deal right now. Would you like to do that?
>
> Walt: That sounds great, thank you.
>
> PFT: 'Awright, cool. You just need to say "Pizza! Pizza!"
>
> Walt: ... I need to say *what?*
>
> PFT: To get the deal you just need to say "Pizza! Pizza!"
>
> Walt: No.

PFT: Oh. ... Umm, if you say "Pizza! Pizza!" then it's buy-one, get-one-free!

Walt: I heard you. I'm not saying that.

PFT: But ... okay. Hmm. I think I have to charge you for both pizzas then. Are you sure?

Walt: Go ahead and charge me for both. I'm not saying it.

PFT: ... Please just say "Pizza! Pizza!"

Walt: No. I am not saying it. It's stupid.

The kid probably went on to a highly decorated career as a safety inspector. As for Walt, he could have saved five bucks that day, but he held onto his dignity instead.

That was Walt. Principled and uncompromising. Serious, but selfless. A generous man with a gigantic heart. And utterly unwilling to humiliate himself to get a free pizza.

PART II

The Catholics

A Quick Word About the Irish

My mom's family lives for competition. Games. Contests. Challenges. Tournaments. Debates. Anything with a winner and a loser. My uncles and aunts once organized an event where—I am not making this up—they put all us kids, ranging from age 6 to 15, in a sand volleyball pit for a no-holds-barred, battle royale. Twenty Murphy cousins entered the arena with instructions to eliminate the others by shoving them out of the pit. The last combatant left standing would be declared the winner. Like bloodthirsty Romans in the Colosseum, the adults surrounded the pit and screamed—yes, *screamed*—at their favored offspring, urging us to tackle, incapacitate, and maim our cousins. My cousin Elyse won the event. She was eleven.

That ancestral fervor for competition makes for great family parties but is working against me at the moment. I know there are several Murphys out there who picked up this book and frowned at the title.

"*Some People Call Us Claus?*" they clucked with disapproval. "I thought this was supposed to be about our family. Why not, *Some People Call Us Murphy?*"[1]

The old competitive fire began to flicker.

With egos slightly bruised, these proud Murphys then opened to Chapter One ... only to find a story about some German codger named Hauser. With that Irish dander now hovering up near the ceiling, they quickly flipped through the pages and observed that Part I is devoted entirely to Lutherans and Part II—*second place, hmph!*—covers the Catholics. They began counting chapters. Eight offerings in Part I. A mere four in Part II.

I know what happened next. Pausing briefly to curse my name, the name of the Clauses, and the names of all the Protestants in recorded history, these scorned relatives then skipped over the first eight chapters and, spotting the word "Irish" at the top of the page, started reading here.

---

[1] The title, if you care to know, is explained in the Introduction.

But they remain salty. In their minds, I've demoted our family of great thoroughbreds to the ranks of the also-rans. I've lost the audience before (to keep with horse-racing theme) I'm out of the gate.

Let me explain.

The Irish are a lovely people, known for their poetry, their hospitality, and their zest for life. But they are not known for their recordkeeping. And well-kept records are manna for the family historian.

Not that we should blame them. More than half the Irish population was illiterate for much of the nineteenth century. Most folks spent their days trying not to starve. That's no joke. As one observer of Irish farmers in the 1830s described: "When they have dug the potatoes from the pits, they still have to collect fuel, and to wash them and boil them; in fact, between setting potatoes, digging potatoes, washing potatoes and boiling potatoes, they have hardly time to attend to anything else."[2] And that was *before* the Great Famine that began in 1845 wiped out a million people. Keeping detailed family records was not a priority, or even a possibility. Many of the records that did exist were destroyed by fire during the Irish civil war. Others were intentionally destroyed by the Irish government (I'm sure they had a good reason for this, but for the life of me I can't think of one).

Then there is the problem of names. Ireland is a small, isolated island, and there seem to be only about a dozen names between the residents. Take my great-grandfather, John Murphy. John is the most common first name in Ireland. Murphy is the most common last name in Ireland. Trying to locate one specific John Murphy in Ireland is like trying to find a crooked politician in Illinois. Too many possibilities.

Nothing would make me happier than spending the next decade writing the definitive, multi-volume biography on the life of John Murphy. But the available information about John Murphy could fit inside a fortune cookie. He was born in Cahersiveen, Ireland in 1873. He emigrated around 1893 and eventually settled in Chicago. He married Jennie Sheehan, who also was originally from near Cahersiveen. He worked as a freight checker at the railyards. He wore an excellent mustache. End of biography.

---

2 Author unknown; *available at*: https://sites.rootsweb.com/~irlker/famemig.

John's son, my grandfather, Jerome Murphy, wasn't much help in this area. When asked to describe his parents "in a few words," he took the assignment literally. Jerome said: "Wonderful, loving, caring, and Irish." Which no doubt was true, and glad we are to hear it, but it doesn't give the historian much to work with.

Grandpa Murphy did provide one very enlightening piece of information about his parents, however: John and Jennie were fiercely proud to call themselves Americans. Ireland had not been an enchanted place of song and whimsy. To the contrary, John reportedly told his son that he "never wanted to set foot in that hellhole ever again," or words to that effect. For John, America as The Land of Opportunity was not an outdated cliché to snicker at, but a life-changing reality that improved his lot in ways he never could have imagined back in Cahersiveen.

If you happened to read Part I, you will recall that life for the Klauses and Hausers in Europe—between the diseases, constant wars, and lack of food—was rather grim. "Wretched" was the word I believe I used, and I stand by it. Even without solid evidence, we can safely presume that the experiences of generations of Murphys in Ireland were every bit as miserable, probably worse.

An 1841 census divided Irish homes into four categories. The lowest of these was "Fourth Class," which was described in the census as "mud cabins having only one room." The windowless, mud dwellings were usually only five or six feet high, with no furniture or running water. County Kerry, where the Murphys lived, was one of, if not the, most impoverished counties in Ireland. The census shows that an incredible *two-thirds* of County Kerry homes were of the Fourth Class variety, so it is statistically likely that our Murphys lived in these miserable accommodations. (The Sheehans, from what we can tell, were slightly better off. I sure hope so, for their sakes).

Writing in the late 1830s, the Frenchman Gustave de Beaumont toured the Irish countryside and described a typical County Kerry home.

Imagine four walls of dried mud (which the rain, as it falls, easily restores to its primitive condition) having for its roof a little straw or some sods, for its chimney a hole cut in the roof, or very frequently the door through which alone the smoke finds an issue. A single apartment contains father, mother, children and sometimes a grandfather and a grandmother; there is no furniture in the wretched hovel; a single bed of straw serves the entire family.

Five or six half-naked children may be seen crouched near a miserable fire, the ashes of which cover a few potatoes, the sole nourishment of the family. In the midst of all lies a dirty pig, the only thriving inhabitant of the place, for he lives in filth. The presence of a pig in an Irish hovel may at first seem an indication of misery; on the contrary, it is a sign of comparative comfort. Indigence is still more extreme in a hovel where no pig is found.[3]

You can see why John Murphy had little desire to go back. And you would think that modern society, as it lounges on its sectional sofa passing the time on its smartphone until its food delivery arrives, would have some appreciation for the people and institutions that lifted us out of the mud shack. But no. Those people and institutions are resented and denounced. Surveys show that American happiness has never been lower. Griping is the new national pastime. At the time of this writing, the bestselling book in the world is a whiny, woe-is-me, pity party of a memoir written by—wait for it—an *actual prince*. I wonder what those Murphys trying to live on a single potato a day in County Kerry would think.

The point I was making, however, was related not to the downtrodden Royal's book, but the humble manuscript in your hands. In summary, there are more "Claus" chapters than "Murphy" chapters because the Germans kept better records. And the "Claus" chapters precede the "Murphy" chapters because the "Claus" records are older, so it makes sense chronologically. Neither of these editorial decisions reflect the esteem to which I hold our proud Murphy line. *My* allegiance cannot be questioned.

---

3   Quoted from the FOREIGN MONTHLY REVIEW in THE MIRROR OF LITERATURE, AMUSEMENT, AND INSTRUCTION, Volume 34, ed by John Timbs (J. Limbird, 1839).

To put things in terms a Murphy can appreciate, I just wrote approximately 25,000 words devoted to this family. What have *you* done? In the Who Loves The Family The Most competition, the score is:

Mike: 25,000
Rest of Family: Zero.

I jest, of course. If I have seen anything it is only because I stood on the shoulders of giants. Starting with my great-aunt Yvette (LeCubain) Dwyer. Yvette was a French native who married Robert Dwyer, my grandmother's brother, while he was stationed overseas. In a pre-internet era, she managed to compile unbelievably detailed family trees of not just the Dwyers, but anyone who showed up on the Dwyer family tree, including the Murphys. She spent her entire adult life crisscrossing the United States, Canada, and Europe, visiting the archives of libraries and churches, and sent letters requesting information to places she could not visit. It wasn't even her family! My aunts Erin and Colleen took up where Yvette left off, propelled by her research and the treasure trove of new information available online. Years of my Uncle Mike's entertaining recollections over email put the meat on the bone for many of these characters and inspired others to add their own memories.

My only request of you Murphys is that you start from the beginning of the book. One chapter builds on the next, you see, and a few hours spent in the company of Lutherans never hurt anyone. Enjoy this chef-d'oeuvre as the artist originally intended. After all, would you listen to a half-composed *Moonlight Sonata?* Watch a half-filmed *Maltese Falcon??* Gaze upon a half-dressed *Mona Lisa?!?*

You would, eh? Stubborn to the end. Since there is no moving a dug-in Murphy, at least go back and check out Part I when you're done. There's some good stuff in there. The tale of a one-legged scoundrel. Reminiscences of a strange, extinct holiday in New York City. An old man's battle with a teenager over a pizza. There is even a very touching tribute to cousin intermarriage. In the meantime, enjoy these tales of Oswalds, Primassings, Sheehans, Dwyers, and, of course, ... Murphys.

The handwritten caption reads, "Dad with his Fuller Brush case."

9

The Brush Man

"Hi! I'm your Fuller Brush Man."

If you are my age or younger, chances are those words mean nothing to you. I had never heard of the Fuller Brush Man, but I surveyed my parents and they knew the reference immediately. In fact, there was a time when nearly every adult in America listened to the Fuller Brush Man introduce himself.

Between 1906 and 1956, the Fuller Brush Man knocked on nine out of every ten doors in the country.[1] To be more precise, said knocking was accomplished not by one man, but by thousands of door-to-door salesmen peddling merchandise for the Fuller Brush Company. They carried black cases full of samples and booklets and worked their territories, frequently on foot. Brushes were their trade—household cleaning brushes mainly—but expanded into hygiene and grooming products as well. Their inventory also included mops, brooms, driers, cloths, and dusters—but brushes were the star. They had brushes for dishes, brushes for stairs, brushes for stoves, brushes for hearths, brushes for radiators, brushes for walls, brushes for the bathroom, brushes for antique furniture, brushes for silk hats, and multipurpose brushes for everything else but the kitchen sink, which, of course, had its own special brush.

If a housewife opened the door for the Fuller Brush Man and allowed him into the home, she was given a free gift—a small brush designed for cleaning vegetables—whether she bought anything or not.[2] Even better, the salesman would demonstrate the products by personally mopping the

---

1 Kernicky, K., "'Fuller Brush Man' a Part of History," *South Florida Sun-Sentinel* (August 8, 1995).

2 https://fuller.com/pages/fuller-brush-history.

floor, brushing the curtains, and scrubbing the toilet to show Mrs. Housewife how her life would improve with a large purchase. The company boasted, "there is a special Fuller Brush for every purpose and every woman needs every one of them."[3] (Note to the Reader: Yes, these cleaning products were specifically marketed to women. No, I did not invent "traditional" gender roles, so don't be mad at *me*.)

A guide provided to Fuller Brush salesmen in 1922 explained how different brushes were essential for different purposes and how the salesmen might explain to their clients why they absolutely could not live without them. Take a look at this proposed "schedule" the company suggested for the ladies:

> Help the women in your territory to accomplish the most thorough cleaning with the least expenditure of time and energy by equipping her to carry through the following schedule:
>
> I. Floors
>   1. Dust with Wonder Mop.
>   2. Sweep with Fuller Broom.
>   3. Scrub with Fuller Wet Mop.
>
> II. Furniture, Stairway or Pictures
>   1. Dust with Wonder Duster.
>   2. For leather, use Furniture Brush.
>   3. For velour, use Furniture Brush.
>   4. For tapestry, use Flesh Brush or Stove and Shoe Brush.
>
> III. Walls, Curtains and Draperies
>   1. Brush walls with Fuller Wall Brush.
>   2. Brush draperies with Wall Brush or Hearth Brush.
>
> IV. Windows
>   1. Wash windows with Window Brush.
>   2. Dry windows with Window Drier.
>   3. Dust windows with Hearth Brush or Wonder Duster.

---

3 *The Fuller Bristler*, The Fuller Brush Company (January 1923).

V. Special Problems
   1. The radiator or hot air register—dust with Radiator Brush.
   2. Stair carpets—dust with Stove and Shoe Brush.
   3. Bathroom bowl—clean with Bowl Brush.[4]

Sheesh. I'm tired just reading that. Not that the salesmen had it any easier. The average Fuller Brush Man walked six miles and visited 60 homes in a day, *and* had to scour and scrub any homes he managed to charm his way into. Despite all that effort, the very best salesmen were successful at only one of every five homes they visited.[5]

In the first half of the 20th century, *everyone* knew of the Fuller Brush Man. He was a legitimate cultural icon—"America's most famous visitor," as one advertisement claimed. He showed up in *Mickey Mouse* and *Blondie* comic strips and even made a cameo in the 1933 Walt Disney cartoon, *The Three Little Pigs*, when the Big Bad Wolf comes to the door disguised as a brush salesman. The 1948 film, *The Fuller Brush Man,* was a murder-mystery comedy featuring (spoiler alert!) a very unusual murder weapon. The movie was popular enough that it spawned a sequel, *The Fuller Brush Girl*, starring Lucille Ball. There were unauthorized stories of the Fuller Brush Man as well, dime store trash novels telling bawdy tales of how the lady of the house, er … "treated" the Fuller Brush Man while her husband was away at work. (Note to self: get to a dime store ASAP.)

The Fuller Brush Company is a great model of American enterprise. Maintaining a house was *a lot* of work and the Fuller Brush Company offered high quality products that lots of people wanted. And the Fuller Brush sales team was the best in the business. The salesmen, *gratis* vegetable brush in hand, would journey street to street, house to house, knock on the door, and introduce themselves.

"Hi! I'm your Fuller Brush Man."

My great-great grandfather Engelbert Oswald (maternal grandfather to Mary Jane (Dwyer) Murphy) probably recited those words thousands of times. How long he worked as a Fuller Brush Man is unclear—my best

---

4 *Id.*

5 "Hartford's Fuller Brush Company Goes Door-to-Door Across US," Connecticut.org (March 31, 2020).

119

guess is that it was only for a few years, from around 1922 to 1925, but perhaps longer. Even if it was just a brief stretch, I think it says a lot about the character of Ol' Engelbert.

Engelbert Oswald's mother was Helena Primassing.[6] She was born in German Prussia in 1826 and came to America in 1846. The Primassings settled in Dubuque, Iowa, a brand-new town on the banks of the Mississippi River. In 1851, Helena married widower Mathias Oswald, a German-born farmer, tailor, and gravedigger who was sixteen years her senior. Both the Oswalds and Primassings were among the first settlers in Dubuque and several sources refer to the families as "Dubuque pioneers."

Helena seems like she was a gem of woman. Her 1906 obituary suggests clear parallels with her great-granddaughter, Mary Jane, who died nearly 115 years later.

> Mrs. Oswald Passes Away
> Another of Dubuque's Early Settlers Goes to the Great Beyond

> Mrs. Helena Oswald, one of Dubuque's oldest and highly respected residents, passed away at her home. ... Mrs. Oswald was known throughout the community as a woman of highest character and Christian charity and enjoyed the esteem of a large circle of friends. She belonged to St. Mary's Catholic church and to the Rosary society and was active in Christian work.

Helena (again, like her great-granddaughter) was fruitful and multiplied, as the Good Book says. Helena had eleven children but, sadly, outlived only four. That she apparently remained charitable and active in church work despite these sorrows is a testament to her faith.

Engelbert was born in 1860, the seventh of eleven Oswald children. He married Margaret Bahl, whose family likewise immigrated from Germany. Like so many of the time, the couple lost multiple children. Andrew (age 6), Edward (age 4), and Frieda (age 2) all died within a period of *three weeks* in 1890, most likely from a diphtheria outbreak. Margaret

---

6 Annoyingly for the researcher, the name has multiple spellings and seems to change with each passing year. Variations include Primassing, Primmasing, Primasing, Primmassing, and Premassing.

was six months pregnant when she buried her children. Three months later, my great-grandmother Irene was born.

Engelbert was not always a Fuller Brush Man. It seems to have been a late in life career change—the last of many career changes. He bounced from job to job and is listed in various documents as a laborer, farmer, watchman, machinist, carpenter, and worked in a brewery for a while. Finally, around age 60, he became a salesman. So, was Engelbert flighty? Did he lack drive? Unable to focus? Possibly, but I think not.

It is clear he was clever. In 1909, he received a patent from the United States Patent Office. His invention was a "Box-Lid Support." It was, essentially, a spring coiled around a metal shaft that was then connected to the lid of a box, which would hold the lid in its open position.

Okay, so it wasn't the iPhone—but it's one more patent than I'll ever have. He must have found it useful for some purpose, perhaps to keep his toolbox open as he fixed machines in a Dubuque factory.

In 1922, the hugely successful Fuller Brush Company was looking to expand its salesforce. It ran print ads in publications like *The Saturday Evening Post* and *The American Legion Weekly*. One such advertisement read:

> Here's Your Chance
>
> We need a limited number of ambitious men, of good character (preferably married), to demonstrate "Fuller Brushes" in the homes. Reasonable security required. Auto desirable. Perhaps one of these opportunities is now right in your own home territory. Previous selling experience is not necessary to sell "Fuller Brushes," because we give every man a special training in our salesmanship methods—the same methods that have developed our 3,500 successful representatives, many of whom came from positions where there was absolutely no chance for advancement or salary. Today they are among the world's best salesmen, making more money and happier in every way. ... Don't wait for it; get in touch with the nearest Fuller office (look it up in the telephone book).[7]

---

7 https://fuller.com/pages/fuller-brush-history.

It's an advertisement targeted directly to someone like Engelbert.

That he held the job with a respected company and had at least moderate success tells us several things. He must have had charisma. He must have worked hard. He had ambition. Both of his parents were native Germans but he had learned English. He was willing to take risks. And like his mother, he was a respected figure in the Dubuque community.

The Fuller Brush company published a monthly newsletter named *The Fuller Bristler*. The journal included sales figures and projections, letters from corporate executives, company updates, that sort of thing. It was also chock-full of banal motivational adages—lots of rah-rah, unlock your potential, Always Be Closing fare. Really nauseating stuff. There were jokes too, anecdotes from the sales trail, and even poems. One absolutely ridiculous offering titled, *When She Says "NO"* provides an enlightening peek into the entertainment of the age. I suppose I should give attribution. The poem's author is listed as "Delaware Diamond Digger," though I have my doubts as to whether that was his real name. (Oh! Time for another Note to the Reader: If you are the hypersensitive, perpetually offended type, with half a mind to send an angry Letter to the Editor to complain of "problematic" sexism from a hundred years ago, just remember that I am but the messenger. Direct all complaints to Digger, D. of Delaware).

>
> When She Says "NO"
>
> When you take your daily trip with your brushes in grip,
> And some lady that you call on has a grouch,
> When you don't quite make a hit and somehow don't seem to fit
> Though at selling goods you think you're no slouch
> Do not let her get away, figure out just what to say,
> Have a story that will make your brushes go,
> If she doesn't buy from you, keep on smiling, don't get blue,
> When the lady where you're canvassing says, "NO."
>
> If your goods you wish to sell, step right up and ring the bell,
> And you'll find she greets you with a charming blush,
> Then you think you've sold a set, but you've lost another bet,
> She's kidding you to get a sample brush.

122

Still, be careful what you say, she may buy a lot some day,
A woman's mind, mere man can never know.
Be respectful all the while, don't forget to wear a smile,
When the lady where you're canvassing says, "NO."

If the Housewife turns you down, smile at her, don't frown,
Don't forget she has her troubles too.
Though the women have the vote, do not let them get your goat,
For tomorrow may bring better luck to you.
Every cloud that comes your way has a silver edge they say,
Buck up Pal, some day things will not be so slow.
There is just one way to win, tip your hat to her and grin,
When the lady you're canvassing says, "NO."

Along with other literary masterpieces, *The Fuller Bristler* also included a list of salesmen who had earned a bonus for the quarter by hitting certain sales targets. I am only able to locate two annual volumes of the *Bristler*—1922 and 1923. Engelbert Oswald's name appears in the February 1923 issue. He sold enough in the final quarter of 1922 to earn a $40 bonus.

The year 1925 was Engelbert's last as a Fuller Brush Man. Charles Dwyer, young husband of his daughter Irene, was killed in a car accident. The tragedy left Irene alone in Chicago with three small children. That is a very sad story indeed, one we will cover in the next chapter. Engelbert hung up his brushes and he and Margaret moved from Dubuque—the only town they had ever known—to Chicago, to live close to the grieving family. This sacrifice also tells us the kind of person Engelbert was.

You don't see many door-to-door salesmen these days, and I, for one, am not complaining. It is a profession mostly relegated to the pages of history, somewhere between the switchboard operator and the video store clerk. There's something depressing about the door-to-door salesman. One thinks of Willy Loman from *Death of a Salesman* trying to convince himself that he is vital to his company, until his son finally says it bluntly: Willy is a dime a dozen.[8]

Was Engelbert's fourth quarter in 1922 the single highlight of his sales career? Did he struggle to hit his number, holding out pathetic hope for just one big score? Was he Willy Loman—a sad old man desperately trying to stay relevant? Again, possible. In fact, that's where I thought this story might be headed. That is, until my mom unearthed an old photograph, long buried in the family files. It is dated April 18, 1924—Good Friday. For me, this picture changes everything.

Engelbert is shown standing in front of a tree wearing a black homburg hat, white dress shirt with tie, a large black sample case in his hand. He is 64 years old but shows no hint of fatigue or cynicism. His head is held high. He looks proud, borderline triumphant. Cheerful. Completely at ease with himself. The handwritten caption reads, "Dad with his Fuller Brush case." Somebody must have asked him to pose with it and he was happy to oblige. Not a trace of Willy Loman anywhere.

There is enough melancholy in our history—no need to manufacture it. I think I know how this story ends. Actually, the more I look at his photograph, I *know* this is the way it happened:

February 1923. A cold, blustery evening in Dubuque. The sun has set and the streets are mostly quiet. Families all across the city are sitting down to supper. Engelbert Oswald rounds the corner and begins his ascent up the familiar path, gravel scattering with each step. He has visited dozens of homes today and is anxious to get back to his own. He is thinking about that Mrs. Bryant—wishing he could have closed the deal on the Wonder Mop—and makes a mental note to try her again in the spring. As the house comes into view, his thoughts turn to other matters. His old legs ache but there's pep in his step this evening. He pauses at the mailbox and anxiously peeks inside. This month's *Fuller Bristler* has arrived—the one he has been waiting for. He suppresses a smile.

Engelbert sets his black case down, right into a mud puddle, and grasps the paper in both hands. He quickly flips through the pages, past the articles and goofy jokes, and stops on page 24. The headline reads *Bonus*

---

8 Miller, A. *Death of a Salesman*, Act II. Penguin Classics (2000).

Winners in Fourth Quarterly Period. He notes the top earner for the quarter—George Harper of California, with over $5,000 in sales. Engelbert shakes his head in amazement. Maybe someday. He flips some more pages, past the $2,000 tier, past the $1,500 tier, down to the $750 - $900 list. His eyes dart back and forth. At last, he spots it:

O'Laughlin, Brian M., Calif . . . $763.30
Osborne, Rufus S., Utah . . . $753.00
Oswald, Engelbert, Iowa . . . $798.05
Quinlan, John A., Maine . . . $752.12

He reads his name twice more, just to be sure, then grabs his case. It will need to be cleaned—that's okay, he has the brushes to do it. He hustles up the steps and opens the door, the warmth providing instant relief to his chilly fingers. Home has never looked so good. Maggie is by the stove cooking dinner—boiled chicken and cabbage tonight. He sets the newsletter on the table.

"Is it here?" she asks excitedly. It is.

She rushes over, beaming. Humbly, he starts to explain that his name is in the lowest bonus tier. One fellow sold more than $5,000. She dismisses him. Most salesmen did not get any bonuses—and here was his name, printed for everyone to see. It might as well be *The New York Times*. She can't wait to show the kids—and the neighbors, especially. She wraps her arms around his neck and hugs him tightly. They share a quiet moment. They have been through so much.

Maggie gets back to the stove and Engelbert sits down at the table, still reading. He thinks of his mother and father and wishes they could see him. That's why they came to this country, wasn't it? To hustle and build a better life. And now he has done it. Engelbert Oswald ... a Fuller Brush Man.

Engelbert Oswald. The thriving, hard-driving, patent-holding, nose to the grindstoning, bonus-winning, American dreaming, Fuller Brush Man of Dubuque!

*"I CRAVE IT MORE THAN A BOOZE PIG DOES HIS LIQUOR,
OR A DOPE FIEND DOES HIS COKE."*

10

Chas and The Cutester

It was already dark when Charles Dwyer left the little brick bungalow on the South Side of Chicago. Irene may have sent him off with a quick kiss after they had eaten dinner and together tucked their children into bed for the night. The three kiddos, Robert (age 5), Mary Jane (4), and Jack (five months) were soon asleep. Irene might have settled down for some much-needed rest herself, or otherwise returned to her sewing.

Charles was looking forward to the night ahead as he and his friend Bill Kuehne journeyed north toward the city in Bill's automobile. Perhaps Chas spotted the twinkling lights of the distant Chicago skyline and sighed contently. His gaze may have settled on the nearly completed Tribune Tower, the architectural marvel that would celebrate its Grand Opening in a few months and was already named the most beautiful office building in the world. Or maybe his thoughts still lingered on the modest bungalow at 8221 Blackstone Avenue—his own architectural marvel. All the work and planning and saving were realized in that humble edifice. The rooms were small and there was but a postage stamp yard, but for the Dwyers and their growing family, the home felt perfect.

In truth, there is no reason to believe Charles was feeling especially reflective that Saturday evening. It is just as likely that his thoughts were on his new set of golf irons, or some project at work, or the cinnamon rolls he hoped Irene would bake for Sunday brunch. Where he went that night has been forgotten all these years later, but it probably was a welcome respite for Charles since his work as Chief Clerk for the Secretary of the Chicago Police Department often kept him busy through the weekend. In the early hours of March 8, 1925, the friends headed for home, Charles riding passenger in Bill's motorcar.

Some hours later, Irene would have received the news that forever shattered the happy life they were building. Then, shocked family and neighbors would rush over to offer any help they could. Word would be sent to Irene's family in Dubuque and Charles' family in Ontario, Canada. Still more friends and colleagues would cry in disbelief when they read the newspaper the next morning.

POLICE OFFICIAL DIES IN CRASH; DAY'S TOTAL 4
Charles J. Dwyer, Chief Clerk
to Secretary of Department, Instantly Killed.

Charles J. Dwyer, 8221 Blackstone Av., chief clerk to Si Mayer, secretary of the police department, was killed early yesterday morning in a motor car accident on S. State St., near Roosevelt Road. The machine, driven by William Kuehne, 1149 W. Sixty-seventh St., struck an express wagon. Kuehne and Charles Bordell, 6028 S. Peoria St., driver of the wagon, were slightly injured. Dwyer leaves a wife and three children.

Other accounts fill in the awful details. Bill and Charles were driving on State Street, in what we now call the South Loop. The sun had not yet risen, and the streets were only dimly lit. Suddenly through the darkness, Bill saw something directly in front of him, just a few yards away. An instant later, their vehicle crashed into a lumbering horse-drawn wagon, then careened into a steel beam under the Roosevelt Road viaduct. Charles was taken to People's Hospital and pronounced dead on arrival. He was 38 years old.

It would not be unusual if that was all we knew about the life and death of Charles Dwyer. So it goes with most of our relatives born before the twentieth century. We have a birth year, a death year, and if we're lucky some general information about the lifetime in between. But for Charles, despite many unknowns, the picture is clearer. He wrote a series of letters to Irene, first from an Army boot camp in 1918, and then during a period when Irene and the children were away in Iowa, while the home on Blackstone was under construction. Irene saved the letters, and they were eventually passed down to her children and grandchildren. Thanks to the Dwyer Epistles (Charles had a first-rate vocabulary and penchant for embellishment; in that spirit, his letters to Irene shall collectively be referred to as the Dwyer Epistles), we have something even better than facts and dates. We have uncommon insight into Charles Dwyer's personality and character. Although we don't know much about his life, we know a lot about the man.

As seen in the Dwyer Epistles, Charles had a way with words. When he took a sentence out for a walk he knew exactly where he was leading it. A few examples to whet the appetite:

Describing a slow, bumpy train ride: "The excursion train was of the vintage 1492 and it was impossible to rest very much."

Explaining his refusal to stay in the Army as a clerk: "I do not especially relish the idea of doing clerical work for 26 and 3/10 cents per day. I am willing to fight but not to fink."

Describing a bad haircut he received from a hillbilly: "The barber was a big apple-knocker who was more at home with a hoe than a razor."

Observing with some gentle sarcasm that Irene had not told him when she expected to return home from Iowa: "You say Hilda and Lee will drive you here but neglect to say on what date. A few particulars in this respect would be greatly appreciated."

Beyond the nimble prose, we can draw three Rock Solid Conclusions upon review of the Dwyer Epistles.

(1) Charles was completely enamored with Irene. Smitten. H. over h.

(2) Charles had a sweet tooth to rival the chubbiest kid in a candy store.

(3) Charles may have been—and I understand the magnitude of what I am about to say and do not say it without the expectation of debate—the wittiest of all our kin.

Charles J. Dwyer, my great-grandfather, was born in Albion, Ontario, Canada in 1887. His parents, Thomas and Mary (Mulloy), and grandparents, Charles and Margaret (Keenan) were also born in Ontario.

Before them, Michael Dwyer, my (4x) great-grandfather, was born in 1787 in the Irish County formerly known as Queen's, now called County Laois.[1]

Michael Dwyer left what was most certainly a difficult life in Ireland and emigrated to Canada in the year 1812, and, well, you know what they say about frying pans and fires. He would have arrived just as the Canadians were staring down an American invasion of Ontario in the War of 1812. In fact, Michael took up arms against the Red, White and Blue, fighting for the British-Canadian side. (I know, *I know*—but he was new to this continent and didn't know any better.) He fought at the Battle of Queenstown Heights on October 13, 1812, a British victory that repelled the American invasion and was a massively significant moment for the future of North America.

Michael Dwyer survived the American hostilities and married Isabella "Kitty" Wells, a Catholic immigrant originally from County Armagh in Northern Ireland. Likely in recognition of his service to the Crown, the British government offered Michael a free plot of land near Toronto where he could settle and start a family. Michael and Kitty surveyed the land and—quite incredibly, it seems to me—turned down the offer. Years later, one of their grandsons, Patrick Dwyer, wrote a letter that explained this decision, and describing his courageous, determined, relentless, scrappy grandparents:

> After looking over the land, about where Bathurst Street [in Toronto] is now, they decided to go further inland in search of better land and timber, which they found and located at a point less than 40 miles distant, which was reached, of course, by the only means of travel at that time—walking and carrying provisions needed. They depended on settlers' cabins or tree shelter at night. The fear of wild animals was not present as there was no knowledge of such in these young Irish immigrants—one from the North and one from the South, united in love for better or for worse, until death alone would part them.

---

1 Pronounced "Leesh," for some reason.

The spot chosen was in the midst of a dense forest of wonderful timber, where a small but lovely creek, or small river (well filled with speckled trout) wound its way toward the Humber River. On this beautiful spot they located and within a few days had erected a comfortable log house. After cutting great timber and burning it, they cleared sufficient for planting potatoes and vegetables, which, with flour procured in Toronto and carried on back to their new home, provided the necessary food to sustain them while they cleared acre after acre. They brought forth a healthy family of four boys and four girls, the descendants of whom are now known in many parts of Canada and the United States.

So began the Dwyer line in North America, and to recap the order of operations, Michael and Kitty beget Charles, who beget Thomas, who beget Charles, who called himself "Chas" and is our primary focus in this chapter. The Dwyers moved to Chicago when Great-Grandpa Chas was a toddler, though the reason why is unknown. How, where, and when he met the pretty girl from Dubuque, Iowa is also lost to history. However it happened, Chas married Irene Oswald in 1917 at St. Ambrose Church in Chicago.

Returning, as history always does, to the subject of wars. The United States entered World War I in April 1917. A month later, Congress passed the Selective Service Act, which required that all men aged 21-30 register for the draft. Among the 24 million Americans who dutifully registered were Babe Ruth, Harry Houdini, Norman Rockwell, Duke Ellington, Al Capone, and Charles Dwyer. In 1918, like a persistent Fuller Brush salesman making his rounds, Uncle Sam knocked on the door of the Dwyer residence.

The Dwyer Epistles reveal no hint that Chas was reluctant to heed the call of duty, but it probably was not tops on his wish list either. He was 30 when he enlisted, older than nearly all his fellow draftees. He was newly married and held a good job as a clerk with the Chicago Police Department. The reckless days of adventurous youth were behind him. But his was not to reason why, and his duty, he did. On November 9, 1918, Charles arrived at Camp Forrest to begin training in the town of Fort Oglethorpe in northern Georgia.

They—and by "they" I mean the same folks who blather about frying pans and fire—also say something about timing. Viz.—that it is everything. Though Camp Forrest was among the last places Chas wanted to be, his timing couldn't have been better. Just *two days* after he arrived and donned his government-issued marchers (military slang for boots), the German and Allied Forces agreed to an armistice, effectively ending the war. (If for some reason you ever forget when Armistice Day is and need a reminder, the ceasefire agreement went into effect at "the eleventh hour of the eleventh day of the eleventh month" of 1918.)

Charles would be spared the horrors and butchery of trench warfare. While he might have been overjoyed, his letters don't show it. Rather, his Epistles from boot camp reflect guarded optimism and a whole heap of uncertainty. Wars, especially World Wars, don't neatly end at the eleventh hour of the eleventh day of the eleventh month, all wrapped up with a bow. It takes a while for the word to get around. Troops have to relocate. Prisoners must be swapped. Men in tall hats need to draw up treaties. The combatants keep a wary eye on each other. So, Chas, along with the rest of his 27th Provisional Recruit Company of Engineer Replacement Troops, had to carry on as if they would be called into action at any moment.

After several upbeat letters to Irene, Charles wrote describing the cold, dreary, difficult life at Camp Forrest. It is far and away his gloomiest dispatch, but is informative of the life of a soldier, and he still manages to work in some humor for the benefit of his anxious wife back home.

Thursday
11/22/1918
Dearest Sweetheart -

I know you are terribly mad at me for not writing sooner but you don't know what an awful task it is to write under the conditions here. Yesterday I did not find time to wash my face or hands until 7:30 p.m. I could wash in 2 minutes but I never found the 2 minutes time. I will give you a day's routine so that you can see what we do.

5:45 A.M. - Arise

5:45 to 6:00 - Dress up (it takes every second to get into these trick clothes)

6:00 to 6:15 - Reveille (Morning inspection in ranks)

6:15 to 6:50 - Breakfast (Most of this time is spent in line à la cafeteria)

6:50 to 7:00 - Police the Streets (Shooting snipes)

7:00 to 11:30 or later - Drill (No let up)

11:30 to 12:30 - Dinner (Such as it is)

12:30 to 4:30 - Formations + Drill (Long marches, etc)

4:30 to 5:00 - Clean up bed + barracks (Police quarters in Army lingo)

5:00 to 6:00 - Mess (No comment needed)

6:00 to 9:30 - To ourselves (Usually we are called out 4 or 5 times during this period for one thing or another)

We have to do all these things at top speed and you can see that we have no time to ourselves at all. When you consider the fact that it is so cold at nights that we are unable to sleep more than 2 or 3 hours and that we work so hard that we are dead tired when we get through, you will realize that if a fellow lays on his bunk for a second during the evening (when it is not so cold) he falls dead asleep. If he sleeps too long there is no chance to write a letter. ... We are worked much harder than they were worked at the camps before Peace was declared. I suppose they think we are going home very soon and they want to teach us all they can in the short time they will have to work on us. The best proof of my love for you is the fact that I am writing this letter to you. It is indeed a labor of love. My hands are freezing and I never was so tired and sleepy in my life. Slept about 2 hours last night. Shivered the rest of the time. ... As for you, send me your love and I will be more than pleased. Taps has sounded. Good-bye little darling, I am terribly lonesome for you.

A literary critic would note that despite the poor conditions for writing and bleak mood, Charles' command of the language remains masterful. And we have our first glimpse of Rock Solid Conclusion #1: his love for Irene. Actually, that one was pretty tame. Some of his letters are positively *gushing* with the lovey-dovey goo-goo.

I pause here and apologize to Grandpa Dwyer. Truly. I would be horrified if anyone ever got ahold of flirty love letters I wrote to my wife. And if they were *published,* I probably would just sell all my possessions, catch the first train to Camp Forrest, and join up—damn the torpedoes. To any of my future great-grandchildren out there, Listen Here: you do *not* have my permission, express or implied, to read, examine, distribute, broadcast, discuss, or even think about any of my cutesy messages to your great-grandmother.

Nevertheless. The Dwyer Epistles are all we have. So, with sincere apologies, and using the least intrusive means available, we briefly examine Charles and Irene's love life, strictly for educational purposes. We need not dwell longer than necessary on his pet names for her, be they "my little sweetheart child," "the Cutester," or "the loveliest little softy in the world." And to reprint his postscript that declares, in third-person, "He loves his little sweetheart ever so much and is awfully glad she is feeling well," would be beyond the pale. One dispatch from June 20, 1917 is sufficient to convey the point. As context, Charles and Irene were set to be married two months later and Charles was not one of those grooms-to-be who gets cold feet.

Dear Little Child-Sweetheart-

I went to the Vista and saw Charles Ray in *The Clodhopper.* It was very good but sitting there made me feel lonely for you, and I did not enjoy it as much as I would have if I was holding a Cutie's hand. ...

The part of your letter where you said that you were invited to stay in Iowa over Sunday aroused my ire because it seems as if Friday will never come and as for Sunday, it is too dreadful to contemplate waiting that long. Last night I did all my bookkeeping and tonight I am going to read the only book out of your collection which I have not previously read, so you can see that my expedients for whiling away the time until my 'Hon returns are just about exhausted. I would just love to feel my sweetheart's nose about now. ...

Convey my respects to your mother and sisters and tell them that you *must* come home Friday or you will receive a severe penalty. I shall be waiting at the station at 9 o'clock with some candy for you and all you will have to do to get a piece of it will be to let me rub the powder off your nose!

I sat on our bench for a while this evening but I did not enjoy it nearly as much as on former occasions. It must have been because I didn't have the little Cutester with me. I am going to tell you a secret – I love my sweetheart! Have a good time but don't forget that I am crazy to have you back.

Yours very truly
Chas J Dwyer,
The Guy who loves you to death

It's sentimental drivel, of course, and I would never lower myself to it,[2] but women seem to go for that sort of thing. I may try out some of his pick-up lines, though, as far as I know, my own little Cutester does not powder her nose. And I absolutely cannot endorse employing a "compliment" that he used on more than one occasion. (It's not the entire sentiment, but merely one phrase that is questionable. See if you can spot it.)

---

2 *Don't* see Chapter 19.

I received your letter yesterday and was much relieved to find out that you are in good health and that Chicago is not full of the flu as we heard down here. I was quite worried, as you are a lovely little fatty and I love you so much that it would make me sick to know that you are not well.[3]

Rock Solid Conclusion #2—that Charles had a major sweet tooth—may seem insignificant compared to the first Conclusion. It was *not* insignificant to Charles.

Like most military fare, the food at Camp Forrest was terrible. Chas absolutely despised the recurrent offering of hotdogs, beans, and cold potatoes. So, when he wasn't pining for Irene, he was pining for sugar. It consumed his thoughts. The man needed dessert.

Americans have apple pie; Canadians, which Charles was by birth, have maple syrup. Blocks of "maple sugar" were unequivocally his favorite. It is not a popular American treat, so by way of background, maple sugar is made by simmering pure maple syrup over heat until the moisture evaporates, leaving a thicker molasses that is then poured into molds until it hardens. Partakers then take the hardened brick of maple sugar and shave or grate flakes of it into oatmeal, coffee, or toast for added flavor and sweetness.

Most partakers do, anyway. Chas lost all self-control in the presence of maple sugar. Upon receiving a care package containing it, he would immediately gobble it up, then write to Irene again, demanding another block. He was fanatical. Of the thirteen Dwyer Epistles from Camp Forrest, *ten* mention the stuff:

> 11/10/1918 ... tell Beatrice that the maple sugar was wonderful. I have it nearly all licked up and I wish you would send me two more bricks of it at once. Send them a day apart so that if one goes astray I will get the other. They give you no sugar here and our cooks–taken from the ranks–are not hep to their jobs as yet; they give you cold potatoes, which I cannot eat. As a result I have a constant craving for sugar which supplies the system with the same chemicals as potatoes.

---

3 Irene was rather slender as a young woman, so perhaps "fatty" held a different meaning in the 1910s. Or maybe Charles was the bravest husband who ever lived.

11/12/1918 ... It was ten thousand degrees below zero here last night and we slept with all the windows open. The kit I brought was a darb, but it lacked two very essential articles: a double thick sealskin blanket and a barrel of maple sugar.

11/22/1918 ... Have not got the maple sugar yet. Please send some more and send a package of it every Wed. and Saturday. I crave it more than a booze pig does his liquor, or a dope fiend does his coke.

11/23/1918 ... Got the maple sugar yesterday. Am sorry to say that it is all licked up now.

12/6/1918 ... Don't forget to send maple sugar. Send it Special Delivery.

12/11/1918 ... You have not said in your letters how you are feeling. Please let me know at once. I have rec'd no maple sugar for a month.

12/14/1918 ... It is so long since I have received maple sugar that I have almost lost my craving for it. I have sent to all the nearby cities for it, but they don't seem to carry it in the south.

12/15/1918 [Momentarily changing tack] ... Hilda has not kicked in with her box of fudge yet but I still have hopes.

12/17/1918 ... I received the maple sugar last night and licked it up right away – it is not as good as the other kind, but very fine for a' that.

12/23/1918 ... They sent all us married rums through the personnel office today and gave us our discharges to date as of Dec. 26, 1918, so you will probably see me about Dec. 27th. Of course, things are mighty uncertain in this man's army and they may change their minds before the 26th and keep us here. The chances are, however, that we will make our getaway on that date. If you are contemplating sending any maple sugar, do not let this news deter you from your purpose.

Rock Solid Conclusion #3, pertaining to Charles' wit and comedic instincts should be evident by now. In a family of writers, his work stands alone. A few more excerpts prove the point. As the war wound down, soldiers were slowly released from duty and returned home. Rumors swirled in Camp Forrest about who might be next. Meanwhile, Charles observed that the clerks tasked with drafting up discharge papers had abysmal penmanship—some barely knew how to write. Being a professional clerk, it got under his skin. With an eye to posterity, Charles vowed to have his own papers written legibly. And in his self-deprecating way, he conjured images of his future self, regaling his family with tales of his illustrious, military career that lasted all of one month:

12/15/1918
Dearest Sweetheart -

The latest latrine news is that we will be home Monday. The latrine is a combined toilet, gymnasium, laundry, and lounging room and all the rumors originate from there. If you spend a half hour there you will hear 19 different stories, each under the seal of secrecy, and supposed to be straight from someone who is acquainted with a friend of the colonel's hatter or barber, and is therefore in a position to know. No let up in the drilling however, so I guess that there is nothing coming off. We sure will be home shortly however, for with all this smoke there must be some fire. ...

I am going to try to select a *human being* to write out my discharge papers, as most of them appear to be written in either ancient Hebraic or in the Indian sign language. Said discharge will be put away in the drawer from which it can be produced in later years by a certain Old Pap named C.J. Dwyer, and shown with great éclat to the assembled multitude of applauding guests. Said O.P. will then remove the marchers and display the wound on his big toe, received at the battle of Chickamauga (this camp being at Chickamauga Park) and thus prove conclusively that the Dwyers are of an heroic clan and did their bit for democracy.

Five years later, Charles wrote another letter that is both entertaining and relatable, particularly for, as he would put it, "us married rums."

It's a tale as old as time. A household item is misplaced and the parties to the marriage, otherwise living in domestic bliss, blame each other. Husband asks Little Cutester where she might have put the item. Cutester denies knowledge of whereabouts of said item and suggests that Husband lost it. Husband provides at least twenty-seven reasons why that is not possible and quite fairly puts the ball back in Cutester's court. Cutester stares at Husband as if he has two heads, declares that she has moved on with her life and refuses to spend another millisecond thinking about it.

For the Dwyers, it was an alarm clock. Irene had packed up the kids and temporarily relocated to Dubuque while their new home was under construction, leaving Charles in Chicago at his mother's house. Somehow the family alarm clock was lost in all the shuffling and Charles had an idea who was responsible. In a J'accusing letter, he detailed the great sacrifices he was making without the precious timepiece.

Chicago, Ills.
7/5/23
Dear Child –

I have been somewhat busy since you left and have not visited the bungalow (an edifice, by the way, that would be fit for Potter Palmer[4]) so I cannot report progress on the same, but I have no tee time on the golf course for this evening so I will have a look at it and will submit a full and complete report in my next epistle. -- *Alarm clock* -- I wrote that down so that I would not forget it! Aunt Ellen and I have searched the house completely but can find no trace of same. I am going to hire Bill Collins, the famous Detective, and if he cannot detect where you have hidden it, I will have to admit that you certainly know how to hide alarm clocks.

If you care to let me in on the secret I would appreciate it, as I find it somewhat wearying to stay up all night so as not to miss the four-thirty A.M. car for the golf course. To make it a little more complicated, Ma also stays up all night so that in case I should drop off to sleep from sheer exhaustion, she will be able to wake me in time. As I say, I would

---

[4] The Chicago real estate developer responsible for much of the city's classic architecture in the 1800s.

appreciate it very much if you would tell me where the alarm clock is hidden. ...

When you write, if ever, tell me all the doings of the kids and of yourself, not forgetting to mention how much wine you licked up at the barn dance, and tell me if the children went swimming yet. With all my love to you and the children I remain,

Yours very truly

    Chas. J. Dwyer

P.S. - Alarm clock.

Once Chas found a gag he liked, he stuck with it. Irene's return letter apparently ignored his allegations—not an uncommon tactic among cutesters—but that only encouraged him.

7/7/1923

I received your letter and was glad to note that you are all okay. There was no reference to an alarm clock in it, but no doubt the whereabouts of same is one of your most cherished secrets. I stayed up all night last night but fell asleep at 3:55 and did not wake until nearly 5 o'clock, so I was a little late in reporting at the golf course. ...

The final letter we have is from August 28, 1923. No mention of the alarm clock, so that mystery must have been solved. Chas gave the usual updates on the construction of the bungalow and his fledgling progress on the golf course. It appropriately concludes:

Write and tell me about Bobby and Mary Jane and tell me when you are coming home.

    Your loving husband,
    Chas J. Dwyer

Irene returned with the kids, and the family moved into their new home sometime in the Fall of 1923. In October 1924, baby Jack was born.

Charles was killed five months later.

He was a casualty of rapidly changing technology in a world too slow to adapt. Busy city streets were still primarily for pedestrians and horses. Automobile collisions were truly a national crisis—more than 20,000 died in 1925 alone. Newspapers kept totals of traffic fatalities like they would baseball scores. One account of Charles' accident noted bleakly, "Three more names were added to Cook County's automobile death list yesterday, the total for the 67 days of 1925 reaching 105."

Charles was gone, but of course the Dwyer/Oswald story does not end there. Irene was left to raise and provide for Bob, Mary Jane, and Jack—but she was not alone. Her sisters, Edith and Irma, left Dubuque and moved into the bungalow permanently. The cozy house built for Chas and Irene became the home of the Oswald sisters. The impact of these two women on the family's trajectory—women who uprooted their lives for their sister and her children—cannot be measured. Irene's parents, Engelbert and Margaret, had also come to Chicago to be close to their daughter and grandchildren. As examples of how we ought to lift up our families, the Oswald clan is Exhibit A.

Irene lived in the house at 8221 Blackstone for the rest of her life. As a mother she was loving, kind, and sensible. She had been a homemaker but worked as a secretary after Chas died. She was an extraordinary seamstress who made most of her own clothes, from professional suits to church dresses to nightgowns. The loss of Charles surely devasted her, but the Blackstone bungalow was filled with warmth, laughter, and the delicious smells of the Oswald sisters' home-cooked meals.

The end of Charles and Irene's story is among the saddest in our family. There is no way to sugarcoat his untimely death, not even with a brick of maple sugar. Yet there is a triumph buried in the tragedy. Charles and Irene's legacy lives on in the Dwyer Epistles, which show an intelligent, affectionate, playful couple in love. And it lives on in their family tree, which sprouted in ways they probably never imagined.

In their short time together, Charles and Irene were blessed with three children, Bob, Mary Jane, and Jack. From them, the grandchildren of Charles and Irene: John, Jan, Joe, Colleen, Mike, Kerry, Tim, Kevin, Erin, Sally, Brian, Shannon, and Terry; their great-grandchildren, solely considering Mary Jane's line: Chas, Jenny, Dan, Mike, Pete, Matt, Elizabeth, Jessica, Patrick, Shannon, Maggie, Cara, Jerome, Dan, Jackie, Leah, Sean, Becca, Elyse, John, Lauren, Kerry, Jim, Jack, Erin, Reaghan, Cassidy, Killeen, Grace, and Shane; *and* their great-great grandchildren: DeCody, Allison, Gianna, Addison, Owen, William, Molly, Megan, Zoe, Jaden, Noah, Otis, Sean, Ryan, Anna, Nick, Natalie, Jack, Ben, Joel, Caroline, Samantha, Tanner, Emmaline, Dylan, Beau, John, Bernadette, Domenica, Joseph, Louie, Landon, Lawler, James, Maureen, Sally, Winston, Peter, Arthur ... and counting!

NO MIDDLE SCHOOL BOY WANTS TO LOSE AN ATHLETIC COMPETITION TO HIS GRANDMA.

11

Love, Laughter, and Scorpions

One Sunday after Mass at Notre Dame, my grandmother turned to me, grinning. Something during the service had caught her attention and she was eager to discuss it. It was a reading from the Book of Luke—right after the bit about asking and receiving, seeking and finding, etc. The passage poses a series of questions, meant to be rhetorical.

"Which of you fathers, if your son asks for a fish, will give him a snake instead? Or if he asks for an egg, will give him a scorpion?"[1]

The punchline is that *no one* would ever be so cruel to their children—not even we sinners—so imagine the great things our loving God will do for us if we just ask. But Grandma seemed to miss the point altogether. In fact, she was absolutely delighted by the scenario.

"If they are whining about eggs ... just pass them a scorpion! Ah, that would be a riot!!" she said, lifting both hands in the air and laughing. She mentioned that it might teach the ingrates a lesson and I'm pretty sure she made a mental note to try out the gag sometime.

She hadn't really missed the point, of course. For more than ninety years, Grandma was a weekly, then daily churchgoer and had heard the passage many times. Whip-smart and a voracious reader, she could decode a sticky metaphor with aplomb. Nor was she a cruel mother—quite the opposite. She raised ten children, all of whom adored her. But with so many kids of varying ages and levels of cooperation to manage, she was forced to employ unusual tactics to keep the house running and herself sane.

For example, as youngsters, two of her more rambunctious sons, my uncles Tim and Kevin, had a habit of getting out of bed and "rassling" in the middle of the night. That wouldn't have bothered her so much— *"let*

---

1 Luke 11:11-12.

them work it out," she might say—but the racket would wake up the rest of the house. Using heavy straps, she fastened the boys to their beds until morning. It was a clear violation of the fire code and possible grounds for child endangerment charges, but an effective sleep aid. It also shows that, while she preferred to bestow the fish and eggs to her children, she would not hesitate to unleash a scorpion if needed.

Mary Jane Murphy was four feet, eleven inches of perpetual motion. She wrangled children and grandchildren, cooked daily meals for dozens, distributed the Eucharist at church, wrote letters while she waited for the laundry to dry, organized photo albums, entered bridge tournaments, brought meals to shut-ins, got the gossip at the neighborhood coffee klatsch, played tennis every day possible, golfed on days she wasn't playing tennis, pored over books and crossword puzzles, hosted countless parties, and volunteered what remaining free time she had. As a young woman, she attended an endless series of her childrens' sporting events, concerts, banquets, and graduations. As an old woman, she drove what she referred to as "the old people" (they were 80, she was 85) to weekly Mass at St. Cajetan.

One part of Grandma's charm was her distinctive voice.

"If they are whining about eggs ... just pass them a scorpion! Ah, that would be a riot!!"

Although this is not an audio book, I guarantee that anyone who read that line and knew Mary Jane *heard* her saying it. She was inimitable in many ways—her energy, her spirit, and her attitude among them—but her voice was endlessly, well ... imitable. Everyone in our family has a "Grandma Murph" impression. Her voice needs no description for us. But for the benefit of those who never had the pleasure, her voice was a sort of—not high pitched—but a high, friendly, *scratchy* tone; her words punctuated with lots of extra *"ahh's."* Like an elderly cat might sound.

Her unforgettable voice, along with her trademark white curly hair and diminutive frame, puts her in the running for most physically memorable member of the family. But it was her personality, kindness, and that wonderfully wacky sense of humor that we remember most.

Mary Jane Dwyer was born October 22, 1920, on the South Side of Chicago. She likely had only vague memories of her father, Charles, who was killed in an automobile accident when Mary Jane was four and a half years old. Her mother Irene, who had been full-time mom and homemaker, took a job as a secretary. The family got along with the support of aunts Irma and Edith Oswald who moved from Dubuque to live with the Dwyers and help look after Mary Jane and her two brothers, Bob and Jack.

Irene taught her children that, just as her job was to work as a secretary, their job was to study hard and earn scholarships to high school and college. Mary Jane did just that, earning a scholarship to Mercy High School in Chicago. Upon graduation, she turned down a scholarship from Northwestern University in favor of one from Clarke College, an all-girls Catholic school in Dubuque. After two years at Clarke, she completed her teaching degree at Chicago Teachers College—while working forty hours a week. She gave most of her wages to her mother.

As a young grade-school teacher in Chicago Public Schools, Mary Jane devised unconventional schemes to tackle behavior issues in her classroom. For example, and for reasons I have not discerned, her students persisted in removing their shoes at recess. Over and over, she reminded them that *shoes must stay on their feet*. But no matter how many times she exhorted, the children would return from their play as shoeless as Joe Jackson.

What to do? Mary Jane first initiated a "root cause analysis" of the issue, then applying trendy new "restorative justice" principles she had learned from career administrators with *very* impressive education degrees, she created a "safe space" for the students where they had no fear of punishment, which in turn empowered the individual child to make his or her own choices about when shoe wearing is appropriate.

Sounds ridiculous, doesn't it? I'm afraid today's "progressive" educators would be none too impressed with Mary Jane's methods—and the feeling would be mutual! What *actually* happened is that, in true Mary Jane fashion, she raided her Science lesson supplies, gathered a bunch of sea urchins (I guess there were no scorpions handy) and when the kids inevitably removed their footwear and ran off, she stuffed the spiky creatures in the toes of their shoes. When the students came back from recess and slid on their shoes—*youch!* Problem solved, with no harm done, other than a few tender toes. (Grandma told this story with her customary throwing of the arms in the air while laughing. She was quite pleased with her ingenuity.)

Alright, so we covered the scholarships, we covered the teaching, and the sea urchins—what else? ... Oh! One thing I ought to have mentioned up front. Mary Jane singlehandedly saved Western Civilization. Silly me for burying that little detail.

World War II was raging. Mary Jane's brothers joined the military, and she also did her part for The Cause, working as a secretary in a factory that manufactured airplane wings. One evening when the office was mostly empty, she was approached by an unfamiliar coworker. The man's name was Elmer Hartzell. Elmer claimed to be some sort of manager with high-level security clearance. He flashed a million-dollar smile, complimented her, and announced assertively that he needed to borrow her keys to the locked file room to check on something.

If Elmer thought he had found an easy mark in the seemingly naive young secretary, he was mistaken. Mary Jane politely declined, then alerted her supervisors. Herr Hartzell was escorted out under guard, never heard from again, and America's top-secret airplane wing designs remained secure.

When she wasn't saving humanity from fascism, young Mary Jane Dwyer was social and loved parties, music, and dancing. As a 16-year-old, she attended a New Year's Eve bash that changed her life. There she met Jerome T. Murphy, a fellow South Sider with a similar affinity for socializing and music, with a beautiful voice to match his passion. Both had arrived at the party with dates (Mary Jane's cousin, Dorthea Dwyer, had brought Jerome) but were quickly chatting each other up between songs. According to Mary Jane, *"we were each with someone else, but I was impressed with his wit and singing!"* He later proposed to her on her twenty-third birthday, after first securing Irene's blessing, of course.

"MJ" and "Jerry" married in 1946. This was the era of the Baby Boom and the Murphys boomed with the best of them. Together they welcomed Colleen (1948), Michael (1950), my mother Kerry (1952), Timothy (1954), Kevin (1955), Erin (1957), Sally (1959), Brian (1960), Shannon (1963) and Terrence (1964).

Just as her own mother had, Mary Jane stressed the importance of education and could be a taskmaster if she felt there was excessive "goofing off" at the expense of studying. But a helicopter parent she was not. If the kids weren't doing homework, they were expected to keep themselves entertained—at local Kennedy Park, in sports leagues, in the backyard, or in the basement. No TV on school nights for the Murphy kids. She never spoiled them but made sure they had plenty of life's essentials—roller skates, hockey sticks, baseball gloves, bicycles, golf clubs, volleyballs, and basketballs for outside, and for inside, books—*lots* of books.

The Murphy home on South Bell Avenue was the neighborhood gathering grounds for parties and picnics and Mary Jane documented these great events with home movies and photographs. For decades she asked, nay, *demanded* that her guests pose for pictures—the goofier the better. If a relative brought a new "significant other" to a picnic, the S.O. would soon be donning a comical hat or posing with a plastic skeleton. If Father Hurley dropped in for a visit, MJ would grab her camera and make the good reverend pose with a butcher knife, pretending to stab someone. Newly engaged couples were forced to reenact the proposal, with the groom on one knee and the bride feigning surprise. During the South Side Irish Parade on St. Patrick's Day, she famously would halt the entire procession by standing in the middle of Western Avenue with her camera, conjuring images of Tiananmen Square. Confused gapers watched in amazement as Mary Jane "got some good shots" of the float from St. Cajetan or pressed some aspiring politician to wear novelty sunglasses for a photo. Then she laughed and sent them on their way, waiting for the next marching band or group from the Knights of Columbus she could stop in their tracks.

Mary Jane brought unique perspectives borne of a unique mind. You often left a conversation thinking, "*Huh* ... I never thought of it that way." Here are just a few examples.

On biology: Her son, Tim, told her that the family cats might carry fleas and tried to convince her to put flea collars on them. *"Tim says the fleas will get on people and eat their blood—sounds a little far-fetched to me. Besides, we've all got plenty of blood."*

On football strategy: She was perplexed as to why teams struggled in short yard situations, especially near the goal line. *"Why not just give the ball to a dwarf and have some of the big guys grab him and toss him over the pile?"*

On theatre etiquette: Carrying her trusty video camera, she attended her daughter's performance at Mother McAuley High School. *"Sally's play was a great big hit—standing room only. I took some movies even though they said 'no pictures.' Since I was sitting in the front row, I'm sure it didn't bother anyone."*

On politics: During an election season, she had two political signs displayed in her yard. Canvassers had been out canvassing and she recognized some names from the neighborhood (O'Malley and Kelly, possibly). *"Ahh, sure,"* she said amicably, the O'Malley people could put up their sign in the yard. And when the Kelly team showed up, they too were welcomed to display a sign for their guy. The problem, several of her sons and grandchildren later pointed out, is that O'Malley and Kelly were opponents—running against each other for the same office. When asked which sign she wanted taken down, she replied, *"Ahh, what do I care? Let them fight it out!"* Both signs stayed put.

As her children headed off to college, started jobs, or got married, she kept everyone informed of the goings-on at Bell Avenue with letters from home (several are excerpted in this chapter). The letters were so treasured by her children that collectively they saved, literally hundreds of them, ranging from 1971 to the late 1990s. "Mom" often began her correspondence with her favorite salutation. She had read it as a child in letters sent to the Dwyer house by some ancient relation and it stuck with her all those years. *"It has a nice old-fashioned ring to it!"* she wrote of the greeting. I agree. Few things gave her adult children greater delight than opening an envelope and reading the words at the top of the page:

"Dear Ones All."

Between her archived correspondence, and the collective memories of ten children and thirty grandchildren, there's no shortage of Mary Jane stories. All of us experienced countless moments where she made us laugh or feel special. Nine of her kids are happy to recount those occasions when their mother reassured them, cheered them, or taught an enduring lesson. Those nine are a very chatty crowd indeed—verbose even—and always ready with the story of that time in 1977 when MJ did such and such. Ask them for a Mary Jane Murphy story and they may never shut up. So, rather than try to tell too many of their tales, we focus now on Mary Jane's youngest—the tenth of the Murphy children.

Terrence John Murphy was born January 1, 1964. Doctors informed MJ and Jerry that "Terry" was born with Down syndrome. Over time, it was apparent that he was severely disabled. We now know that Terry's mental capacity is in the range of a four-month-old or lower. With some difficulty, he can walk short distances, but cannot speak, use the bathroom, feed himself, or control any aspect of his behavior. He requires 24-hour supervision to keep him safe. Since 1988, he has lived at Misericordia home in Chicago. But for the first 24 years of his life, caring for Terry was a round-the-clock job for MJ.

Mary Jane probably had a pretty good handle on things somewhere around the sixth or seventh kid. She was in a groove. But Terry's challenges were brand new to her and, sadly, there were few measurable milestones in his childhood. With each passing year, his needs grew more demanding. In essence, Terry was a growing boy, then teenager, then man—with the mind of an infant. He needed to be monitored for every meal, bath, and bedtime, day after day, year after year, with no letup.

There is no cure for Down syndrome, but Mary Jane always hoped for some breakthrough. An educator by trade, she researched teaching methods that might trigger some improvement for Terry. When he was still a toddler, she and Jerry visited a facility in Philadelphia called the Institutes for the Achievement of Human Potential, which had devised a new system for treating disabled children—the Doman-Delacato method. Doman-Delacato was premised on the idea that a damaged brain could be "rewired" through highly repetitive physical exercises and sensory stimulation. "Patterning" exercises involved maneuvering the child's arms, legs, and head in a specific order, which would, said Messrs. Doman and Delacato, strengthen healthy brain cells and improve unhealthy ones over time. During a session the child's left leg might be bent, followed by straightening the right knee while simultaneously turning his head from side-to-side; then the sequence reversed, and so on. Creeping on the floor was added to the patterning regimen, then crawling, then grasping, all with the critical requirement of repetition in the proper sequence.

Only MJ could answer whether she *truly* believed the unusual system would help Terry. But she was willing to try if it meant even a small chance her son would improve, so she introduced the Doman-Delacato treatment into Terry's routine.

It was an extraordinary commitment. The patterning exercises required three people manipulating Terry's limbs in the prescribed order—15 minute sessions, four times a day, 365 days a year. For crawling, Doman and Delacato stressed that repetition in voice was just as critical as repetition of movement. Mary Jane spent months repeating the mantra, "*Crawl, Terry! Crawl, Terry!*" at specified intervals, until she had the brilliant idea of making a recording of her voice. She still needed to physically maneuver him, but a cassette tape handled the vocals.

"*Crawl, Terry! . . . Crawl, Terry! . . . Crawl, Terry!*"

Whatever the advantages of Doman-Delacato—considerable skepticism has since emerged in the medical community regarding its effectiveness—the system was not of significant benefit for Terry. His deficiencies were simply too severe.

As he grew older, the mere act of moving him was exhausting. Terry could not be left at home alone, which meant that Mary Jane spent her days carting him along on errands or staying home when others went out. One of her letters summarizes a representative weekend for MJ when Terry was home:

> It's a peaceful Saturday again—everyone is out except Terry, the cat, and me. I just gave them their lunch and now I'm having some cheese and crackers and am watching the finals of the Women's Tennis Open—Chris Evert is winning so far. A little later the Notre Dame - Purdue game will come on and I'll try to find Brian, Erin, Mike and Kevin on TV. They're all at the game—wish Dad and I were, too! But Dad had work to do and I have Terry to worry about.

She wasn't complaining or looking for sympathy. It would be understandable if she had some solitary moments of frustration and tears. Actually, it would be surprising if she didn't. But she never made her duty anyone else's. She loved her son, so she adjusted her life. The other kids helped out as often as they could. Erin stayed with Terry so Jerome and

Mary Jane could go on vacation. Sally brought her own young children over to the house so MJ could spend the afternoon golfing. Mike accompanied them on trips to the doctor. Kevin helped fetch his brother off the school bus. Mary Jane appreciated the assistance, but she also understood that they had their own jobs, children, and lives. The responsibility of minding Terry was primarily hers and she handled it with her typical compassion and humor.

Bringing a fully-grown Terry anywhere could be a daunting project for his sub-five-foot-tall mother. He was incredibly strong and equally stubborn. He could walk, but usually was against it, and there wasn't any convincing him otherwise. When he did not want to move, he would simply sit down, cross-legged, and remain in place. MJ called these his "sit down strikes." If one of the kids or a friendly neighbor was not around to help pick him up, she could sometimes coax him along with saltine crackers, his favorite food. She employed this method so often that she turned it into a verb, i.e., *"Terry wouldn't budge but I crackered him into the house."*

When Terry was in his late teens (while he still lived at home), Mary Jane applied for a "respite program" at Misericordia. The facility would house patients for a week during the summer so their parents could go on vacation. However, for this particular program, none of the patients were supposed to be capable of walking and Terry, for all of his problems, could walk a bit. Accompanied by her daughter Shannon, MJ brought Terry to be seen by a social worker who would evaluate him for the program. She later explained in a letter:

> I had told the social worker that Terry could walk, but not too well and only for short distances. They didn't want anyone who could walk around and knock other kids over. So I told Shannon we didn't want him to walk *too* well when we brought him in. We had to park about half a block away and Terry simply would not walk to the building. I was on one side and Shannon on the other, dragging him and prodding him along. Shannon said, "My, he certainly is playing his part well!" Anyway, we got him into the program for a week in August.

That was nothing compared to Terry's legendary medical appointments. Another letter from Mary Jane tells the exasperating tale of a trip to the dentist when Terry was 18 years old:

> Yesterday was a lost day—I had to take Terry to the dentist. Nancy Boles went with me to help. I had to give Terry a Valium tablet the night before and was supposed to give him another in the morning to make him agreeable. When I got him up at 8:00 he was like a zombie, couldn't walk, was white as a sheet, gagging, falling down. So I was afraid to give him any more dope. But by the time we got to the dentist at 16:00 he was full of pep. The dentist was only going to clean his teeth and there was no pain involved, but you know how Terry won't let anyone near his head or mouth. It ended up with six people holding him even though his body and arms were in restraints. They couldn't believe how strong he is. The dentist, his assistant, his wife, Nancy, myself and another dentist had to come in and sit on top of him. So they never did complete the job and now I have to bring him back in October. Terry didn't let one cry out of him, but just tried to pull their hands away.

Still another dispatch, this one from 1985, describes the misadventure of Terry's eye and ear examinations. Terry was 21 years old at the time. MJ's ability to find silver linings and humor in the most frustrating situations is truly remarkable:

> We spent the day going from doctor to doctor—seven in all. We were up and down halls and elevators like trained robots, except one of the robots didn't want to move. In the middle of the hearing test Terry managed to wet through his diaper, his pants, his shirt, etc. I had to wrestle him to the carpet for a complete change while the hearing machine was clanging gongs, simulating waterfalls (how appropriate) etc. He had the wax removed from his ears while I and three or four attendants held him. The ear people decided he could have some hearing loss but no one can really tell because of his lack of response. Even if he had a hearing aid, he would pluck it out and dash it to the ground before you could bat an eye. Eyes were next—his were examined as the eye doctor fought off his grabs for the instruments and his vicelike grip on the doc's hand—verdict—he doesn't need glasses. If he did they'd go to the ground with the hearing aid. Anyway, it went on until

we got home at 3:00 with nothing to eat or drink. Have to go back for the psychological exam—I'm looking forward to that! The people were all very nice and certainly have patience and kindness to work with the disabled all day. We must take our hats off to them—or as Brian would say, *doff our chapeaux!* That includes Colleen and Benote for all the work they've done with the disabled—hats off!!

In 1988, Terry was accepted as a full-time resident at Misericordia. It was a godsend for the family, and Mary Jane and Jerome could take comfort that Terry was not just in good hands, but the *best* hands. Part of Misericordia's mission is to give their residents a purpose—or *raison d'etre* to stick with Brian's French theme from 1985—to maximize the individual's potential and self-worth. For many at Misericordia, that means working in the bakery, serving tables in the cafeteria, contributing artwork to sell in fundraisers, and working in the laundry facility. Terry's abilities are very much lower but that doesn't stop the incredible staff from trying to find some goals for him.

After a month or so without Terry in the house, MJ wrote explaining what he was up to and how they both were adjusting.

> It's very strange around here without Terry. He goes to workshop at Misericordia every day from 9:00 until 3:00—it's about half a block away, on their grounds. He has to walk there and back. I guess he has lots of sit down strikes. I asked them what he could do in a workshop since he can't even put on his own shoes. They said they are trying to get him to put balls in a bucket. They will attempt to toilet train him by running him to the bathroom every hour. So it looks like he has his work cut out for him! He doesn't even recognize us when we go to see him so I'm sure he doesn't miss home. I miss having him after 24 years. We had him home for a week in July and will have him for another visit soon.

When Terry was born, the life expectancy of someone with Down syndrome was between 10 and 25 years old.[2] My Uncle Terry is now 60 years old, still living at Misericordia. I'm no doctor, but I believe this

---

2 National Center on Birth Defects and Developmental Disabilities, Centers for Disease Control and Prevention, https://www.cdc.gov/ncbddd/index.html.

miracle is due in large part to the love and care shown first by Mary Jane and her family, and then by Misericordia. It has long been the Murphy family's most cherished charity, and we are very grateful for the incredible, compassionate work that happens there. For folks like Terry of course, and for their parents too.

With an empty nest, Mary Jane finally had more free time to devote to her hobbies. One of those hobbies was playing innocent jokes or pranks on her friends and relations. Nothing meanspirited—she wanted to laugh with people, not at them. Had she gone through with her scheme from the Book of Luke, I am certain the scorpion would be made of plastic, or at the very worst, sleeping.

One of her favorite tactics was to utilize the United States Postal Service in furtherance of her frauds (a federal crime).[3] Often aided and abetted by my own mother, she would send letters and postcards from undisclosed addresses under false pretenses. There was the time MJ and Kerry sent out invitations for a formal party—and then a couple of weeks later mailed only half the invitees a separate note from an address that could not be traced, stating that the plan was changed—and it was now a *costume* party. Naturally, they played dumb when the folks who showed up in costumes demanded answers. They also sent silly Valentines back and forth, *incognito,* to people who had absolutely no romantic interest in each other. And they were quite pleased when their efforts to confuse the guests at an out-of-town weekend getaway hosted by their old friend, Chuck Fetter, paid off:

> When Kerry was here, she and I sent all the guests notes asking them to bring goofy things for the weekend and we signed Chuck Fetter's name. He didn't know what was going on. Some of them fell for it, others figured it was a joke. Tim Lynch did plant his forget-me-not seeds in 8 little peat pots as his note told him to. He gave the pots to Chuck and Chuck thought he was wacky. Boleses were all set to bring two large electric fans but they weren't able to go. Marie S. brought a delicious chocolate cake for Ed Burke's retirement but Ed wasn't there. Blanche Kelly brought 15 blindfolds and Harrington brought his rags and Spic-and-Span so he could clean up afterwards. They were all confused

---

3 18 U.S.C. ¶ 1341.

when Fetter said he didn't send any notes! I told everyone Heneghan did it.

I also was the target of Grandma's postal chicanery. At least, I think I was. She never owned up to it, even when directly challenged.

While in college at DePauw, I received a mysterious piece of mail. It was a postcard with a picture of a French maid on the front and a bizarre message on the back:

Dear Handsome-

Eyeballed you at the ND - Michigan St. game. Whoop de doo! Woweee and oolala! (I'm French!). We'd make an awesome duo!! Meet me at the Moses statue after the USC game for some French cookin.'

   -Suzette

It seemed like Grandma's handiwork, but the handwriting didn't match. I tossed it in a shoebox and returned to my studying. Then, a few weeks later, I received another postcard—this one with a World War II era sailor holding a rifle and bayonet on the front, and a more sinister message, in *different handwriting*, on the back:

Handsome-

This rugged sea boy reminded me of you but I'm sure he's nicer. Actually, I'd like to use his bayonet on you. Why didn't you meet me at Moses after the USC game as we planned? – Another dolly?? Where will we rendezvous next? How about a trip to Baghdad together soon?

   XX – Suzette

I later learned that my brothers and several cousins had, during their college years, received similar cards from increasingly scorned admirers. Suzette was not alone, apparently. "Peaches" and "Trixie" had also stalked MJ's grandsons through cryptic postcards bearing Chicago postmarks. Either Grandma had a hand in it, or it is one of the world's strangest coincidences. When confronted with the evidence, she just threw up her hands and laughed and said she didn't know who it could be ... I guess we'll never know for sure.

There are other moments I shared with my grandmother that I will always personally cherish. I don't claim these stories are funnier or more interesting than anyone else's. They would probably not make the *Grandma's Greatest Hits* album or even the Hot 100. But hopefully they capture some of her spirit and perhaps prompt others to smile and chime in with their own tales of the woman we called MJ, Mom, Ma, and Grandma Murph.

In 2010, I had been living with my cousin Patrick on the north side of Chicago. In an odd twist of fate, we lived on North Bell Avenue, the very same street as our grandma's house, twenty miles due north. It was a blast. We had youth, few responsibilities, and enough money to entertain ourselves—but not enough money to do any real damage. We threw a couple of parties that I maintain rivaled some of the legendary affairs on South Bell Ave. But when Pat decided to get married and I decided to go to law school, the world's greatest roommate combination (self-proclaimed) was torn asunder. There were a few months between the time our lease was up and when I would start classes at Notre Dame, so I packed my things and moved from 3500 North Bell to 11333 South Bell, where my new, 89-year-old roommate waited.

We too were a great combination. I think Grandma felt safer having someone younger in the house and we both enjoyed chatting while watching a ballgame or reading the newspaper. Plus, she did my laundry.[4]

She asked me about books I was reading—biographies, usually. I asked about books she was reading—stories about cats who solve mysteries, usually. But she also dabbled in stories about priests who solve mysteries, and when she ran out of cats and priests solving mysteries, she turned to ordinary detectives solving mysteries.

Still, there is no such thing as *perfect* roommates. Eventually, disagreements will arise. For example, from years of living alone after Jerome died, Grandma had developed an obsessive habit of locking doors. Many is the time I would make a quick trip to the basement to shower or

---

4 It's true, and no, I'm not ashamed of it. *She* offered and why would I say no?

158

grab a drink from the refrigerator, only to find that she had locked me down there. If I was lucky, she would hear the pounding on the basement door and free me. But she was deaf in one ear and the other was nothing to brag about, so more often than not I was forced to go outside via the back door, walk around the house and rap on the front windows to try to get her attention. When she finally noticed me, she would open the door with a laugh and say, *"Ahh, I guess I locked you out!"* It became part of our routine.

As for my flaws (if you can even call them that), several of my roommates over the years have observed that I can be a touch untidy. For example, when I am through with an article of clothing, I simply discard it on the floor with tentative plans to retrieve it later. The system works just fine for me, but my cohabitants are less impressed. Grandma was stunned when she discovered my habit of leaving dirty socks around the house. Couldn't wrap her head around it. And when she saw the state of my bedroom, she was *aghast*. One day after coming home from work, I was greeted by a large, yellow, handmade sign posted on the door of my bedroom.

CONDEMNED
By Order of the City of Chicago

> This location has been deemed unfit for human habitation due to extreme messiness. All occupants must vacate the premises until toxic waste crews are able to clear the area.

It seems I had earned a scorpion.

It was during my tenancy at Grandma's that I witnessed one of the most infamous moments in sports history. June 2, 2010. We were sitting together in the TV room. Grandma was, as usual, reading a novel about a mystery-solving cat—it may have been called *The Cat Who Knew a Cardinal.* I also had felines on the mind as I watched the Detroit Tigers baseball game on TV.

My beloved Tigers have a long and storied history from Ty Cobb to Miguel Cabrera, but no pitcher for the team has ever thrown a perfect game. In over 120 years, it has never happened. As I sat next to my grandmother on that fateful day, it appeared that the wait for perfection was over. The game was down to the final out. The Tigers' pitcher, Armando Galarraga, had retired 26 batters in a row. The sold-out stadium crowd was on its feet, cameras flashing. My heart raced as I gripped the arms of my chair.

Galarraga delivered a curveball. The batter hit a slow roller toward first base. This was it! The first baseman collected the ball and tossed it to the covering pitcher, who stepped on the bag a half-step before the runner. The crowd erupted. History made!

"Safe!" the umpire called, emphatically.

"... Safe? Safe?! *Safe???* ARE YOU KIDDING ME?!!"

I flew out of my chair in a rage. I screamed at the TV. I pulled my hair out. I fell to my knees and pounded the floor. The weeping, the gnashing of teeth—the whole bit. Meanwhile in Detroit, the crowd was apoplectic. The announcers were speechless. The first baseman had to be restrained from assaulting the umpire. Even the batter held his hands on his head in disbelief.

As the broadcast showed the replay (close calls were not reversible in those days), I thought, *maybe the first baseman pulled his foot off the ba—* No! No! No! No! No! No! No! No! ARE YOU KIDDING ME?!? He was out by a mile! Back to the floor I went for some more screaming and writhing in agony.

I eventually sank back into my chair, completely disgusted, not just with the call, but with life itself. Finally, I glanced over at Grandma, who had been watching the spectacle in silence. She looked at me sympathetically, but I detected a suppressed, barely perceptible smile. Histrionics over sports were the norm in the Murphy house. For decades she had witnessed similar exhibitions from her late husband and offspring in that very same room. Perhaps the scene reminded her of seventy years of blown calls, clanked free throws, pathetic tackles, double-faults, botched field goals, pushed putts, swings-and-misses, and inexplicable coaching decisions that came before.

"*Ahhh,*" she sighed, lifting her hands in a consolatory shrug. "*He* was out."

Sigh. That he was, Grandma. That he was.

Speaking of sports (as Howard Cosell would say), Mary Jane enjoyed watching them but not as much as she loved playing them. She was a true tomboy (an expression that has fallen out of favor despite being a perfect descriptor. Anyway, the label was self-applied). Like her own father, she played golf whenever she had time. She did not have much distance off the tee but played smart and consistent. And unlike most amateur golfers I've come across, she did not take herself too seriously. She carried just four clubs in a flimsy cloth bag—a driver, long iron, short iron, and putter—and really that was probably one club more than she needed. She also had a wonderful knack for getting on the course for free. I guess the managers at the pro shop took a liking to the friendly, little white-haired lady with the tattered golf bag and clubs from the 1950s.

Tennis was her first love, athletically speaking. As a young girl, she watched players at the local tennis court and collected any tennis balls they were willing to part with. She took up the sport as a child and continued through her teens and into her twenties. Raising ten children limited her playing time until the house emptied out; then she played at least twice a week until beyond the age of 90. MJ's letters from home would always include details about the friends she played with and the result of the match:

> I played tennis again with Ginny Kaiser and she beat me again. However, I'll not give up. I expect to be able to beat her when I get back into playing shape. Can't play tomorrow as I have to play golf.

I played against Grandma a few times as a cocky youngster and found myself humbled. Having had no formal lessons, she was not a model of textbook fundamentals, but she was tricky. Her shots had unusual spin and you never could predict which way the ball would bounce. She would wind up to blast a powerful forehand only to, with a last-second twist of the wrist, place a beautiful drop shot. A ball that looked out of her reach turned into a lob over my head. And when I stormed the net expecting a short one, she swatted a backhand right past me. No middle school boy wants to lose an athletic competition *to his grandma*. Yet there I was, congratulating her on the match. She laughed and said I better practice up for when we played next time.

She was delighted for the opportunity to watch "the Virginia Slims," a group of professional women who toured the country in the 1970s and put on tournaments. The Slims were sponsored by the cigarette maker of the same name (who better to sponsor professional athletes?). MJ marveled at their skill—and some of the pros even marveled at *her*. She wrote:

> Thursday two of the players from the Slims came to our tennis club to give us some tips. About 20 of us were in the group and we got to take turns hitting with the pros and they would give us pointers and tips. One pro said she didn't know what to tell *me* because she'd never hit with anyone who hit exactly like me, and we all had a big laugh over that. She said she wished she had my topspin, and everyone clapped.

The episode with the Slims—MJ laughing along with her friends at her unorthodox playing style—not only shows her modesty but how popular she was with her tennis pals. She was a challenging opponent and played to win, but it was always fun. She was gracious in victory and defeat and the most important thing was getting the next match on the schedule.

In 2010, MJ's friends arranged for local media to come out and witness the 90-year-old tennis-playing sensation. Bashfully, she agreed to be interviewed and filmed by local news outlets. On a sleepy day in November, the extended Murphy family woke up to a series of news stories like this one:

90-Year-Old Says Tennis Keeps Her Young

Mary Jane "Tiger" Murphy, 90, still plays with the same spirit she started with 80 years ago.

"When we went out to play we didn't have lessons like the kids do now. But, I probably do everything wrong," said Murphy. But she really does everything just about right. Murphy has a good serve that's almost always on target. And her 90-year-old legs still get her where she has to get on that court. Mary Casserly has been playing with Murphy for 40 years.

"We call her the Energizer Bunny. She has a lot of great drop shots. A lot of great lobs," said Casserly.

"Tough, tenacious. She just never gives up. She'll run into the net. Through the net," said Elaine Tryjefaczka, tennis friend.

"She's very challenging," said Glenda Capuano, tennis partner. "That's why we call her Tiger."

Murphy began playing as a young girl in Avalon Park in Chicago at the local tennis court with used tennis balls collected from players, now she's a local legend with no shortage of potential opponents. She admits that a lot has changed in the sport since she began playing as a young girl.

"When we started they were all wooden rackets," she says looking at the one in her hand and cracks a smile. "Now they're mostly metal and I don't know, uranium? titanium? Or something or other."

Tennis and a healthy diet, she says, are a big part of her good health. That--and Murphy never sits still.

"Just keep moving. Keep doing something. On the days that I don't play tennis or golf or something, I go out and rake the leaves or cut the grass," said Murphy.

Tiger got her start in tennis when she was just a cub in 1930 at Avalon Park on Chicago's South Side. In those days, little girls weren't supposed to be such active athletes.

"I think I was a tomboy. I used to play football out in the street with my brothers and the boy next door," said Murphy.

How long does Murphy intend to keep it up?

"Well maybe another eighty," said Murphy.[5]

---

5 The entirety of the article from ABC Chicago is included and *available at* https://abc13.com/archive/7808614/. For the sake of readability, I also inserted a couple of paragraphs from the original NBC Chicago story, *available at*

The story ran on the local news in Chicago and then it hit the wire. Boy, did it hit the wire! For the next week, dozens of outlets from New York to LA and everywhere in between ran some version of the tale of the tennis-playing grandmother. It was shared on Facebook and blogged in every corner of the internet. To our great surprise, Grandma had gone viral.

For her part, MJ thought all the attention was a little silly. She put her foot down when late-night television hosts offered to fly her to L.A. to appear on their shows. For us, it was a perfect exclamation point to Grandma's athletic career and a fitting final chapter of her life. It was a way for us to share—literally with the whole world—this exceptional woman we loved so dearly. A woman who gave us more laughs than we can count, more stories than we can tell, more love than we can measure, and yes—a few scorpions when we deserved them.

Mary Jane Dwyer Murphy died in 2019, two days shy of her 99th birthday. In some ways it feels like she's still around—hers was such a life force. I can still hear that unforgettable voice (though that may be owing to the fact that her five daughters sound more like her every day). Her spirit lingers over family parties—still held at the Murphy House, with my Aunt Shannon now assuming the role of spirited hostess. Conversation among Murphys invariably turns to memories of MJ. We can't stop talking about her. I don't think we ever will.

> Remember when Mom ordered two desserts every night at Tabor Farm?
>
> Remember when Grandma would hide that rubber witch in the cabinet to scare us?
>
> Remember when MJ bought those goofy hats at the flea market?
>
> Remember when Grandma gave me that plastic, bloody foot for Christmas?

---

https://www.nbcchicago.com/news/local/grandma-90-dubbed-tiger-on-tennis-court/1862035/.

Remember when Ma played golf with that man who called himself "GOD"?

Remember when Grandma made us climb onto the museum exhibit for a picture?

Remember when Dad hit MJ in the leg with his tee shot?

Remember when Grandma made us see who could stand on one foot the longest?

Remember when Mom ate the full box of Fannie May?

Remember when Grandma would chase us around with the gigantic pacifier that she called "The Plug"?

Remember when we used to sing the "Grandma Fight Song?"

Remember when Ma falsified our birth certificates so we could get jobs?

Remember when Grandma rollerbladed down Bell Avenue?

Remember when Mom dispensed sulfa pills for any and all ailments?

Remember when Grandma would creep forward at us when she took pictures?

    Remember when . . .

        Remember when . . .

            Remember when . . .

It was not a swanky place, very much off the beaten path, and the cottages were refurbished railroad cars.

12
What We Have

Zzzzz . . . Zzzzz . . . Zzzzz . . .

Miiike Clauuuuuus! Miiike Clauuuuuus!

What? What's that? Who's there?

Wake up, Miiike Clauuuuuus!

Agh! It's a g-g-ghost! . . . Who are you, spirit?!

I am the Ghost of the Family's Histoooryyy.

Why are you talking like that?

I told you. I am a ghoooost. This is how we taaaalk.

Why are you here, Ghost of the Family's History?

I show you shadows of the things that have been.

Come again?

I show you scenes from the past.

Oh, do you? And the present and the future as well, I presume? This should be a lot of fun!

Noooo. Just the past. Now, pay attention. Tonight, you will visit a scene of old faaaaamily loooore. You shall journey to--

I know what I want to see.

Please don't interruuuuupt. You will visit the scene of an old Irish schoolhouse--

No, thank you. I know where we should go. Take me to--

You are not in charge here! You don't get to make wishes. I'm not a genie!

Why can't I choose? Look, your whole act is all over the place. We've got the Ebenezer Scrooge routine going but it's the middle of July! The readers are completely confused. You're just making it up as you go along, so I can too. Now, are you going to help me or not?

Ugh ... Fine. Grab hold of my robe and I shall take you.

Really? Your robe? Aren't you supposed to be more of the Jacob Marley figure, foretelling what the other spirits have got cooked up for me? Marley didn't wear a robe. He wore the chains he forged in life. The book was very clear on that point. It was the three spirits that wore--

I SUPPOSE you'd prefer a pair of ruby slippers to click together and magically transport you there! Or shall I call Doc Brown and have him swing by in his DeLorean? I really don't have time for this. TAKE THE DARN ROBE! Err-- taaake the rooooobe." Very well, then. Where to?

Spirit, take me to Sodus, Michigan. 1961. 10:00 p.m.

A starry night in August. A company of around fifteen people, most sitting in lawn chairs, is gathered outside a small, white cottage. A dozen or more similar cottages can be seen scattered throughout the wooded area, but this one has drawn the crowd. Golf clubs lean against the wall of the cottage near a couple of aluminum coolers. The smell of cigarettes fills the air. Despite the balminess, some of the men are in sport coats, while the women wear bright sundresses in stark contrast to their rustic surroundings. Their bellies are full—earlier tonight they were in the dining hall, scarfing down roast beef, vegetables, homemade rolls, mashed potatoes with gravy, and freshly baked pastries for dessert. After dinner, they sent the kids to the "lodge" for ice, then made the short walk back to the cottage. A few cases of beer waited for them there, in the same spot they had left them when they had all met before the dinner bell rang. Soon, the youngsters were tucked into bed and the older kids ran off to enjoy themselves.

The ensemble has grown since the pre-dinner gathering. One of their number met some nice folks from Ohio at dinner and invited them back to join the fun. The conversation is lively—aided by the beer and cocktails, sure—but mostly by the spirit of friendship and family that binds them. Their laughter echoes across the grounds, over the swimming pool and tennis courts, and out beyond the golf course. Every now and again a song breaks out. Later, many will return to the dining hall for yet another feast at the resort's famous "midnight snack" hour when the guests are allowed free reign in the kitchen. Some will call it a night after that; others will return to their lawn chairs.

One of the revelers attracts more attention than the rest—the same man who befriended the strangers from Ohio. He is not boisterous but when he speaks, everyone listens. He introduces the newcomers to the group and makes sure they have drinks and comfortable chairs. He asks about their line of work and how they ended up here in Michigan at the summer resort called Tabor Farm. The conversation drifts from the news, to sports, to the real estate market. Before long, someone asks the man to sing an old song and he obliges with *Walking My Baby Back Home*, or perhaps *Sentimental Journey*, or *I Found a Million Dollar Baby*. Sometimes the others join in; other times they just sit, listen, and enjoy. The vocalist is named Jerome Timothy Murphy. They affectionately call him Jerry, Jer, or Murph.

Jerome and Mary Jane first visited Tabor Farm on their honeymoon in 1946. It was not a swanky place, very much off the beaten path, and the cottages were refurbished railroad cars. But it had everything they wanted. Delicious food. Tennis courts. A swimming pool. Plenty of friendly guests to meet. Best of all, a free, nine-hole golf course. They enjoyed themselves so much that they invited their friends and went back. For many years it was the only place the Murphy family vacationed. On rare occasions later in life, Jer and MJ checked out other, more exotic locales. There was a weekend in Las Vegas. A golf excursion to Florida. On a trip to South Carolina in 1989, Jerome saw the ocean for the first time (at age 73!). For Jerry, none compared to Tabor Farm.[1]

Of the grandparents I had a chance to know, I spent the least time with my Grandpa Murphy. Gipper, as his older grandchildren often called him,[2] lived in Chicago and we lived in Michigan, so most of our interactions were limited to holidays and summer vacations. Dad would cram our bags into the plastic car top carrier and strap it to the roof of the family station wagon. Optimistic plans to "make good time" to Chicago were inevitably derailed by bathroom breaks and a stop for dinner, turning a five-hour drive into a seven-or-eight-hour slog. At Gary, Indiana—it was always at Gary—our progress would go from slog to sloth. There we would sit for another hour or two, parked on the highway amongst thousands of incensed travelers, breathing in that distinctive local brew of carbon monoxide from the cars' exhaust pipes and sulphur dioxide from the city's steel plants.

When we finally arrived at "Grandma's house," she would greet us at the door and bring out the snacks, ready for a party. Grandpa usually would emerge a while later and give us all big hugs. He would ask us about school

---

1 As a detail too strange to go unmentioned, the owners and proprietors of Tabor Farm—the same couple who served the food, manicured the golf course, rationed the ice, and made sure everyone had fresh sheets—would go on to become the President and First Lady of Lithuania. The country! Do with that information what you will.

2 The name is a nod to the Notre Dame Fighting Irish football legend, and is, as it happens, how his oldest grandchild (my brother Chas) pronounced the word "Grandpa" as a toddler.

and how our sports teams were doing. Then, a few minutes before 8:00, or 9:00, and *definitely* by 10:00—he would drift to the TV room to watch the nightly news on a strange channel we did not get at home, called WGN. Then he would fall asleep in his recliner with his crossword puzzle on his lap.

Unlike Grandma, she of boundless energy, Gipper always *seemed* old to me. He had survived several major heart and cancer scares in the 1970s and 80s, but his body never really recovered. He still went to his law office every morning and always made sure we were all up for church on Sundays, but he moved slowly, and you got the sense that the daily grind was just that. Looking back, I think he was a guy who got old faster than he had expected and certainly faster than he had hoped. He died when I was a freshman in high school, more than twenty years before his wife.

It's a shame we didn't have more quality time together in his healthier years because, of all my grandparents, I think we are probably most alike in temperament and interests. Granny was much sweeter than I could ever hope to be. Walt and Ralph were more serious, deep thinkers, with little interest in sports. And my default setting is grumpier than Grandma Murphy on her worst day. Gipper was a lawyer, a sports nut, and a night owl. I suspect that he was at his best when he could unwind after the responsibilities of the week were finished. I imagine us out together late on a Friday night at the bowling alley or staying for one more round at the bar—after dusting the competition in a men's 16-inch softball game. We might run into some of his buddies from the South Side's NFL team—not the Chicago Bears, but the Chicago Cardinals—who often asked him to sing at the piano. Or maybe we'd just find a quiet table and discuss some legal case or bit of local news while he enjoyed a cigarette and I, a cigar.

Whenever I discuss memories of Jerome with his children—my mom and aunts and uncles—the refrain is always the same:

"I wish you could have known him when he was younger."

He was, all report, fun and magnetic, friendly and charming. A charismatic man who would command a room. So that's why if I ever am visited by a cantankerous, time-traveling vision ghost, I already know exactly what I want to see first. Jerome sitting outside a cottage at Tabor Farm. Grandpa at his healthiest, in one of his favorite places, with some of his favorite people—relaxed, chatting, and singing. Completely in his element.

Jerome Timothy Murphy was born October 20, 1916, arriving in the world with his twin sister, Catherine. There were no ultrasound machines at the time, so his parents were surely surprised and a little sad to see that baby Jerome was born without a left arm.

Yes, Grandpa Murphy only had one arm, and it might be odd to introduce that fact so late in the story. After all, it was a physical handicap that could have defined his life. Think of the many ordinary activities we perform that are best done with two arms. Tying shoes, paging through a book, and writing, to name a few (his handwriting was notoriously poor, with no second hand to hold the paper steady). And when he was older—changing diapers, raking leaves, and tying a tie. Pouring a hot cup of coffee was always a risky venture. He once botched a pour that sent more coffee on his son Brian's lap than in the cup. Brian cried, "Dad! You're spilling on me!" Prompting Jerry's now infamous response, *"I'm* not spilling it! It's spilling *itself!"*

Jerome's handicap *could* have defined him, but he wouldn't allow it. Nor would his mother, Jennie (Sheehan) Murphy. When he was eight years old, Jennie gave her son some advice that he remembered for the rest of his life. Perhaps he was upset that he couldn't climb trees with the rest of the boys in the neighborhood, or play piano, or some other youthful frustration that came with being different. His mother sat him down and told him, "Do the best you can with what you have."

That's another moment I'd like to see. The tough old Irish gal giving her youngest son straight, frank guidance, but with a mother's compassion.

"Jerome," she may have said, pulling him close. "God only gave you one arm and nothing is going to change that. But the arm He gave you is strong, and you have two good legs, and a great mind, and a big heart. Now, do the best you can with what you have."

That is what defined Jerry's life. Not that he had just one arm, but what he could do—and did do—in spite of it.

"Do the best you can with what you have." Young Jerome loved sports. He could not swim and wasn't much on the basketball court. But he could bowl, play softball, (he was a pitcher and could crush the ball, one-armed, at the plate), and golf (with left-handed clubs, swinging backhand).

172

He also loved music, but there would be no piano or saxophone lessons. Because he was blessed with a great singing voice, he made music that way. In high school he joined the Glee Club, and for years after he wrote, directed, and performed in variety shows to help raise money for his parish and community.

As for a career, his father, John Murphy, worked loading freight for the railroad. Manual labor was not going to be an option for Jerome, but he figured he could rely on his brain to make a living. In the end, he chose to do neither ... and decided to become a lawyer.

Get it? That is what is known as a "lawyer joke." It's about as amusing as lawyer jokes get, which means it may elicit something between an eye roll and a polite chuckle. Lawyer jokes just aren't very funny (as opposed to the always uproarious Pomeranian jokes[3]), so I generally avoid telling them. However, there is a lawyer joke that always makes me think of Gipper:

> An exasperated CEO calls his secretary into his office.
> "Get me a one-armed lawyer!" he yells.
> The confused secretary asks, "Why do you want a one-armed lawyer?"
> The CEO replies, "All these guys I hire from big law firms keep telling me, 'On the one hand you should do this. But on the other hand, you shouldn't.' I need a one-armed lawyer to give me a straight answer!"

It turns out that lots of people wanted the advice of this real-life, one-armed lawyer. For more than fifty years, the one-armed lawyer was one of the most well-known and respected attorneys on the South Side of Chicago. Even more impressive because he was not a flashy trial lawyer whose name splashed the newspaper headlines. He was the trusted neighborhood solicitor on everything from real estate deals to child adoptions, and was elected the first president of the South Side Bar Association. Incredibly, Jerome's grandson—also named Jerome Murphy—also a Chicago lawyer—is still approached by old attorneys and judges (some thirty years later) who recognize the name and recall what a great man the one-armed lawyer was.

---

3 *See* Chapter Five.

Jerry's earliest clients were friends looking to purchase a home or needing help handling the estate of a deceased relative. He built a thriving practice through word-of-mouth and referrals. Folks trusted his advice—the hallmark of a good lawyer—and were happy to recommend him. In Jerome's first year he made $500, which, even adjusted for inflation is only about $9,000. By 1955, he had saved enough to purchase the large house on South Bell Avenue for the bargain price of $27,500.

Real estate and probate were specialties, but Jerry was also willing to take risks if he liked an opportunity. He invested in properties that looked promising and in 1963, built and founded a secretarial training school called the Southwest School of Business. His work kept him at the office on many nights and weekends, but he appreciated staying busy. It meant his services were valued.

Now that I'm a father and provider, I have found one of the most difficult aspects of life is transitioning from "work mode" to "home mode." I'm not very good at it. I might spend nine or ten hours at work thinking about some thorny legal issue—up to and including during my walk home from the train station. Then I open the door and am greeted by my beautiful wife and adorable kids who are eager to discuss the happenings of their day—only to find their long-awaited husband/father is staring off into space, still brooding on whether my client has complied with Rule 4, or Rule 26, or, heaven help us, Rule 11.

Jerome probably experienced something similar, except he came home from work each night to the world of *ten* children and whatever problems or issues they may have. Kerry was still looking for a summer job. Tim wanted to borrow the car. Kevin needed new basketball shoes. Sally hurt herself on the monkey bars. The tuition check for St. Cajetan school was due. He would sit down to dinner, address any domestic problems needing his attention, maybe read the newspaper, and then, because work was so busy, he often went back to the office—back to the world of closings and escrow and statutes and disclosures. It must have been exhausting.

During a major health emergency for Jerry in 1981, Mary Jane wrote a "Dear Ones All" letter to her children, expressing a wife's concern and reflecting on all "Dad" did for the family. Here again, I can relate. Aspirationally, I mean. I might not be the best father around (though my

"#1 DAD" coffee mug says otherwise) but if someone ever says this about me, I'll have done my job:

> It's a big worry and should make us all stop and think about Dad. He's always been there to help when there's trouble and never blames anyone. He just gives good advice and strong support and hard-earned cash if needed.

Jerome's hard-earned cash put his children through Catholic elementary and high schools, and then nine colleges. It was especially generous because he had little use for ivy-walled institutions of higher learning, having himself only had a year or two of junior college before law school. He referred to expensive, four-year universities as "playgrounds" and was not interested in visiting campuses unless it was for a sporting event. Despite his reservations, he always sent the checks to Dayton, Notre Dame, Hillsdale, Lewis, and DePaul. As someone who understood cost-benefit analysis, he knew that in those days a 4-year degree was one of the surest ways to put his children on the path to success. The playgrounds got their money, and the kids got their degrees.

Jerry was a man of strong opinions and took a rather curmudgeonly attitude to activities and events he deemed to be "goofy" or a waste of time. Long-winded priests and youth coaches endlessly babbling at end-of-season banquets were particularly irritating. As were graduation ceremonies, which combined the pretention of the college playgrounds with the long-winded babblers. MJ described Jerry's reaction when Sally's husband Peter, trying to be polite, invited them to his graduation from Business School:

> Dad declined not very graciously, saying he *hated* graduations and had been to too many of them already!

He held a similar view of wedding rehearsals. He felt that his role as father of the betrothed was not difficult and certainly did not require rehearsing. It was this self-assurance—some might call it pigheadedness—that produced a great moment in family history.

It is known in some circles as The Battle of the Blusher. To others it is The Trial in the Aisle. The Falter at the Altar. The Sacramental Scrap. Jerome's daughter Erin provided her first-hand account of the Tale of the Veil:

> Dad refused to go to the church rehearsal for my wedding. He said that he had already been to plenty of them and he already knew what to do ... walk me down the aisle, give me a kiss, and give my hand to my husband-to-be. So he stayed home (and probably had a few minutes of much deserved peace and quiet) while the rest of us went to the rehearsal. The big day arrived, and I wore a long white gown and a veil with a blusher. The blusher is netting which falls in front of the bride's face. Dad walked me down the aisle in front of many family and friends. When we reached the altar, he lifted the blusher and pushed it back over my head, and gave me a kiss. Then he reached back and pulled the blusher back down over my face. I grabbed the blusher and started lifting it, but he quickly batted it down, almost like he was swatting a fly. I was startled, but regained my composure and lifted the blusher again. Just as quickly, he swatted it down again! Up, down, up, down, arms swinging so quickly that it was beginning to look like a karate match. I lifted the veil, gave him a dirty look, and said to him through clenched teeth, *"It's supposed to stay up!"* Dad gave my hand to Joe, who smiled and said to me, "You look beautiful." I graciously responded by scowling back, "He should have gone to the rehearsal!"

Yes, he was stubborn and could be impatient, but it would be a disservice to linger on those traits. What set Jerome T. Murphy apart was his caring heart. His clients, friends, and family all felt it. If someone had a problem, they knew Jerry would set aside what he was doing and find a way to help. As he grew into a man, Jerome developed a fondness for people, kids especially, who might be lonely or feel left out. I have no evidence of this, but my hunch is that it was a product of growing up different than the others. By the time he was an adult, nobody gave his missing arm a second thought. But kids can be cruel. When he was young, he may have been teased or banished to the sidelines. As an adult, he quietly kept watch for anyone who might be experiencing something similar.

We see this remarkable quality on display during a fourth-grader's birthday party in the basement of the Murphy house. Jerry and MJ had a rule about birthday parties: *all* the kids in the class got an invitation. After the party, a father pulled Jerome aside and earnestly thanked him. This was the only birthday party his daughter had been invited to that year and he so appreciated the Murphys' kindness.

We see that quality in the gymnasium at Mother McAuley High School. The Father-Daughter Dance was the event of the year for ninth graders at the all-girls school. For weeks the girls gabbed excitedly about dresses, shoes, and hair, and crossed their fingers that their fathers would not embarrass them. When the evening finally arrived, Jerome brought *two* dates—his oldest daughter Colleen, and her classmate Joann. Joann's father had died when she was in third grade, and she had no one else to take her. Jerry would not let that girl be left out.

We see it in the kitchen of the Murphy home too, where the family telephone rested on the high radiator. Every homecoming or prom season brought a steady ringing of phone calls from teenagers looking for dates to the dance. The House Rule, instituted by MJ and enforced by JTM, was controversial: If someone has the courage to ask you to the dance, you say "yes," or you don't go at all. No waiting for someone cuter or more popular. Never mind if they have the personality of a wet noodle and look like Eleanor Roosevelt. Jerry wouldn't allow his own children to ruin someone else's night. The Murphy teenagers *hated* this rule, but the central location of the phone meant there was no weaseling out of it (they sometimes tried). I think most of them have now grown to appreciate the sentiment.

Yet again, we see this quality in the Murphy dining room, absolutely overflowing with guests on Thanksgiving, Easter, and Christmas. It was not just his large, immediate family that he welcomed to his table. Places were set for the elderly bachelor and his sister, for the widowed cousin, for the lonely client, even for a couple of old nuns he had met at Misericordia. If you had nowhere else to be, you could be with Jerome and his family.

That may have been Grandpa's greatest quality—his ability to find humble ways to make folks feel special and loved. I include myself among those on the receiving end of his quiet kindness, though I almost did not bother recounting for the reading public one of my favorite memories.

There really isn't that much to it. Spoiler: it ends with Grandpa buying me some candy. A nice gesture, I'm sure all would agree, but not exactly earth-shattering. Grandfathers have been plying their grandchildren with sweet treats since old Father Abraham bounced Jacob on his knee and slipped him a honey-coated locust when Isaac wasn't looking.[4] So, as I say, I *almost* didn't bother telling it. But in the course of researching, I came across something that gave me the proverbial goosebumps.

Two years after his death, Jerome's children and grandchildren shared some memories of Gipper in an email thread. My Uncle Mike compiled the emails and had them printed for future readings and future readers. It's a fantastic tribute, with the advantage that many of the Murphys are excellent writers. For example, the story of Erin's epic blusher battle, reprinted above, is included in the accounts. But what struck me with the aforementioned goose b.'s, was a very sweet memory shared by my mother:

> I always liked taking walks around the neighborhood with Dad. It was very social and you felt important just being with him because everyone seemed to like and respect him. We'd stop and talk and laugh at about every other house, taking about an hour just to go a couple of blocks! Sometimes we had the "little kids" with us, but often it was just the two of us. Our walks together always ended at the drugstore and Dad would buy whatever—a pair of shoelaces, some Dr. Scholl's footpowder, some aspirin; then he'd buy me a Snickers bar to eat on the way home. We didn't have candy all that often, so it was kind of a secret treat between the two of us. You may have noticed that to this day I have a love of fine chocolate—Snickers bars remain one of my favorites!

Now, my story, that I almost didn't tell: We were spending Easter in Chicago. It may have been Good Friday. As usual, the Murphy house was jammed with about fifty people, including twenty of us grandchildren. It was a loud, chaotic scene. I was probably around ten years old.

I was in the kitchen for some reason—perhaps just passing through on my way to the basement, when my mom stopped me and looked me right in the eyes.

"Grandpa is going to the store. Do you want to go with him?"

---

4 Probably.

Just me?, I thought. This was an unusual ask. As the eighth of an eventual thirty grandchildren, there weren't a lot of moments alone with Gipper. It was a problem of sheer numbers. And I don't think I'd ever *gone* anywhere with Grandpa, just the two of us. I'm not sure why I was selected. I may have just been the closest to the door where he was gathering his coat.

Judging by the preposterous heights to which Mom had raised her eyebrows when she asked if I wanted to go with Grandpa, I knew the answer should be in the affirmative. So, I said yes. The truth is, though, I wasn't just being polite—I was excited.

It played out a little differently than my mother's special trips with her dad to the drugstore. The neighborhood had changed and so had Jerome. We drove in his big Buick, rather than walked. There were no stops to chitchat with neighbors, though he did have lots of questions for me as we rode. Our destination was not the charming, locally owned Bercier-Henning drugstore of my mom's youth, but a generic Walgreens. We were gone less than half an hour.

I followed Grandpa around the store. He grabbed whatever it was that he needed, then turned to me.

"Why don't you go pick out some candy you like?"

I hurried over to the candy section and not wanting to look greedy, picked out a small bag of Skittles. He smiled.

"Is that it? Come on! Get something big too."

I didn't need to be told twice. I grabbed the biggest bag of Sour Patch Kids I could find.

"That's more like it!"

Back at the house, a group of cousins gathered around as I enjoyed the fruits of my trip to the store with Grandpa. Naturally, I started with the big bag, right there in the playroom for all to gaze upon in wonder.

"Whoaa! Where did you get that?!"

"Grandpa got it for me," I said, nonchalantly as I could.

"Whooaaaaa!"

It wasn't about the candy, of course. Well, it was, and it wasn't. I *did* enjoy that candy. But really, it was about feeling special. Jerome had a wife, ten children, dozens of grandchildren, and scores of clients and friends, all, in a way, vying for his attention. On that day, in a house practically bursting at the seams with people he loved, I was the one Grandpa took to the store.

I understand now that it's the same feeling my mom felt when she got her secret treat on their walks through the neighborhood. And the same feeling that little girl experienced when she finally got an invitation to someone's birthday party. It was the same feeling for Joann when she learned someone would take her to the Father-Daughter dance. As I think about my own children, I can only hope there is someone in their lives like Grandpa Murphy. Someone who will protect the shy ones and take care that the lonely ones get to play too. I'll have to make sure I surround myself with good people who could fill that role.

Heyyyy, wait a minute! That's not the lesson here. I shouldn't hope for someone like Grandpa to show up—I should be that person!

Jerome Murphy set a great example. It's up to us to follow it. Look out for the little guy. Work hard. Keep family close. Do the best we can with what we have.

What we have ... it's easy to forget, isn't it?

The happiest people you will ever see in the City of Chicago can be found in the lobby of my office at the downtown federal courthouse. A few times a month, dozens of immigrants of varying ethnicities and ages are sworn in as American citizens at a naturalization ceremony held in one of the courtrooms. Sometimes I linger for a while and observe. They hug their families and pose for photographs, often waving tiny American flags and beaming—plainly with the optimism that this nation will provide something their native lands did not.

And the rest of us? It seems we live in a country that is grateful for nothing and angry about everything. If there is a way to be offended, folks will find it. Old-fashioned virtues like hard work, overcoming obstacles, and forgiveness are out, replaced by victimhood, tattling, and narcissism. Social media makes it worse, of course (social media makes everything worse). Any perceived slight, no matter how minor, is broadcast to the world, and the surest way to get attention is to claim the mantle of victimhood. Oh yes, the grievance business is booming. Never mind that by any objective measure we live in the richest, most accepting, most comfortable civilization, for virtually every segment of society, in the history of the world.

Jerome was never a victim. If he ever mentioned his disability, it was matter-of-factly.

"I couldn't work at the freight yard like my dad because of my physical limitations."

That was it. No demands for sympathy or special treatment. He'd rather no one even notice it. To be sure, that attitude reflected the times he lived in, but it also reflected the man. He appreciated that his parents had the courage to leave Ireland. He was grateful for his country and the freedom and opportunity it afforded, and deeply saddened that he could not join his friends to fight in the Second World War. He valued his clients and worked long hours to keep them happy. He loved his large, Catholic family, and insisted that we all stay close. He knew landing Mary Jane was his biggest accomplishment. Jerome T. Murphy knew what he had. Pray that we do too.

Shall I get you a taller sooooaap box?

Agh! Spirit! You're still here?! I thought you'd gone.

Oh no, just waiting for my release. Shall we leave this place?

Please, just a few more minutes? It looks like they're nearly finished.

Back at Tabor Farm, Jerome and his old pal Bill McCummiskey remain, still yapping and laughing, covering much of the same ground from hours earlier. The rest of the crowd has dispersed. Mary Jane retired a few hours ago, reminding her husband that she planned to be back on the golf course early in the morning and he better be ready. And then there were two. Bill suggests cracking one more beer, but Jerry is tired and he knows Mary Jane wasn't kidding about the golf course. The young man says goodnight, hoists himself out of his chair, pats his friend on the back, and disappears into the silent cottage.

PART III

The Big Mix-Up

Oh, it is the biggest mix-up that you have ever seen.
My father, he was Orange and me mother, she was Green.

My father was a Pontiac man, proud Protestant was he.
My mother was a Catholic girl, from county Cook was she.
They were married in two churches, lived happily enough,
Until the day that I was born and things got rather tough.[1]

---

[1] The Irish Rovers. "The Orange and the Green" (parodied).

SOMEONE WAS CRAWLING AROUND ON THE FLOOR THAT DAY.

13

The Trial of Chuck Claus

Order in the court! Order in the court! Re-calling case number 24601, The State vs. R. Charles Claus. *This court is now in session. All the evidence is in. Are the parties prepared for closing arguments? Very good. Counsel for the defense, you may begin.*

Readers of the jury. The facts in this case are distressing. You all know Chuck Claus as the father of your author—a genial, white-haired fellow whose only fault is an unhealthy fixation with catching the weather and traffic report on the radio. But he was once a mere ninth grader, just a lad, trying to chart his path at Eastern Junior High School in Pontiac, Michigan. This trial is about a rather ... *awkward* incident that occurred within those hallowed halls back in 1966. An incident for which, the evidence will show, Chuck is entirely blameless.

One moment Chuck is innocently selling candy bars at a school basketball game. He's helping raise money for the chess club (or something), trying his best to be a forthright and model citizen. The next moment he is sitting in the principal's office, confronted on charges of voyeurism.

Yes, voyeurism! Peeping on a modest woman in a state of undress, a member of the faculty, no less. A shocking accusation levied by the school's gym teacher, Ms. West.[1]

How to describe Ms. West?

Ms. West looked exactly how you would expect a female gym teacher in 1966 to look. Solidly built. Like a Sherman tank in sweats. One could correctly call her "top heavy," but it would be a disservice to her bottom

---

1 The names have been changed to protect the innocent.

half. She was pushing age 60, but could still pommel a horse, if you know what I mean.[2]

According to Ms. West, she was in her office after the basketball game, changing from her sweats to … whatever gym teachers wear when they are not in sweats. The gymnasium was on one side of the closed door and Ms. West's office was on the other. Near the bottom of the door—this part is important, so please pay attention—near the bottom of the door was an open vent that provided some air circulation in the windowless gym. However, in the extremely unlikely event that someone happened to be crawling around on the floor near the door, they just might be able to see into her office from the gymnasium, and anyone in the office could see out.

Well, someone *was* crawling around on the floor that day. As I mentioned, Chuck was working the concession stand at the basketball game. Earlier that day, he had dragged a folding table across the gymnasium floor over to the doorway where he set things up. After finishing with his sales duties, Chuck, being that forthright and model citizen, returned to the gym after the game to make sure he had not scratched the floor. He walked back and forth, his eyes trained on the floor, scanning for the slightest mark. He even got down on his hands and knees to get a good, close look at things. Having performed his inspection and found all satisfactory, he skipped off to his next adventure.

A few minutes later (I think Chuck was clapping erasers for the Science teacher at the time), the school principal, Mr. Lopez, approached.

"Chuck. Will you come to my office, please?"

How to describe Mr. Lopez?

Mr. Lopez was a passionate educator and administrator and took his vocation seriously. If there was a problem in his school, he would get to the bottom of it. Mr. Lopez also was barely five feet tall, balding, and weighed about 110 pounds. Any of the girls on the Eastern Junior High School basketball team would have dominated him in the paint. An imposing figure, Mr. Lopez was not. So, while getting called to the principal's office rarely portends good news, Chuck was not exactly scared. In fact, Mr. Lopez looked considerably more shaken than Chuck as they shuffled into the headmaster's sanctum.

---

2 I don't think *I* know what I mean.

Chuck sat across from Mr. Lopez. The man, usually a picture of dignified professionalism, was visibly uncomfortable. He fidgeted. He fidgeted in his chair. He fidgeted with his tie. He fidgeted with a pen. After what felt like several minutes of silent fidgeting, he addressed the accused.

"I've just been speaking to Ms. West."

Mr. Lopez peered over at Chuck, hoping the words would trigger some sort of reaction. There was none. He cleared his throat and tried again.

"I've just been speaking to Ms. West," he repeated. "She seems to think that, eh, well..."

He winced and trailed off, apparently wrestling with some dark thoughts. An even longer silence than the first set in. Mr. Lopez sank deep into his chair and stared at the ceiling fan. More fidgeting. Finally, he composed himself and had another go at it.

"Eh, Chuck ... you didn't, eh--you didn't try to, er--you didn't watch Ms. West ... changing her clothes, did you?"

Chuck was aghast.

"*The gym teacher?!* No, sir!"

Mr. Lopez leaned back and released a loud sigh of relief.

"I didn't think so."

Now it was Chuck's turn to fidget. He simply couldn't comprehend the line of questioning.

"But why would I--I mean, why would *anyone?*"

Another pause. Mr. Lopez stared at the ceiling fan. Chuck stared at his shoes. They both shuddered.

"Well, she was getting dressed in her office, and she thought she saw you, er, peeking, eh, through the vent--eh. And I didn't--well, she's not really, um ... You can go now, Chuck."

Chuck staggered to the door, not quite sure if he was awake or in a nightmare. Mr. Lopez opened a window for some fresh air. It had all been a gross misunderstanding. Case closed.

Some of you readers of the jury may be thinking that Mr. Lopez could have done just a little more due diligence before concluding his investigation. Yes, it is true that his enquiry consisted of a single question. But nobody understood his pupils better than Mr. Lopez. Chuck was the son of a preacher. A good student. Well-behaved. The forthright and model Cit. In summary, not the type of boy who goes around trying to peek at aged gym teachers in their undies. If Chuck's denial was good enough for Mr. Lopez, then darn it all, it's good enough for me!

Do you know where the term "peeping Tom" comes from? It's the legend of Lady Godiva. Godiva was, as you may have guessed, a lady. She lived in Coventry, where her husband was the head Earl in charge. The earl loved nothing more than imposing oppressive taxes on the good folks in his earldom. But Godiva was a Lady of the People. She promised to ride a horse, naked, through the streets of the city as a protest against her own husband's policies. To thank her for being such a good sport, the citizens all agreed to cover their eyes as she passed in her birthday suit. When the big day arrived, all went according to script. Godiva rode, the citizens covered—except for one creep named Tom. He peeped. Tom was struck blind for his offense, but at least he had a good excuse. Have you ever seen a statue of Lady Godiva? *Whoaa mama! Ow ow owwww! Hubba hubba! Awooooga! Awooooga!*

(Panting) ... I apologize, Your Honor. I got a little carried away there. All I'm trying to say is that Ms. West was no Lady Godiva, *ergo,* Chuck was no Tom.

Thank you for that, Counselor. Clearly, you make a very compelling argument. I, for one, am convinced. Does the prosecution even wish to proceed, or can we declare this poor man innocent and go home?

Just a few words for the prosecution. Like all of you, I was moved by the words of the learned defense attorney. Everything about Chuck's story seems to check out. Ms. West was no pin-up girl, we can all agree on that. And Chuck did have a perfectly plausible reason for crawling around on the floor. Why was it again that Chuck returned to the gymnasium after his work was done? Ah, that's right. To see if he had left scratches on the floor when moving the concession table. That certainly makes sense. And yet ...

This trial is about a junior high school gym teacher. But let us fast forward a few years. Chuck is now in high school. The Pontiac Central

High School baseball teams are on a bus, coming home from games in Midland. It was a long drive, about three hours.

If you have ever been on a team bus, you know it's rocking after a big win. Songs and chants rattle the walls, guys are hanging out the windows, and you're home before you know it. In contrast, after a loss, the bus may as well be a hearse. A 15-minute drive can feel like an hour, and a three-hour drive is absolute torture.

As the season drew to its end, the Pontiac Central varsity team was playing well, in serious contention for the league crown. The junior varsity team, on the other hand, was not contending for anything other than their pride, something they had abandoned by the third game of the season. The JV was full of scrubs, goof-offs, and, worst of all, belly-itchers—the combination of which had managed to scrape together a grand total of *zero wins* on the season. Unfortunately, things had not gone well for either squad that afternoon in Midland, with both the varsity and junior varsity taking bad L's.

The varsity team sat at the front of the bus, appropriately in silence, pondering what had gone wrong. The junior varsity, meanwhile, sitting in the back of the bus, did not seem especially fazed by their defeat. Actually, they were having a ball. Anticipating the interminable bus ride, they had brought along coolers with snacks and refreshments. They passed around the supplies. They clowned, they laughed, they traded comic books. Someone told the old joke about the Italian grandmother who goes to the ballgame to watch Joe DiMaggio, and they laughed louder still. Their latest loss on the baseball diamond could not have been further from their minds.

All of this did not sit well with those mourning at the front.

One of the varsity team captains—this guy was a real try-hard—came sulking to the back.

"Hey, guys. Coach says no more talking."

The referenced coach was an old school, no-nonsense kind of guy named Ness. He did not tolerate goof-offs and he *despised* belly-itchers. Coach Ness was all business. The headline in the newspaper after his death many years later legitimately read, *"Coach Ness Epitomized Discipline."* So, if Coach Ness said no more talking, he meant no more talking.

189

"Got it," said Chuck. (Did I mention that Chuck was one of the JV guys?) "No more talking, fellas."

The captain moped back to the front of the bus to rejoin the funeral.

The silence was golden but fleeting. Coach Ness had said no more talking—but he didn't say anything about *singing*. Abiding by the letter, but certainly not the spirit of the law, the JV team started in again. A melody began to drift from the rear of the bus. This is not confirmed, but I'm told they did a lovely rendition of *Scarborough Fair* in four-part harmony.

The captain, now joined by the co-captain, sprinted to the back and this time they were not messing around.

"Seriously, shut up guys! Coach is ticked!"

"Hey man, we aren't talking," said one of the wise guys. "We're just singing."

"No more singing!"

Then with great indignation, they reclaimed their seats.

Now Chuck and his teammates were really flummoxed. No talking. No singing. Were they really sentenced to sit in silence for the next 90 minutes? Would they actually have to spend some time contemplating how to improve their game?

I wish I could tell you that the story ended right there, with lessons learned and respect shown and a JV team with a newfound appreciation for the game. My friends, the story does not end there. Because that's when the JV team started *whistling*.

They had only gotten to the third bar of the *Colonel Bogey March* when the crimson-faced figure appeared in their midst. It was not the team captain this time, but none other than the man who epitomized discipline: Coach Ness.

Coach Ness was not pleased. He took a deep breath. What followed was one of the most epic tirades in the history of Michigan high school athletics. He questioned the JV squad's character. Their manhood. Their dedication to the game. Their intellectual capabilities. He observed that they had not been particularly successful that season. He predicted failures in all aspects of their futures. He compared the team's pitchers, unfavorably, to belly-itchers. He dedicated several minutes to hissing personal insults at each of the ringleaders—really cutting stuff. Finally, when things reached a crescendo and with Coach Ness about to run out of breath, he brought forth his final threat, loudest of all, as he thundered,

"Just keep this up and *as God as my witness,* none of you will EVEN SMELL A VARSITY LETTER!!!"

For a few seconds, the only sounds that could be heard were the bus engine and Coach Ness panting. He turned and started the journey back to his seat, exhausted but confident his message had, at last, gotten through. A stillness fell over the bus.

But then—a sound.

Clap.

Clap clap.

Clap clap clap.

Others joined in now.

Clap clap clap clap clap clap clap.

Thunderous applause echoed from the back of the bus. The whole JV team was on their feet now, giving their coach a standing ovation. They began shouting words of mocking approval.

"Great speech!"

"Bravo!"

"You tell 'em, Coach!"

"Author! Author!"

And there was Chuck, cheering with as much gusto as any of them.

Decades later, completely by chance while shopping for flowers on Mother's Day, the Claus family spotted Coach Ness. He was admiring some chrysanthemums, enjoying the company of his family. The old disciplinarian still looked proud, yet there was a sadness in his eyes, as if he had never fully recovered from the indignity of that bus ride so many years ago.

Ladies and gentlemen of the jury, I have some very simple questions for you.

Does the Chuck we just heard about seem mature beyond his years? Does the Chuck we just heard about seem like a boy who holds uncommon respect for authority figures? Does the Chuck we just heard about not only do the right thing, but go out of his way to do the right thing? Does the

Chuck we just heard about seem like a boy who would walk all the way back to the gymnasium ... *just to make sure he did not LEAVE ANY SCRATCHES ON THE FLOOR?!?*

(Gasps! Murmurs! A woman fainting in the front row!)

Order! Order! Order in this court! Mr. Prosecutor, you have made your point. In light of your observations, I believe there is enough evidence to send this case to the jury. What say you, readers of the jury? Just what exactly was Chuck doing on the floor of that gymnasium? You have heard the evidence. We await your verdict.

The locals still talk about the delirious lunatic spotted running through the campus that night.

14

To Hillsdale and Beyond

or

How I Met Your Mother

Kids, I'm going to tell you an incredible story. The story of how I met your mother.

First things first.

I'm standing on the deck of a cottage in Indiana on a cool Fall morning. My wife (she was pregnant with you, Sally) is next to me. It is the weekend of her college Homecoming—a time to see some familiar faces and catch up with her old classmates. Yesterday, the campus was a constant hum of young, recent grads singing their refrain of, *"you look so good!"* and *"this is my husband"* and *"whad'ya hear from so and so?"* Today, however, we are the youngest people at the party by a wide margin. We are surrounded by Boomers.

Just a short drive from the Hillsdale College campus, the white cottage on Clear Lake has been a rallying point for a group of friends on Homecoming weekend and other reunions since the 1970s. As a child of Hillsdale alums, I have been to Clear Lake a handful of times. But as an adult, non-alum, it has been over a decade since my last visit. I married into this.

At the moment, we are being arranged for a photograph. It is a picture that everyone claims they want, yet no one wants to cooperate. Among the non-cooperatives are my parents and my new in-laws, plus a dozen or so of their buddies from the classes of 1974 and 1975 and their spouses. The photographer is instructing this person to crouch down and that person to shift over but no one is listening. They shout, they hoot, they jostle about. Finally, after much cajoling, everyone is in place.

As is tradition, the folks in front are holding a faded painted sign—pilfered from the football field long ago by someone in more reckless days—that reads, "No Alcoholic Beverages in Stadium." In a break with tradition, we are standing with our *backs to the house,* looking out over the lake, while the photographer positions herself in front. Back on the "Traditions Observed" side of the ledger, my dad is stirring the pot.

"Gee, Marion, why would we ever want that stunning view of the lake in the picture? This *blank wall* is a perfect backdrop!"

Marion Griffiths has drawn the short straw and is photographer today. She ignores my father and readies her camera. But then Fred Schultz—he along with his wife, Jan, own the place—announces his agreement.

"Hey, yeah! Why are we facing this way?! What kind of amateur picture is this?!"

A few more voices chime in. Pretty soon the entire group is laser focused on one question: *Why isn't the lake in the picture?*

The crowd—not adolescents, mind you, but retirees with perhaps a head-and-a-half of their original hair color between them—begins chanting in unison.

"We want the lake!"

"We want the lake!"

"We want the lake!!"

"WE WANT THE LAKE!"

Marion is used to the antics of this lot. Like a guard at Buckingham Palace, she is completely impervious to their jeers. In workman-like fashion, she snaps a few photos with six or seven different cameras and dismisses the assembly. The subject of the lake's presence in the photograph is immediately forgotten, replaced by discussions of the new buildings on campus, their preferred brand of CPAP machines, and who is next in line for a knee replacement.

Hillsdale is a tiny college in rural southern Michigan, with an enrollment about half that of my high school. The school is not just a part of our family—it shaped it. My parents, Chuck and Kerry (Murphy) Claus, are alums who met at Hillsdale. As are my brother Chas and his wife Emily (Sawyer), my mom's sister, Shannon (Murphy) Shannon, and Kelly

(Avenall) Pinner, who is not blood-related but may as well be my second sister. My wife, Class of 2011, is even more connected. Her grandparents, Robert and Virginia "Ginny" (Hungerford) Donovan, her father Mark Donovan, her aunt Kerry (Donovan) Cummings, and two brothers, Ross and Jake Donovan, all called themselves Hillsdale Chargers.[1]

Back at Clear Lake, Jan is offering me a cup of coffee when she stops abruptly, literally midsentence. The old friends have begun singing. It is a melody they have sung together many times and Jan adds her voice to the chorus. The song refers to Albion College, a nearby school and one-time rival of Hillsdale. The slow ballad, sung with passion and sentiment, goes like this:

> Don't send my boy to Albion,
> A dying mother said.
> Don't send my boy to Albion,
> I'd rather see him dead.
> But send my boy to HILLSDALE!
> I know he'll do right well.
> But rather than to Albion,
> I'd see my boy in Hell.

The song *is* amusing, but as is so often the case, the historical truth is more nuanced. In reality, my father was just one capable administrator away from attending Albion himself. Indeed, if just a single competent bureaucrat could be found in the Admissions department at Albion, or for that matter within the federal government, Chuck never goes to Hillsdale, never meets Kerry, and this book vanishes from your hands—erased from existence.

Back in 1970, Chuck had been accepted at Albion and was prepared to go. All that remained was his scholarship award. The school assured Chuck they had money allocated for him but required a specific form

---

[1] While technically not an alum myself, my photograph appeared on Page 1 of the Spring/Summer 2023 issue of the Hillsdale alumni magazine, which some would argue is as good as a degree.

verifying his parents' income to make it official. The form they needed, call it Form 4506-T or whatever it was, could only be obtained from the federal government (an institution famous for its efficiency and responsiveness). Despite repeated requests over the course of months, Albion never got the correct documentation from the feds. Rather than honor the scholarship until the government produced the verification it so jealously guarded, Albion simply pulled the scholarship, with just a few weeks before classes would start.

I don't think I overstate the case when I say that it was a crummy thing to do. Yes, I call it crummy, and I mean it. Thankfully, Hillsdale stepped in to give refuge to the persecuted and light to the distressed. *Hillsdale*, not Albion said, "give me your tired, your poor, your Form 4506-T-less." Dad "settled" for Hillsdale and the entire Claus family as we know it was saved ... by a verification of income form!

Mom's path to Hillsdale is even more improbable, given that she lived in Chicago and had never even heard of the school. By complete chance, she read some marketing materials in a catalogue at a neighbor's house and thought it "looked nice." Never bothered to visit. It "looked nice" and that was enough. The first time either Chuck or Kerry saw the campus was when they arrived for freshman orientation in the Fall of 1970.

Chuck's roommate freshman year was an old pal from Pontiac named Grigor "Scottie" Hasted. A few weeks before classes started, their mothers got together to help furnish the room and came up with a brilliant idea to help their sons make an impression on the lads in the dorm. When new classmates stopped by Chuck's and Scottie's room to introduce themselves, the first thing they beheld was the appalling sight of *matching* brown, yellow, and orange plaid-patterned bedspreads. It would be cute, their moms had assured them. "Cute" was *one* word for it.

With time, Chuck's social standing would recover from the bedspread blunder, and he even managed to impress some coeds. To entertain his new friend Kerry and her dormmates, Jan and Diane, he rigged a nifty rope system with wheels and pulleys that allowed the girls to pass things back and forth across a courtyard, even on different floors. The items couldn't be heavier than an apple and it would obviously be quicker to just walk down the stairs and deliver said item—but what is college for, if not trivial pursuits? Eventually campus security ordered the contraption removed.

Both Chuck and Kerry joined clubs and were active on the campus Greek scene. Kerry pledged Kappa Kappa Gamma, a sorority with a beautiful residence known for its refinement and class. Dad hung out at Tau Kappa Epsilon. *Their* house has since been demolished because the fraternity was banned from campus. Growing up we heard all kinds of stories about what a filthy pit the old TKE house was, with its sticky floors, stale smells, and peeling walls, not to mention the animals, both human and non, that inhabited it. (Imagine my surprise when some years later my parents were visiting my own fraternity house and Dad told me—with disgust and not an ounce of irony—that I *should be ashamed of myself* to live there. "Do as I say," I guess.)

Their first date was a party at the TKE house. Chuck's (not that serious) girlfriend was out of town, so he asked Kerry to join him instead. Apparently, it went well. On their first official date, Kerry informed him that they would be getting married. I would say that she was prophetic, but it sounds like he didn't have much choice in the matter. (By the way, if you think this is the only Claus male who was told on a first date that his bachelor days were finished, stay tuned!)

Chuck was what is colloquially known as a "theatre kid," performing in multiple productions per year, and was awarded Best Supporting Actor for his role as Snoopy in the musical, *You're a Good Man, Charlie Brown*. Kerry assumed several sorority offices and played varsity volleyball, earning the title of—ready for this?—Most Outstanding Athlete! If you're surprised to hear it, you're not alone. If *I* ever won "Most Outstanding Athlete" of anything, you can bet I would never shut up about it. It's just about the highest honor I can imagine.[2] I would wear a sweater with the words, "Most Outstanding Athlete" knitted on the chest. I would demand that my title be announced, like some important dignitary, whenever I entered a room. But my mother is humbler. She is quick to point out that the modern version of volleyball was ubiquitous in Chicago but brand new in Michigan, so she had more experience than anyone on the team,

---

[2] I did win a Hillsdale alumni pickleball tournament, an achievement that landed my photograph on the first page of the Spring/Summer 2023 issue of the Hillsdale alumni magazine.

including the coach. Still, someone had to be the Most Outstanding and it was her. She really should be more boastful.

Mark Donovan arrived on campus a year after Chuck and Kerry. His accomplishments at the college were equally remarkable. He was crowned champion of a beer chugging contest. His caricatures of his professors earned campus-wide acclaim and were featured in the college newspaper and yearbook. His senior year he was named, by popular vote, "Most Useless Greek on Campus."

Despite these triumphs, and I think he would admit this, Mark did not always put forth his best effort in the classroom. This perturbed his mother, Ginny, who was monitoring her baby boy's academic progress with keen interest. Ginny had been a *bona fide* whiz at Hillsdale, earning what was then the highest GPA of any female graduate in the history of the college. Indeed, she received only one B at Hillsdale ... in field hockey ... while she was pregnant.[3] After a few disappointing report cards, Ginny wrote Mark a series of letters gently advising him that if he did not begin applying his genetically inherited intelligence, she would haul him out of school, drop him off in the woods, and leave him for dead. Mark's grades improved.

Another extracurricular of interest: Chuck was Program Director of the Student Activities Board, which included selecting movies and showing them in the auditorium. This is strange to me, as I have never known Dad to sit still for longer than a few minutes at a time, and certainly not for the duration of a full-length picture. He has never once watched a complete movie with me. He just wanders off. As a teenager, I asked him to take me to see the new *Star Wars* movie. He kept leaving the theatre to add more self-serve butter to his popcorn. When he bored of the butter, he wandered into a few different theatres and tried to estimate how many patrons were at each, then came back to report his findings.

"*Never Been Kissed* is packed! There must be 120 people in there."
"Okay, Dad."
"About 40 people watching *Sleepy Hollow*."
"Okay, Dad."
"Only seven for *Mickey Blue Eyes!* What a bomb!"
"Dad! Shhh!! I can't hear what Jar Jar Binks is saying."

---

3 To be fair, Mark also earned only one B. The rest of his grades were lower.

Yes, he was such a film buff that he was the person responsible for showing movies on campus, but just a few years later swore off movies altogether. Very strange.

Back in those days, showing a movie was indeed a responsibility. You didn't just select a film, press play, and relax for 90 minutes. The reels had to be loaded and swapped out at the proper time to ensure a seamless transition between them. The film had to be threaded through the projector, just so. Movie projectors were complicated devices, and a lot could go wrong. The light might burn out. The heat from the light could burn a hole in the film. If the film was loaded in the wrong spot, it might fray. Finicky machines, projectors. On one occasion, when Chuck was sick, Mark substituted for him and ran the projector. He showed the classic thriller, *Wait Until Dark* to a packed theatre. Everything went brilliantly, until the dramatic climax of the film, when the dialogue suddenly started playing *in French* for the bewildered, then quickly irate audience. You never knew what those old projectors would do next.

In 1973, in his official capacity as Program Director of the Student Activities Board, Chuck arranged for the famous Hollywood director, Frank Capra, to come to Hillsdale to give a guest lecture. Capra was a household name, directing iconic pictures like *It Happened One Night* (1934) and *It's a Wonderful Life* (1945), among others. Capra was to offer insights on his most famous movie of all, *Mr. Smith Goes to Washington* (1939). The film stars Jimmy Stewart as an idealistic young senator determined to take on political corruption and is considered a masterpiece of cinema. A screening of the film would follow Capra's speech—with Chuck manning the projector.

The school did not have a copy of *Mr. Smith,* so Mr. Capra generously offered to bring his personal copy, which was neatly stored in those circular metal containers you used to see ("cans," as they say in the biz.) As the great legend handed the precious cans over to the Program Director of the Student Activities Board, he issued a word of caution.

"Okay, young fella. This is my personal copy of *Mr. Smith Goes to Washington.* Me, Frank Capra. The director of the movie. My own, personal, cherished copy. I'm sure that you know it's irreplaceable. Be extra *extra EXTRA* careful, okay?"

The Program Director of the Student Activities Board nodded eagerly. "Sure thing, Mr. Capra! I'll take real good care of it."

A few hours later, the Program Director of the Student Activities Board was knocking on the door of Frank Capra's hotel room. In his arms were paper grocery bags overflowing with the tangled mess of the great director's irreplaceable film. It had gotten caught in the projector and spun off the reel, shredding every inch of it as it fell pathetically to the floor. The movie continued uninterrupted for the audience, but the film itself died a slow and tortured death. There was no chance of repairing it. The best he could do was gather it all up, stuff it into bags, and return it to its maker.

It must have felt like a death march as Chuck shuffled to Capra's hotel, grocery bags in each arm. Wisely, he brought Kerry along, hoping she might provide a calming influence, or, if things really went south, serve as a witness to a justifiable homicide. But as it turns out, the Hollywood icon could not have been more charming and understanding.

"These things, happen," he said, after Chuck had explained. "Don't give it a second thought. Come on in."

Then Chuck and Kerry spent a wonderful evening discussing great films with Frank Capra in his hotel room. When they rose to leave, Mr. Capra shook Chuck's hand and kissed Kerry on the cheek—a smooch she has been bragging about ever since.

The locals still talk about the delirious lunatic spotted running through the campus that night. Most agree that it was the extremely relieved Program Director of the Student Activities Board sprinting back to the TKE house to tell his buddies the unbelievable story. But others could swear it was George Bailey, with a new appreciation for his friends and family, dashing through the snowy streets of Bedford Falls on Christmas Eve. Whichever version is true, all agree that the young man surely believed that his was a Wonderful Life.

On the topic of classic movies, something in *Willie Wonka and the Chocolate Factory* has always struck me as peculiar. Charlie lives in a room with his mom—and *both* sets of grandparents. How on earth did that arrangement come to be? And if that isn't odd enough, the grandparents all share a bed together, two on each end. Bizarre. Yep, I think we can all agree that Charlie's grandparents' living situation is the strangest aspect of that particular film.

It *is* weird ... but perhaps not unprecedented. Let's put a pin in that for the moment.

Chuck and Kerry were married in 1976 and many of the Hillsdale crowd attended. A year later, Mark and Jeannette Piro exchanged vows before God, family, and Chargers. The full account of that wedding can be found in Mark's book, *7 Brides for 2 Brothers*. For those in need of a refresher, here are the Cliffs Notes: Mark got into hot water at the wedding reception for singing the Hillsdale fight song with his friends (that's bad?!). Some folks—most importantly the bride, but my mother strongly concurs—thought his priorities that evening were misplaced. Heated words between bride and groom were exchanged in a parking lot, apologies were offered, all was forgiven, Mark became a thoughtful and attentive husband, and they lived happily ever after.

Missing from Mark's book is the story of their honeymoon. As a wedding present, his mother Ginny had booked them a lovely cottage on Bass Lake, near Traverse City. She knew it was lovely because the family had vacationed there years ago and had a lovely time. The brochure advertising the cottage looked lovely. The late summer weather would be lovely. It was a lovely gift from a lovely woman to a lovely couple.

After four days of basking in all that loveliness, Mark and Jeannette called up Chuck and Kerry and begged them to come visit. It turns out that the Bass Lake cottage did not exactly match the brochure. The room wasn't so much a cottage as an attic above a garage. It was paradise on earth for the thriving community of spiders that called the place home, but for Mark and Jeannette, it left much to be desired. There was no view of the lake. No TV. No chairs. Just a tiny bed in a cramped loft. They were blessed with a dresser but the drawers could only be opened part way, on account of the bed obstructing it. Air conditioning? Please. There was a shower available if one was willing to descend to the garage and squeeze past a labyrinth of industrial shelving.

To entertain themselves they could go outside and look at the lake. It was a nice enough lake, but how much lake gazing can you do? There was always the radio. That is, until three days after their wedding, when Elvis Presley died. Every station on the dial became the 1970s equivalent of the Elvis channel on satellite radio. It was All Elvis, All the Time, and Jeannette quickly wearied of Mark's (spot-on) impersonation, imploring her to "*oh, let me be ... youurrrrrr teddy bear.*" They were desperate. With no other options presenting themselves, they located a telephone and called my parents.

Chuck and Kerry were newly married themselves and did not have much money. Booking their own room would have been a poor use of scarce resources. So, a decision was made. All four of them squeezed into the "honeymoon suite" with Chuck and Kerry sleeping on the wooden floor.

I think we can all agree that my parents sharing Mark and Jeannette's miniature love nest ranks somewhere between "unusual" and "disturbing." I know my children reading this are struggling to understand. After all, these are their beloved grandparents we're talking about. Kids, I know this is all very confusing. Just rest assured my dear ones, nothing about Mima and Pipa's honeymoon is any weirder than the story of *Willy Wonka*.

Mark and Jeannette (especially Mark) did get the entertainment they had so desperately craved when Chuck threw out his back after one night's slumber on the unforgiving floor and was incapacitated for the rest of the trip. To Mark's endless amusement, Chuck could not bend, lift anything, and could barely walk. The bumpy dune buggy rides, a popular attraction for anyone under the age of 60, were out of the question—they had to content themselves with the "scenic" bus tour. Chuck was not shy about who he thought was to blame for his condition. Jeannette was sympathetic. Mark was not, and when Chuck started moaning too much, he would break into his signature happy dance, merrily singing:

"*Hey! Hey! My back feels great! Hey! Hey! My back feels great!*"

Apart from the accommodations and Chuck's debilitating injury, the situation improved with good friends there to share it. They never told Ginny that her lovely cottage turned out to be a run-down attic.

I admire the great group of friends my parents made at Hillsdale. Their names are a part of the family story: Mark, Scottie, Fred, Jan, Diane, David, Marion, Witt, and more. They genuinely care about each other and always seem to be laughing, whether it's recalling the story of their road trip to California in 1973 or demanding that a lake appear in a photograph in 2017. I have also learned that many of these friends were not only close with each other, but close with each other's parents as well. *Don't Send My Boy to Albion*—that song from back on the deck at the cottage—was taught to them by Mark's father, Robert Donovan. It's all pretty cool.

Mark and Jeannette moved to Carol Stream, Illinois, while Chuck and Kerry settled in Clarkston, Michigan. There is no direct route between the towns. It took a real commitment to schedule somewhat-annual visits. Despite it being completely inconvenient, the Donovans made the six-hour drive to Clarkston frequently enough to make those memories an integral part of my childhood.

It helped that the four oldest Donovan children, Drew, Ross, Luke, and Jake, were roughly the same age as the Claus kids. When they visited, we could expect hours of Nerf gun fights, boxing matches, and cartoon-watching marathons. They were fascinated by the "King Kool" pinball machine we had in our basement—the same model that sat in the student union building at Hillsdale in the 70s. On one visit our parents took us to see the oldies band, The Turtles, who were playing an afternoon concert for what was billed as a "Family Friendly" event at the local music venue. It was a pretty good show. We kids were particularly delighted with the profanity-laced jokes between songs. Kerry and Jeannette hauled us out of there well before the *Happy Together* reprise encore.

True story. I have a vivid memory of standing in the kitchen at my house with Mark and Jeannette's son, Luke, during one of the Donovans' many visits. We are probably six years old, in the heat of a spirited discussion about dinosaurs. Unfortunately, I'm having trouble making my point about the brontosaurus due to the constant interruptions—screams actually—from a baby in a carrier in the corner of the room. Being the youngest in my family, I'm not used to babies.

WAHHHHH!
What is that? I think to myself.
WAHHHHH!
Why is this thing crying so loudly?
WAHHHHH!
Why won't anyone stop it?

Luke sees the bewilderment on my face.
"Don't worry about her," he tells me. "That's just Cortney."

And that, Kids, is how I met your mother.

THE WATER IS STILL. THE FISH ARE STUBBORN TONIGHT.

15

One Summer Night

A hot night in August. Late 1980s. A small nightlight dimly illuminates a hardwood floor littered with books, trucks, baseball cards, toy guns, WWF wrestlers, and discarded socks. A warm breeze drifts in through the open bedroom window—it would be a few years before Dad finally sprang for central air conditioning. The air is thick and muggy and the whole house is sweating. Dan, my older brother, is in the lower bunk. A few minutes ago, he was fiddling with a plastic dagger but has been quiet for a while.

A radio sits on the dresser, its antenna fully extended and angled for optimal reception. The volume is not too high, but loud enough that I can hear it from the top bunk. The Detroit Tigers game is on, and the smooth, grandfatherly voice of Ernie Harwell is calling the action, as he did every night for more than 40 years. The Tigers are getting clobbered by the Minnesota Twins, but with the naïve optimism of a six-year-old fan, I'm confident we still have a chance. It is a hot night in August in the late 1980s. Or maybe July in 1990. Or June 1991. It is one night, and it was hundreds of nights in my youth.

Just when I think Dan is asleep, I hear a whisper from the bottom bunk.

"Hey. You awake?"

"Yeah."

"... You wanna go fishing?"

I don't need to answer. In a flash I sit up and gather my fishin' equipment. It is a special design—a rod, reel, line, and bait all in one—fashioned by rolling my blanket tightly into a sort of rope. I hold on to one end of the blanket and cast the other end over the edge of the bed into the depths below.

Then I wait.

No bites. Undeterred, I reel it back in and cast the line again. The water is still. The fish are stubborn tonight. I am about to reel it back in for a third time, when suddenly—a twitch on the line. Then another. Would he take the bait? I give the blanket a quick shake. Suddenly, my arms are nearly ripped from their sockets. *I've got one on the line!*

A tremendous battle ensues. An epic clash between predator and prey. I'm pulling the line with every ounce of strength in my little arms, but the fish has gravity on his side. At one point I think I have him, but he manages to wrap the blanket around his forearm and gains the advantage (a pretty dirty trick for a fish). Back and forth we go in a tug-of-war, neither one of us considering surrender.

I scream, "Aghhhhhh!"

The fish screams, "Aghhhhhh!"

I laugh hysterically.

The fish laughs hysterically.

I brace my feet on the top bunk's safety bar for leverage and dig in. The tide has turned. The fish is hanging from the blanket, swinging around in the air like a gilled Quasimodo.

"I've got you now!" I scream in triumph.

Just then a sound from the hallway paralyzes us.

Thump. Thump. Thump. Thump. THUMP. THUMP. THUMP.

Kids can tell which parent is approaching just by the sound of their footsteps. *This* thumping is unmistakable. It shakes the ground and rattles the light fixtures. This was the thunder, and the lightning would soon follow. I haul the blanket up and frantically try to cover myself. Dan shoots back into bed just as the door tears open.

Dad bursts into the room, clad only in his underwear. *The whites.* His legs look like gigantic, hairy tree trunks. He has work tomorrow and the sauna-like conditions in the house are not helping his mood. Commence the tirade.

"*What are you guys doing in here? You're supposed to be asleep! Why do we go through this every night?! It is way too late for this! I'm trying to get some sleep! I don't want to hear another sound, do you understand?! That is ENOUGH!*"

Except for the radio, the house is quiet again. The Tigers had managed to score a run, but I didn't hear how. A full ten minutes pass and I figure Dad must be asleep ... but is the fish? Without a word, I toss the blanket back over the side of the bed. A moment later, a quick tug on the blanket gives me the answer. He's back on the line!

We're more cautious now, shhh-ing and doing our best to muffle the laughter, but the fighting remains spirited. Then, the line goes slack. Did he get away? Still grasping the blanket, I peer over the side of the bed. The wily old catfish was bluffing! With one great yank of the blanket, he sends me airborne, over the safety rail, plummeting down to the floor. The impact of my crash landing shakes the walls and knocks a large ceramic eagle—a Christmas present from Granny the previous year—down to the floor, shattering it to oblivion. An earthquake would have been more peaceful.

We look at each other, unable to move. Dan's eyes are as wide as a couple of frisbees. The remnants of the ceramic eagle are scattered among the books, trucks, baseball cards, toy guns, WWF wrestlers, and discarded socks. And just a few seconds later ...

THUMP. THUMP. THUMP. THUMP. THUMP. THUMP.

Dad just about rips the door off its hinges. Mom follows shortly after him, carrying a dustpan and broom. Dad is bellowing at full volume. I don't hear many specifics but he's getting the message across. My sister wanders in to see what all the commotion is about but is quickly shooed away. Dan, of all things, has his head buried in his pillow, pretending to be asleep. A selfish act of betrayal, even if entirely unconvincing. I scurry back up the ladder to the top bunk and take the scolding like a man. Dad exits, still steaming. Mom, who has remained silent, gives us one last glare and shuts the door.

Now we dare not even whisper. It's *so hot,* and I move my blanket to the side. I'm sad about my eagle and wonder if Granny will get me a new one. The radio is still on, having somehow survived the chaos. I listen for a few more innings. The Tigers are down to their last strike. Ernie dutifully relays the events to the remaining faithful.

Here's the 1-2 pitch ... he GOT HIM on strikes. He stood there like the house on the side of the road and watched it go by. Final score, Twins - 6, Tigers - 1. We'll be back for the postgame show after station identification. This is your Detroit Tigers radio network.

Dan is asleep. I'm thinking I should shut off the radio, but it's so ... far ... away. Maybe I'll just listen a bit longer.

Another sound from the hallway—this time softer.

Thump. Thump. Thump. Thump. Thump. Thump. Thump. Thump.

Dad opens the door. He tiptoes over to the radio and switches it off. I lift my head.

"You're still up?" he whispers.

"We lost again," I tell him.

"I heard. We'll get them tomorrow."

He pulls the sheet over me.

"Go to sleep now, Bud. I love you."

Dad returns to bed and is soon snoring. The whole house is sweating but is calm at last. A warm breeze drifts in through the open bedroom window and I close my eyes.

It was ugly, perhaps the ugliest car I have ever seen.

16

My Senior Moment

Sometimes in the course of events, a moment presents itself, and there to meet the moment is the perfect person for it. The stars align, an exceptional confluence of factors coalesces, and the right man for the time and place emerges and etches his name in history. Winston Churchill during The Blitz. The Beatles on *The Ed Sullivan Show*. Kirk Gibson in the World Series. Me, my senior year at Clarkston High school.

Boastful, yes, but allow me to state my case. The Churchills, Beatles, and Gibsons of the world are rightfully remembered for what they achieved—inspiring the spirit of his nation, ushering in a new era of the rock and roll star, and blasting two clutch home runs, respectively. Meanwhile, I am not remembered at Clarkston High for anything. Nary a noteworthy accomplishment to my name. Still, I tell you that I was the perfect man for the moment and the moment was perfect for me.

Senioritis. Everyone gets it. With grade point averages already established and college acceptance letters in hand, the soon-to-be graduates inevitably check out. The bare minimum becomes the standard, even for the overachievers. My experience with the disease was hardly unique. Nevertheless, I'll put my record of accomplishing nothing against anyone's. My lack of accomplishment was my greatest accomplishment.

Starting with my class schedule. Senior year is no time for Chemistry. I spent my final year of high school studying Television Production (where we produced and broadcast the daily announcements), took a couple of Gym classes, worked an hour as a teacher's aide (for the TV Production teacher), and to close out the day, an hour-and-a half of Student Council. My only "real" classes were in subjects I liked—courses in History and English that I would have taken just for the fun of it.

The "manageable" courseload gave me loads of free time and plenty of excuses to be out and about while the rest of the suckers were stuck in a classroom. Being a teacher's aide came with an unlimited supply of hall passes, as did Student Council. I did a lot of wandering. In fact, I did little else. I'd wander to my locker. I'd wander into the cafeteria to meet friends on their lunch period. I'd wander into the gymnasium and shoot hoops. I'd wander to my car and go pick up food. I'd wander to the front entrance and dish the latest gossip with the security guards. I'd wander into the natatorium—for some reason, that is what we called the pool—and dangle my toes in the water.

In retrospect, it's really quite strange. I spent more time in the halls than I did in the classroom. Why didn't anyone tell me to get back to class? Oh, every now and then I'd come across an unfamiliar teacher looking sideways at me.

"Aren't you supposed to be somewhere?"

But I had my supply of trusty hall passes and rolodex of explanations, and any one of them could technically be true.

"I'm working on a story for the morning announcements," I would say, unfazed by the interrogation.

Or, "I need to get supplies for the assembly," casually twirling a hall pass in my fingers.

And the always effective, "Got some, um, Student Council stuff I gotta do." Then off I'd wander.

It helped that I was on chummy terms with most of the faculty. I was a good kid—not out to make trouble. See, that's the biggest mistake troublemakers make: they make trouble. They don't realize that staying lowkey wins the day. It's a lot of effort dealing with a troublemaker. A troublemaker means paperwork for the staff. But a harmless dork moseying around the hallway never bothered anyone. Even the principal, known as something of a battle-axe to much of the student body, would just shake her head at me and smile as if to say, "Michael, *you're incorrigible.*"

The single greatest factor in my ability to do as I pleased, however, had nothing to do with my class schedule or making nice with the administration. It was something totally out of my control.

Before my senior year, I was just one of thousands of generic students. I had no gateway into the world of teachers. They were in charge, we were their subordinates, and ne'er the twain shall meet. But all that changed in 2002—this is what I mean about stars aligning. I had a connection. A man on the inside. Like an inmate that befriends a prison guard who turns around and sneaks him the ripest fruit for the toilet wine. The momentous turn of events was this: My brother Chas was hired as a teacher at Clarkston.

Chas is the oldest of my siblings and I am the youngest, but we have always been close. As a teacher, he maintained an aura of professionalism but despite his best efforts, I did not consider him an authority figure in any sense. He was a pal, just five years older, and I was now the only student with a pal on the faculty. It was not an opportunity I intended to squander.

One day I had neglected to pack a lunch, so I wandered over to Chas' classroom. He was delivering a well-researched lecture on the Industrial Revolution to a class of freshmen. It was early in the schoolyear and said freshmen were not aware that Mr. Claus had a brother in the school.

Chas was standing in the middle of the room, busy with his professoring. I walked right up to him and leaned my elbow on his shoulder.

Nervous laughter from the freshmen.

Chas didn't even acknowledge my presence—he kept right on lecturing about the conditions in meat packing plants or some such. Finally, I noisily cleared my throat. He stopped and looked over.

Complete silence from the freshmen. You could hear a pin drop.

"Listen," I told him in a voice loud enough so those in the back wouldn't miss it. My tone was conversational but firm. "Here's the deal. I forgot my lunch. And I don't have any money. So ... I'm going to need you to give me some cash."

Chas didn't hesitate. He pulled out his wallet, passed me a $10 bill, and continued with his lecture. I greedily snatched the money and left the room.

The freshmen were astounded.

"Mr. Claus ... *who was that?*"

Chas's eyes went wide. "I have no idea," he said in complete deadpan. "I thought you all knew him."

"What?!"

"I've never seen that guy in my life!"

We had a hearty laugh about it at home that evening. He was fresh out of college and still living with our parents. Again, it's hard to take someone seriously as an authority figure when you spend your evenings with him arguing over whose turn it is to play on the computer. What I remember most about that era was the two of us, along with my best friend Kirk Hanna, spending weekends in the basement, staying up until dawn watching sports and playing video games. (None of us had too much going on.) When Chas selected Kirk for the coveted position as his teacher's aide, we continued our hangouts in his classroom. I hung around so much that even Chas began to ask me why I wasn't doing something more productive.

Since my children will be reading this someday, I do feel I owe it to them to set a straight record. I've been hyperbolizing *a bit*. Sprinkling in some "narrative enhancers" to help things along. Truthfully, while I did engage in an extraordinary amount of senior-year-wandering, I enjoyed high school and its associated extracurriculars. I played varsity football and tennis and was on the Student Council. Kirk and I led the student cheering section at basketball games and swim meets. I had plenty of friends, though I don't think anyone ever considered me "cool." (For example, Kirk and I once donned costumes and filmed ourselves in a choreographed, "professional" wrestling match that started in the back yard, raged through the shopping mall, into friends' homes, and down Main Street through town. We stayed in character the entire time. So, no, we didn't get many invitations to party with the popular kids.)

Then, there was the matter of my automobile.

In every movie chronicling high school days, you can tell who the cool kids are by their cars. Whether it's Harrison Ford's black 1955 Chevrolet 150 in *American Graffiti*, McConaughey's 1970 Chevelle in *Dazed and Confused*, or even Alicia Silverstone and her Jeep Wrangler in *Clueless*, part of the essence of the character is what they drive.

I have yet to come across a film where the cool kid rolls around town in a rusty, pockmarked, olive green 1987 Pontiac Grand Prix.

My dad had purchased the car on the cheap from an aging aunt who had kept it stored for about a decade in a dirty garage. This frumpy, broken-down old rattletrap (the car, not the aunt) was presented to my brother Dan a few months before his graduation and was getting worse by the day when I inherited it the following year. The tires were bald, the hubcaps were mismatched, and its vinyl top, called a Landau roof—presumably once an attractive accent piece—was rotting and covered in mold. Portions of its body were rusted completely through. It was ugly, perhaps the ugliest car I have ever seen. Still, I've never been choosy about cars, and I did not complain.

Let me repeat that. *I did not complain* about the aesthetics of the vehicle. I did, however, have some concerns about its operation. Maybe I was just nitpicking. You can be the judge.

Topping the list of what you might call Mission Critical issues was the steering wheel. The Grand Prix's steering wheel column was not fixed in place. If not actively held upright, the steering wheel would slide downward onto the driver's lap, and it also floated side-to-side. To be clear, I don't mean that the wheel would lock into place but come loose—*it had no resting place at all.* So, driving required gripping the wheel with both hands, arms extended, constantly trying to keep it stabilized, vertical, and in a centered position. It was as terrifying as it was exhausting. Stoplights were actually a treat, when the steering wheel could be safely dropped onto the lap for a moment of temporary relief.

Next, consider the car's doors. They were each about five feet long, and *heavy.* Unfortunately, especially when the weather was cold, the passenger door would not latch, so the door wouldn't stay closed. You'd be puttering along, already on edge from the task of keeping the steering wheel aloft, when suddenly the immense slab of steel would fly open, and upon reaching the end of its radius, would whip back to the closed position with a thunderous crash that rattled every nut and bolt in the vehicle. Any soul brave enough to ride along was expected to take hold of the door handle and do their best to keep it secured. For the passenger's convenience, we eventually tied a section of ski rope to the inside of the door and asked them to pull on the other end while the vehicle was in motion.

The ski rope system was all well and good when carpooling but I'm sure you can spot the even bigger problem for solo flights. If *both* hands are required to keep the steering wheel from falling into your lap, how could you, at the same time, pull on the ski rope to keep the door shut? When you found yourself in that predicament, the only solution was to tie the loose end of the ski rope to your wrist and try to puppeteer the whole rig as safely as possible.

As you can imagine, folks weren't lining up to ride shotgun in the ol' Grand Prix. Our neighbors had a daughter who was just starting as a freshman, and they asked if I could give her a ride to school. On the first day of classes, I dutifully pulled into their driveway and blared the horn. The young lady stepped out, looking slightly uncomfortable. Probably just first-day jitters, I supposed. Nothing to do with the embarrassment of showing up to her first day of high school in *that*. She reluctantly climbed in.

Thinking I might calm her nerves, I greeted her extra cheerfully.

"Hiya, Lauren! First day of high school, eh? Excited to meet all your new classmates? I'm sure you'll make a great first impression. Now, just grab ahold of that ski rope next to you. That's the one. You're going to want to pull on that as hard as you can, or you might tumble out into the road. We wouldn't want that on your first day, would we, hehehe! Seat belts on, please."

A couple of days later Lauren's mom called and said there was no need to drive her anymore. She had found another ride.

Some kids might have grumbled about the car, but I knew better. Vehicle expenses were a touchy subject in the Claus House. Dad was not about to spend his public servant's salary outfitting his teenage children with better cars than his own. The cars we drove to high school were reclamation projects from—along with the aging aunts—friendly neighbors, shady neighbors, and on one occasion, a dead neighbor.

That's a horribly sad story that always makes me laugh. An old lady that lived a few houses down from us had died in her home. Apparently, she was not in regular contact with her children and nobody discovered the body until several weeks later. Dad came home one night and reported the grim news. He also reported some happier news. The dead lady's car was parked in our driveway. Somehow, he swung a deal with the poor woman's estate, and we were now the lucky owners of a sputtering 1991 Toyota Tercel with a bad transmission—another prize piece in the Claus Collection.

Now, for some reason Dad had gotten it into his head that his children were not appreciative of the vehicles he provided. To my knowledge it was entirely baseless—I know that I never complained and I don't recall hearing anyone else complain either. Nevertheless, he simply insisted that we were ungrateful. And nothing set him off faster than the mere suggestion of a problem with a car.

Be that as it may, I felt that if there were some legitimate safety concerns with the Grand Prix, Dad would want to know. I thought he might at least be *interested* to hear that, if not actively managed, the steering wheel would plummet onto the driver's lap. So, while I dreaded the conversation, I thought alerting him was the right thing to do.

I waited for the right moment, trying to catch him in a chipper mood, and settled on a lovely family dinner on a Sunday evening. I tried to sound casual.

"Delicious chicken, Mom! Some of your best work. Can I get you a drink, Dad? You must be beat after all that yard work today. The lawn really looks great! By the way, the car is acting kind of funny. Beer, or something stronger for you?"

There was a pause, then he carefully placed his silverware on the table and looked up from his chicken.

You've probably heard about people's eyes narrowing when they get angry. That is exactly what Dad's eyes did now. Just moments ago, they had been wide and bright, but at the mention of the word "car," his appearance was ninety percent eyelids.

"*Oh?* Is there a problem with the car?" Dad replied, his voice oozing with contempt. So much for the chipper mood.

I sighed. I knew exactly what was coming next. It was a speech I'd heard him deliver many times to my siblings in response to any vehicular problems brought to his attention. It was always the same bit. He launched into it again now.

"Don't worry about the car ... you can just ride to school on the Big Yellow School Bus."

I resented the implication. I resented it then and I resent it now. My automobile needs were low priority and rightfully so. But I wasn't asking for a trendy Jeep Wrangler or a '55 Chevy. I wasn't even asking for a Grand Prix that wasn't the most hideous shade of olive green anyone had ever laid eyes on. I merely preferred that the door not fly open every time I turned left. I tried to cut him off.

"No, I—"

"The car isn't good enough for you. That's fine. I bet you'll make lots of new friends on the Big Yellow School Bus!"

"Dad, I'm just saying that the steering wheel—"

"That Biiiiiiiiiiig Yellooooow School Bus," he continued, really dialing up the sarcasm, "she's a-waitin'. It's pretty chilly out there at the bus stop so be sure you wear your wittle mittens."

I could see it was a fool's errand. I dropped the subject, hoping to cut my losses and finish the meal in peace. He went quiet, and for a moment I thought I had been spared the worst. But then he broke into it. The routine I feared most. The ultimate humiliation. Doing his best imitation of a Kindergarten teacher, Dad began to sing:

"*Theee wheels on the bus go round and round! Round and round! Round and round ...*"

As I cried myself to sleep later that night,[1] my only comfort was the thought of how wonderful it would be to drive a car with a steering wheel that stayed in one place. Some day, I promised myself. Some day.

Some Day came sooner than I thought. A week later, somebody borrowed my mom's car, so she needed to use the Grand Prix for the day. She came home white as a ghost.

"Chuck, what is wrong with that car!? *NO ONE* should be driving that! It needs to be fixed!"

And wouldn't you know it? My car got repaired.

I have come to appreciate the Grand Prix and everything that clunky monstrosity represents. I said that I was the perfect man for my senior year moment and the moment was perfect for me. I should amend that. I was the perfect man to drive an ugly 1987 Grand Prix my senior year and the car was perfect for me. I had plenty of confidence in high school. Enough confidence to wander the school halls for hours on end without fear of reproach. Enough confidence to demand lunch money from a brand-new teacher in front of his students. *Too much* confidence—I see that now.

---

[1] Narrative enhancer.

Those white-knuckle drives to high school in the world's worst car were the only thing keeping my ego from ballooning to the size of the Big Yellow School Bus. Maybe the old man knew what he was doing.

The fox head fit perfectly.

17

Rocky Mountain Low

I rolled over in bed and stared at the cellphone vibrating angrily on the table next to me. Closer inspection of the device revealed that I had seven missed calls. Seven?! What time was it?? I sat up, and as I did I suddenly became aware that someone was driving a railroad spike into the front of my skull, or at least that seemed the only reasonable explanation for the sensation in my head.

I played the most recent voicemail and was greeted by the exasperated voice of my supervisor.

"Claus. Where are you?? Get into work, NOW. ... *Bring the fox head.*"

It was Spring of 2006, a beautiful morning in Colorado Springs. Birds were harmonizing, the sun shone brightly, Pikes Peak stood majestic in the distance, and I was exceptionally, outstandingly, *impossibly*, hung over.

My roommate Kyle was across the room, struggling to pry his eyes open. His phone was also buzzing in reproach. The rest of the house was still—our roommates' alarms, unlike ours, had apparently been set and proved equal to the job. Outside the bedroom, red plastic cups littered the counters, along with the playing cards, dice, ping-pong balls, and other essentials for any college party. An empty beer keg sat on the porch where we had left it no more than four hours ago.

We staggered out to Kyle's car and started toward the office in silence. Sweat bled through my shirt despite the cool mountain air. Kyle looked like he had spent the night with his head in a blender. I glanced behind me. Sitting in the backseat was a gigantic fox's head, with an elongated snout and a permanent smile plastered on his face. *Ughh boy.*

A hundred scenarios flashed in my mind. Would I be fired? Kicked out of school? Hauled off to jail? I had done some dumb things over the past five months, but this seemed bad. And as bad as it was, whatever tale *she* was telling about us would be far worse. She had hated me from the start. It was all *her* fault! If she could manage to be even slightly agreeable, I wouldn't be in this mess. Why did we have to oversleep? We had given her an opening and she would strike.

The fox's stupid face was still staring at me as we pulled into the parking lot. We exited the car and shuffled past the banquet hall, past the oversized, concrete baseballs that decorated the pavement, past the shuttered ticket window, inching ever closer to the stadium's main entrance. My supervisor was no doubt waiting in his office for us, like a judge mulling over the record in chambers before pronouncing his sentence. I would soon learn my fate. My entire future in jeopardy. My reputation very much in question. A fox's head in the backseat. *Ohh,* how did it come to this??

My brief tenure with the Colorado Springs Sky Sox baseball team was part of a required semester-long internship my junior year of college. The Sky Sox (similar to a White Sox or a Red Sox, but at a high elevation) were a minor-league affiliate of the Colorado Rockies. Picturing an enjoyable semester of watching baseball in the mountains, I took a job with the team's Media Relations department.

I use the term "job" loosely. Kyle once forcefully argued from a barstool that the gig was "a sin." Yes, declared Kyle, the Colorado Springs Sky Sox internship program was a transgression against God himself. By the end of his speech, I completely agreed, and clanked my pint glass in a show of support.

To start, interns were unpaid. That's understandable. Minor league baseball teams operate on thin margins and even the executives make less than you might expect. Grind it out, content yourself to live on pennies, and you just might make it in the biz. From 8:30 to 5:00, interns were expected to make phone calls to local businesses in an attempt to sell advertising space (on signs or in the program, for example). The same applied to regular employees, so, again, not too much to complain about.

When things got truly evil was after hours. On non-game days, the office cleared out at 5:00—all except the interns. The interns—*unpaid* interns—were required to log *another* two hours from 6:00 to 8:00, now making cold calls to people's homes peddling packages of discounted tickets. These ticket packages weren't exactly hot items. That there was a local baseball team came as a surprise to most people I talked to. Colorado Springs, for all its charms, was not a baseball town. A hiking, skiing, and rock-climbing town, yes—but not baseball. The average attendance at Sky Sox home games was about 4,000 people, dead last in the Pacific Coast League. Because there was never any danger of a sellout, anyone could easily get inexpensive single game tickets at the gate. And if that wasn't bad enough, we made our big sales pitch just as most of these fine folks were sitting down to dinner.[1]

The team's General Manager approached Kyle and me one afternoon and asked if we wanted a break from phone calls. We sure did! I thought he might offer to take us to lunch, but he had something else in mind. He went on to say that several owls had made their home in the stadium rafters and were making a real mess of the concourse. Owls, I was about to learn, swallow their prey whole, then regurgitate the leftover bones, fur, teeth, skulls, and anything else they cannot digest. We could find some brushes and buckets in the storage room.

To summarize: we worked full days unpaid, a substantial portion of that time spent scrubbing regurgitated mouse carcasses off the concrete, and were rewarded with evenings of talking to annoyed citizens of Colorado Springs who had zero interest in baseball and even less interest in purchasing tickets in bulk. This went on day after day, night after night, week after week, without so much as a "thank you" from Management. It wore me down.

The team did secure free housing for the interns, a nice three-bedroom, two-bath apartment for the four of us. Kyle and I shared one of the rooms. He was a recent graduate from Texas A&M and we got along right away, united, in part, by our fascination with the absurd cast of characters around us. A Japanese man in his late thirties who barely spoke English took the room across the hall. Kazuo's primary interest seemed to

---

1 The ballpark itself was no attraction, either. A local columnist described the stadium as "bewilderingly modest," "ridiculously unambitious," and, summing things up, "a nice destination for a high school game, but a joke for a team competing one step below the Bigs." See Ramsey, D., "Triple-A baseball was never built to last in Colorado Springs" *The Gazette* (June 26, 2017).

be showering. He absolutely loved it. He would shower early in the morning, go on a bike ride, shower again after his ride, head to work, then shower again at night. A weird dude, but harmless.

Free housing with young-ish, normal-ish, coworkers might sound like a grand setup for a broke college kid, but the living arrangements grew nearly as depressing as the cold calling. Because occupying the third bedroom was a horrible, fiendish creature, the likes of which I had never encountered before or since. She was nasty. She was rude. She was pompous. She did not like most things, she hated most people, and the person she hated most of all was Yours Truly.

I'm sure you're saying to yourself, "How could anyone dislike Mike? He's a good-natured fellow!" I happen to agree with you. Even so, I will admit that, as a 21-year-old, I lacked some of the polish and tact I learned later in life. I probably could have let some petty insults go unchecked or turned a cheek or two in my dealings with her. Maturity. I lacked maturity. Nevertheless, it remains the case that of the hundreds of people I met while living in Colorado, only one of them ever had a cross word to say about the Undersigned.

Was she really that bad?

She bossed us around and insulted "the interns" even though she was one herself. She resented it when we left for a night out with friends but complained if we decided to stay in and watch a game. If there was a door in striking distance, she would slam it. Whenever we tried to introduce her to a guest, she would glare at the person and storm away without saying a word. Lest you think I am exaggerating, my brother Chas, who possesses far more grace than I, visited for a few days. He tried to engage her but received only icy scowls in return. Forty-eight hours into his visit he dubbed her "The Queen of Unpleasantness," which was one of the kinder monikers that she earned.

I'm still afraid to speak her true name. My greatest nightmare is that this book somehow falls into her hands and she sees everything I've written about her. Then she hunts me down, corners me in a dark alley, and uncorks one of her signature lectures about what a jerk I am. So, to be safe, let's just call her Cruella.

I was sitting on the couch one morning, watching the classic comedy film, *Robin Hood: Men in Tights,* minding my own business. Cruella emerged from her bedroom and shot her patented Cruella Glare in my direction. A cold greeting, but not unusual. Feeling inspired by the movie, I received her presence with enthusiasm.

"Ah! Good morrow to you, my Merry Roommate!" I thundered in a fantastic British accent. "I trust thy slumbers were restful?"

My charming medieval pleasantries were not reciprocated. The bit flopped harder than Robin Hood doing stand-up at the Sheriff of Nottingham's Comedie Clubbe. She completely ignored it and cut right to the fight scene.

"Take the garbage out," she hissed, pointing at a bag in the kitchen.

I was accustomed to her authoritarian ways, but this took me aback. There were four interns in the house, and I didn't generate more garbage than anyone else, so why was I being picked on? I abandoned the Robin Hood routine.

"Pardon me?"

Another glare—a real sour one.

"Take. The garbage. Out."

A rude man might have offered several suggestions for things she could do with that garbage bag, but I remained calm and responded courteously.

"It's not really my job, Cruella, but I would be happy to take the garbage out. If you ask nicely."

I hadn't actually expected her to accept my offer and she didn't. There was the Glare, there was the Door Slam (a Classic Cruella Combo), and she was gone. And from then on, *nobody* took the garbage out. When my parents arrived later that summer to help me move back to school, there were more than 40 full garbage bags piled in the kitchen. In an act of treachery that I have never completely forgiven, *my own parents* forced me to take the garbage out, and I'm certain Cruella listened from inside her room with smug satisfaction as I wrestled with the bags.

Despite the burnout at work and Cruella's daily death glares, Kyle and I tried to squeeze as much fun as we could out of a bad situation. We taught ourselves to snowboard and went to concerts at Red Rocks. We made a good group of friends both at the office and around "the Springs." And, at least when the team was in town, working for a minor league team could actually be a lot of fun. As the Media Relations intern, I watched games from the comfort of the press box where I argued with the local writers about bad calls and debated baseball trivia. Down on the field, the Promotions interns, Kazuo and Cruella, had the more humiliating assignment of trying to energize the empty bleachers with t-shirt slingshots and silly contests. Kyle was an intern in the Operations department. I rarely saw him during games, but from what I gather he spent most of the time smoking and playing cards with the grounds crew.

Our apartment became a hostel for goofballs and characters. Kazuo's mom arrived from Japan and stayed for a month. She cooked dinner for us once, an authentic Japanese recipe I wouldn't dare even smell that sent one coworker racing to the toilet to do his best impression of an owl after lunch. Kaz Matsui, a famous major leaguer from Japan, was also a houseguest. Matsui had just been traded from the Mets to the Rockies, and his first stop was a rehab assignment with the Sky Sox. Kazuo was apparently the only person in Colorado Springs who spoke Japanese, so he was temporarily assigned as Matsui's interpreter, though Kazuo only spoke about fifty words in English himself. Meanwhile, Cruella's older sister moved in and quickly established herself as "the nice sister."

Then Kazuo disappeared. Literally overnight, he left without a trace. It turns out that the Sky Sox coaches wanted an interpreter who could actually speak English, so a proper one arrived from Denver. Kazuo was demoted back to intern, which he perceived as a great dishonor. He refused to come to work and left the country, I guess to think things over. Some weeks later he resurfaced, disgraced and frustrated and looking for his old job back. But the other intern in the Promotions department (guess who?!?) objected. Kazuo had abandoned his post, argued Cruella, and to permit him to return to his unpaid job throwing t-shirts would be unfair to her. At Cruella's insistence, he was terminated. It was sad, but with 21 fewer showers taken per week, we did save a lot of money on our water bill.

The internship brought unique physical challenges as well. In the minor leagues, everyone from the interns to the General Manager helps the grounds crew pull the tarp over the infield during bad weather. If the radar warned that rain was imminent, a "tarp pull" was called and all staff gathered our raincoats and headed down to the field. Usually tarp pulls were an annoyance. Maybe you got a little wet and dirty but nothing beyond that. One epic day in late May, however, the tarp pull was a *war*.

The outlook wasn't brilliant for the Sky Sox team that day; the score stood 9-2 with but one inning left to play. It was one of those interminable games that featured about a dozen pitching changes and everyone involved had lost interest hours ago. Even the team's perpetually grinning mascot, "Sox the Fox," looked like he'd rather be back at his den with the wife and pups. As the eighth inning came to a merciful close, we took some solace that after just six more outs we would be released from the torture and could go home. But just then the General Manager's voice on our walkie-talkies jolted us from our comas.

"Tarp pull!" he called out. "All hands on deck for a tarp pull."

You could hear our collective groan from the top of Pikes Peak. Pulling the tarp meant *at least* an hour delay—and it hadn't even started raining. The skies were clear. Why not at least wait until the showers started? Why not just play the final inning in what was probably a small sprinkle? The game was a blowout, so why not just declare it over? Yes, it was a disgruntled group that descended from the stadium concourse down the stairs and onto the field. However, we soon understood why the call for a tarp pull was made.

Before we could even begin unraveling the tarp, the deluge hit. It was a *shocking* amount of rain. In mere seconds, I was completely drenched. We all scrambled into position, grabbed the handles, and started to pull. The winds came roaring down from the mountains—violent gusts that threw the rain sideways and set the light poles swaying. The tarp, acting like an enormous sail, took flight. I watched in horror as it lifted and dragged 200-pound men too frightened to let go. Complete confusion now. Guys were screaming for people to get off the tarp, while others were attempting to unravel it, and still others were trying to reposition themselves to fasten the corners. A couple of cowards simply ran off the field to safe ground. I managed to avoid liftoff but was dragged around for yards at a time as I struggled to keep an edge secured.

At some point, the tremendous weight of the water on the half-deployed tarp became a more powerful force than the gale winds. The tarp was impossible to move, and the infield was completely exposed and flooded. The day was lost. The General Manager looked like Pickett leaving the battlefield after his doomed charge at Gettysburg. He was shellshocked.

He looked to the heavens—I will never forget this—he literally looked to the heavens and cried out in a quavering voice, *"We've got no chance!"*

Our waterlogged group stumbled to the shelter of the dugout, exhausted and beaten. We sat and watched the storm in pathetic silence. As the wind began to slow, one of the guys from the Sales department shook his head in disgust.

"So, we're just going to give up?!?"

He took one courageous step towards the tarp, and I followed right behind him. Together, we methodically began to unravel the massive canvas, inch-by-inch. We pushed and pulled and scraped and clawed and sprained our fingers and slipped in puddles and got up again. It was grueling work but gradually we made some progress. Fifteen minutes later second base was covered. We could feel the momentum turning. Clearly inspired by our valor, folks started to trickle back onto the field.[2] An hour later the tarp was in place and secure and it was all hugs and handshakes from there. I cannot say that Man conquered Nature—but we picked ourselves up off the mat after an early knockdown and went a full 12 rounds with the champ—victory awarded to Nature on points.

A senior executive who had been with the team for decades called it "one of the most perilous tarp pulls in club history." The public address announcer who had watched the events from the booth said it was "horrifying to watch." It was the highlight of my internship.

The low would come a few months later.

The end of a homestand was always a tremendous event. Teams usually play six to nine games in a row at their home stadium before leaving on a road trip. Following each homestand, the sleep-deprived staff would gather on the concourse or bleachers to unwind after a week of late nights. As a bonus, all perishable food was free to eat, and all tapped kegs were free to drink. It was a private party in a baseball stadium. Around midnight, the boss would shut off the stadium lights to let us know, "you don't have to go home, but you can't stay here."

After one particularly grueling homestand, we weren't quite ready to call it a night. We loaded the cars with a couple of leftover kegs and invited

---

2 Kyle hates this part of the story. If I recall, he was one of the *last* people out of the dugout.

the entire staff back to our place to keep the party going. It was an absolute rager. We blared music and played games. It seemed like half the office was there and I could have sworn that I saw some of the Sky Sox players milling around the kitchen. Somebody—not me—had grabbed the mascot's head before leaving the stadium and revelers were taking pictures with it on their digital cameras.

Admittedly, we all kind of forgot about Cruella. At some point, she appeared from her room and started gesturing wildly. It was so loud that I never actually heard what she was saying but I gathered that she was agitated about something. She eventually returned to her room with the traditional door slam, this time to little effect.

Those who happened to witness the display had a good laugh at her gloominess. But it was at this moment that I, being a good-hearted person, decided that enough was enough. No longer would she have to mope and moan and live a miserable existence. I would extend the olive branch. We would forget our differences and welcome her as one of us. I stood up, resolute in my cause, and made a bold announcement to the room.

"I'll take care of this."

Yet, I knew that sheer determination would not be enough. I needed something extra to bore through that hardened, nay, *metamorphic* exterior, and win her favor. I made my way toward the beast's lair, stopping to collect the prop I needed to seal the deal.

The fox head fit perfectly.

I had a vision of how things would play out when Cruella realized that the person she considered her worst enemy would go to such great lengths to cheer her up. I could see it all clearly: The knock on her door. The opening of the door. The instinctive scowl. The eyeing of the fox's head atop my shoulders. Then, the breakthrough. The suppressed smile. The involuntary chortle. The unrestrained belly-laugh. The friendly hug. The profuse apologies. The "fault-was-all-mine's." The hearty handshake. The welcoming her to the party. The *auld lang syne* group sing-a-long.

That was the plan. The actual events are a little hazy. Visibility was poor inside the fox head, and I wasn't necessarily of sound mind. I was able to piece together some details later with the benefit of eyewitness testimony and some grainy, very-early cellphone video footage.

I knocked on the door for a while. There was no answer, but I persisted. When she finally emerged, she was greeted, *not* by her archrival, but by the happiest looking woodland creature you've ever seen.

And then I gave it everything I had. I did a little tap dance. I rocked from side to side. I waved my arms wildly. I did my very best buck-and-wing. I mashed potatoed. Finally, I threw my arms out, welcoming her in for the warm embrace. The w.e. never came. The door slammed, the most violent slam yet, right in the poor fox's nose.

"Well," I thought, feeling a bit like the General Manager after the disastrous tarp pull. "What more can I do? *We've got no chance.*"

Sometime around 4:00 in the morning, Kyle and I were on the back porch—the last men standing at the party—slurring our way through a conversation about our plans for the future.

"I'm gonna write a book about this someday. I'm serious, man. I'm gonna write a book."

"That's awesome dude. That's just so awesome. Hey, I think that's the sun coming up."

"Oh yeah? We should probably get some sleep, right? Work tomorrow."

Our supervisor, whose office I found myself sitting in the next day, was a former college football player, a laid-back guy who clearly liked us, but just as clearly did not have time for this nonsense (he used a different word for it). I've never seen a man shake his head with greater exasperation. Big, sweeping headshakes that travelled from shoulder blade to shoulder blade.

He told us that Cruella had indeed gone straight to Management, telling disturbing tales and calling for our termination. I wasn't surprised. She already had Kazuo's scalp and nabbing mine would be her greatest triumph. Under different circumstances, I would have sneered at the news. As things were, however, I merely lowered my eyes in quiet remorse. I had forfeited my chance to give a closing argument when I slept in that morning. We were now at sentencing and all I could do was throw myself on the mercy of the court.

234

Mercy really is the right word. Our most merciful supervisor told us that he had intervened, promising Management that he would fix things. A short but pointed speech followed. We were not to be late again ("Not a problem!" I thought). We were to leave Cruella alone ("With pleasure!" I thought). We were to cease and desist with the late night parties at the apartment ("Cruel and unusual punishment!" I thought—but bit my tongue). As I realized that our jobs would be spared, a great swell of relief washed over me. The only thing worse than a dreadful unpaid internship is getting fired from a dreadful unpaid internship.

As we rose to leave, our supervisor had one more question.

"Is the fox head back?"

It was. Kyle had snuck it safely into the locker room before we walked in.

"Good," he replied. "That thing cost $20,000."

And just like that, I sobered up.

Epilogue

Kazuo never returned to the Sky Sox. He now works for a mining company in Peru.

Kyle became an accomplished Program Manager within the United States Department of Defense.

The Sky Sox renamed and relocated to San Antonio in 2018. Colorado Springs' new team, the Rocky Mountain Vibes, has no major league affiliation.

Sox the Fox was retired and replaced by "Toasty," a giant marshmallow with flaming hair and graham crackers hanging from his sides.

Wherever Cruella is, she detests me.

*There were no outfield fences,
just miles and miles of dandelioned grass
that stretched to the ends of the earth.*

18
Keeping Score

We were at the baseball fields, like so many summer evenings, at the park or one of the area high schools. This was one of those operations where the grass is mowed and the baselines chalked once at the beginning of the season and the groundskeeper, satisfied with a job well done, takes the rest of the summer off. With abundant fauna and waist-high flora, one could have confused it with a nature preserve. There were no outfield fences, just miles and miles of dandelioned grass that stretched to the ends of the earth.

It was my second year of T-Ball, coming off (if I'm remembering things correctly) an undefeated season the previous year. Our team was mostly made up of boys from the first-grade class at St. Stephen Lutheran Elementary School. Our sky-blue jerseys bore the beautiful words, *Stadium Coney*, named for a local hotdog joint that sponsored us, and was, not coincidentally, owned by our coach.

The team had no weaknesses—strong in all sixteen positions in the T-Ball field. Each of our seven outfielders were of top quality, fluidly working together in perfect harmony. Our rover could rove. Joe Sternemann was the most natural Shallow-Left-Center Fielder you ever saw. Our Pitcher, Adam Geyer, could pretend-throw a fastball like Sandy Koufax. I reckon that our star First Baseman, Rollin Garcia, could hit the ball over the fence, but as I say, there were no fences.

As for me, I was never much of a power hitter, on account of my being half the size of the next shortest player and weighing 35 pounds. My contributions were on the defensive side, and, unlike most T-Ballers, I knew the rules. I once caught a line drive, stepped on second base to force out the runner who failed to tag up, then tagged out the other equally oblivious runner who was supposed to return to first. *An unassisted triple play!* I don't mean to hyperbolize, but some folks, namely Joe, Adam,

Rollin, and I, say that Stadium Coney was T-Ball's version of the 1927 New York Yankees.

The captain of the *S.S. Coney* was our magnetic skipper, Coach Rollie Garcia. An old family friend, Mr. Garcia had been a multi-sport star at Pontiac Central, the same high school my dad attended. As legend had it, in high school he would light a cigarette, race the 100-yard dash, and then celebrate his victory by finishing the cigarette as soon as he crossed the finish line. He went on to become a cop in Pontiac where he chased criminals half his age through alleys and tenements. He was cool by any measure but compared to most T-Ball coaches (who are positive and encouraging to a fault) he was Steve McQueen.

For years, Mr. Garcia coached my baseball and basketball teams. He was loud, demanding, loud, sarcastic, and loud. He openly mocked us for poor play and taunted us with demeaning nicknames. For an *entire season* of basketball, he referred to me as "Mister Piggy"—not-so-subtly implying that I was a ball hog.

"Pass the ball, Mister Piggy!" he would yell.

"Mister Piggy needs to find the open man!"

"Come on, Mister Piggy, you have four other teammates!"

While Coach Garcia was unquestionably tough, he was not a "no-nonsense" guy in the mold of Chapter 13's Coach Ness. Coach Garcia was a yes-nonsense guy. He adored nonsense. One of Coach's favorite bits of nonsense involved making players run laps after boneheaded plays.

"Take a lap!" he would yell at his target.

Upon the player's circumnavigation of court or field, Coach Garcia would then ask, "Are you tired??"

The player would confirm that he was, in fact, quite winded.

"Then you must be out of shape. Take another lap!"

Now the player, gasping for air following completion of his second round-trip, would think he had it figured out.

"Are you still tired?!" Coach would again demand.

"No, Coach!"

"Then obviously you're not running hard enough! Give me *another* lap!!"

Then Coach Garcia would double over laughing, unable to contain his delight.

His antics made the stuffy Lutheran school teachers uneasy, and we loved him for it. Most importantly, he was effective. Led by Mister Piggy, that basketball team (if I'm remembering things correctly) finished the season unblemished.

Back at the baseball field, Coach was in fine form that day, howling instructions and insults with gusto. Stadium Coney looked sharp—as sharp as a T-ball team can look. A few guys actually caught some throws during warmups and only one player disappeared to pick dandelions.

It was just before first pretend-pitch that I heard the commotion. The moms—who by now should have been well-settled into their lawn chairs, paperback novels in hand—were all standing, gathered in a semi-circle. Some of them looked confused. Others looked angry.

Positioned opposite the moms in the middle of the horseshoe was a man wearing an official Park District hat and shirt. He was standing very seriously, as seriously as one can stand. Arms: behind back. Chin: slightly raised. Face: stone-like. The overall impression was very serious indeed. He could have been a cardiologist delivering the grim prognosis. Whatever it was, any onlooker could plainly see that the Park District Man considered this a very serious matter.

Now one of the moms began shouting, and, to my great wonder, she was not shouting at her son (though she could have, for he was, at this moment, chasing a frog into a nearby creek). Instead, her shouts were aimed in Park District Man's direction. I thought that I must be missing something. Adults, as far as I knew, shouted at kids. They did not shout at other adults. Park District Man apparently countered her shouts with some dismissive remark, which brought loud groans and jeers from several more moms. There was no mistaking it now. Grownup fight! We paused our warmups to watch the fun.

There is some disagreement over the precise cause of the American Civil War. Whether it was slavery, economics, arguments over proper role of government, or some combination thereof, is frequently debated everywhere from tenth-grade history class to the doctoral dissertation. It's a nice topic for debate because there is, you might say, room for debate.

You don't see many dissertations that analyze the war between the Stadium Coney Moms and the Park District Man. The source of the problem couldn't have been clearer. The parties to this conflict stated their positions succinctly and in plain English. The difference in opinion was over ... *pants*.

Arguing for the prosecution, Park District Man stated his case in a solemn tone that reflected the gravity of the situation. Players were permitted to wear shorts, he said. Players were also permitted to wear sweatpants, blue jeans, corduroys, slacks, and pants of any other variety—except stretchy polyester baseball pants. Stretchy polyester baseball pants were absolutely not allowed in this league. *Several* Stadium Coney players, emphasized Park District Man, were wearing stretchy polyester baseball pants. This was a plain violation of the Waterford Park District T-Ball Code of Regulations, Title 12, Section 8.2, Subsection (d), amended by Subsection (f)(2), which clearly states, yada yada yada and etcetera etcetera.

If you're wondering why the contempt for stretchy polyester baseball pants, you are not alone. Sixteen Stadium Coney moms asked this exact question, in unison. Park District Man saved the explanation for his big finale.

"They make you look too much like a real team," he said, and I believe he paused here to dab his eyes. "That isn't what we do in this league. We're here to have fun."

Summing things up, Park District Man's position was as follows:
Our baseball team could wear baseball hats.
Our baseball team could wear baseball jerseys.
Our baseball team could wear baseball gloves.

However, our baseball team could *not* wear stretchy polyester baseball pants—because it made our baseball team look too much like a baseball team.

The moms' position was even more straightforward. The moms' position was that this man belonged in a straitjacket.

One mom pointed out that she had already spent $10 on the stretchy polyester baseball pants and could not return them. Another declared that she would dress her son in whatever clothes she wanted. One rather astute mom explained that wearing stretchy polyester baseball pants and "having fun" were not mutually exclusive propositions. All were agreed that Park District Man was a dope.

P.D.M reiterated that S.P.B.P.'s were forbidden. The moms reiterated that their boys would continue to wear the pants. So, with that all settled, the parties began to disperse.

"One more thing," whispered the Park District Man. He hesitated for a moment, perhaps thinking on whether discretion might be the better part of valor. Then he collected himself and resolved to do his most sacred duty as keeper and enforcer of the Park District T-Ball statutes.

"We have heard that some of your players are keeping track of the score of the games," announced Park District Man. "That isn't what we do in this league. We're here to have fun. No one may keep score."

Several dozen blackbirds that had been lazily nesting in the nearby trees took flight with a great rush of fluttering wings. They were no doubt startled by the roar of Coach Garcia's laughter that echoed through the park like a cannon blast.

He had reason to laugh. The idea was preposterous—as silly as the ban on stretchy polyester baseball pants. The rule didn't bother him personally, but Coach Garcia knew there was someone on our team who *always* kept score. After each inning, he would loudly call it out for the benefit of the crowd, coaches, and players. He considered it a public service. Ominous threats from the Park District Man were not going to stop the kid.

I will note that the task of keeping score in a T-Ball game requires careful attention. Home plate is a revolving door and errors often outnumber outs. It is not uncommon for a team to tally double-digit runs in a single inning, and no, it doesn't count if the runner went the wrong way on the basepath. Of course, there was no actual scoreboard to help keep track of things. I did it all in my head.

"8 to 6 after one inning!" I would call.

"21 to 13 after two innings!"

"34 to 17 after three!"

My mom laid out my uniform on the bed before the next game. The kit included the following items:

Light blue cap, size M.

Light blue Stadium Coney jersey, size XS.

White, stretchy polyester baseball pants, size XXS.

She didn't say a word about it, but I understood. It was Mom's tacit confirmation that, even though he was a grownup, the Park District Man was an idiot and could be ignored. Not all adults are created equal. It was a startling discovery for a child, akin to when I first discovered that, despite all their unusual behavior, I wanted to talk to girls. It changed the whole game.

And ignore him we did. Wearing stretchy polyester baseball pants, Stadium Coney secured (if I'm remembering things correctly) its second undefeated season in a row. From time-to-time Park District Man would show up at our games to mutter and pout. He even brought along an entourage of Park District toadies to intimidate us. The moms would just roll their eyes, but Coach Garcia reveled in it. Always waiting until Park District Man was in earshot, Coach would shout,

"Hey, Mike! What's the score?!?"

"43 to 20. We're *killing* them!"

"Thanks, Mike!"

Then Coach would belly laugh with a force that registered on the Richter Scale.

There's a wonderful irony to the Park District Man's folly. For all his efforts to force six-year-olds to ignore the score, he ensured we would never forget it. Thirty-five years later, we're *still* celebrating our undefeated season(s) and laughing at the Park District Man.

I've been keeping score ever since. It's in my nature. Winning is great, of course, but keeping score is about more than competition. It tracks our progress. Whether in T-Ball or metaphorically in the game of life, if you're losing 43 to 20, it's probably time to change strategies. If no one is keeping score, we may not realize the need for improvement.

My older sister, Jenny, is a nurse. All agree that she is a pillar of the profession. She has been commended for her caring bedside manner, honored by her supervisors and peers, and seems to earn a promotion every other month. "A patient and gentle soul," some have called her.

Patient and gentle ...

Although Jenny has never mentioned visiting Syria, I think she must have bopped along the Road to Damascus at some point and undergone a conversion of Biblical proportions. Only divine intervention can explain her miraculous transformation. It was either that—or fraternal intervention.

Back in high school, Jenny was one of those volatile, quick-to-anger teenagers. A grouch that would make Oscar blush. The slightest thing would send her into an absolute rage. A dinner she didn't like. A question she didn't wish to answer. An imposed curfew. A bird chirping too chirpily in the trees would soon regret it. I was only in eighth grade but was (if I'm remembering things correctly) very mature for my age. Her behavior seemed unhealthy, and I worried about her. I wanted to help.

So, I started documenting her outbursts. Charting them, to be more precise, on a flyer that I hung on the wall in a high foot-traffic area near the kitchen. When Jenny erupted, I, or anyone else who happened to be in the blast zone, would sprint to the "Cranky Chart." Using the provided pen, we would record a brief description of the event and sometimes award a numerical score. A score of 1 was given for mild irritability. 5 meant she was on her way to a meltdown. A 10 was Chernobyl. Naturally, the act of charting usually made her even angrier—but the point was not to cause trouble. I was just keeping score. Another one of my public services.

She should have been grateful. Without the Cranky Chart, no one would ever remember that on February 22, 1999, Jenny "screamed at Mom because she wouldn't let her have chocolate milk"—a tantrum that earned her a whopping 6.0 on the cranky scale. Several more outbursts from the same day and in the weeks that followed included:

February 22
-- Got mad when Mike changed the channel. – 3.5
-- Screamed at Dad and told *him* to clean her room. – 5.0

February 23
-- Yelled at mom because she told her to call Angela.

February 24
-- Yelled at mom because the cereal was all gone.

And so on. It was a lot of work, but we began to see some real improvement.

When it seemed like Jenny was on the verge of uncorking one, we sometimes would raise an arm and slowly twist it in the air, as if turning an invisible crank. The cranking motion was a clever technique to let her know that she was about to be Charted. If she managed to restrain herself, we would all breathe a sigh of relief and let the moment pass. But even with fair warning, the Chart was never lacking entries.

March 22
-- Belched repeatedly and then yelled at Mike, Dan, and Dad for singing the song, *Zuckerman's Famous Pig* at her. – 5.5
-- Mumbled, "I hate this house." – 1.2
-- Yelled at and slapped Mike because he said she was short. – 5.0

April 15, 6:55 a.m.
-- Dad: "Good morning, Jen!"
   Jen: "Shut up, Dad!" – 5

May 18
-- Yelled at Dan to "stop scraping the tongs."
-- Yelled at Dan to give her the balloon.
-- Yelled at her father (*I heard her!*)

That final entry from May 18 was provided by, of all people, Granny. Her Royal Sweetness herself. Even she, a woman who could find the good in a charging warthog, kept score on the Cranky Chart.

The Cranky Chart spawned several additional variations that we hung alongside the original. There were charts that tracked funny quotes and other strange dialogue. Always popular with guests, folks would gather around the charts à la the office water cooler to review and discuss. Jenny countered her Cranky Chart with "Mike's Stupid Chart." It apparently was supposed to track dumb things I said but there were so few entries it's hardly worth mentioning here. (However, I will pause to state for the record that my assertion that "people could live on Venus"[1] was taken completely out of context.)

Eventually the Cranky Chart ran its course and the family moved on to other diversions. Tournament brackets replaced the charts when we decided to hold a competition to determine the *least* funny comic strip in the Sunday newspaper (*Marmaduke* vs. *Cathy* in the semifinals was a titanic battle). After that, we built a wiffleball field in the back yard—complete with functional scoreboard, of course.

A decade passed and the Cranky Chart was a distant memory. That is, until Christmas some years later, when Jenny gifted me one of the greatest presents a little brother could ever receive. It was a black, three-ring binder. Contained within was the original Cranky Chart and all its progeny, bound and preserved in a manner befitting the precious historical documents they are. It was glorious.

Keeping score is a wonderful thing. I would wager my finest pair of polyester pants that this sort of thing doesn't happen in the Park District Man's house. Park District Man would say, "When our sister is cranky, we don't write it on a chart and post it in the living room. That isn't what we do in this family. We're here to have fun." Then the whole Park District Family sits there and frowns, thinking about what fun they are having.

But in our family, we do keep score. Ever since Great-Great-Great Grandpa Andreas Hauser wrote out the family register and mailed a copy to New York City, and probably even before then. That's what this project is all about—recording the score before it's forgotten. Today's score becomes tomorrow's history lesson. When my father-in-law, Mark, set up a cassette-tape recorder and listened to the stories of his Italian grandfather-in-law, it prompted him to write a book. He was keeping score, too. It was a great idea and I'm happy to steal it from him. I hope future generations will do the same.

So, with the score-keeping metaphor stretched and strained to its absolute breaking point, I think that just about wraps things up. There you have it. The family stories in one handy little volume. All the most important pieces have been covered. We've met the key players. We've hit

---

[1] Surface temperature 900 degrees Fahrenheit.

the key events. I really can't think of anything we've missed. So, how to end the thing?

Ah yes ...

Godspeed. Be well. Follow your dreams. Dance like no one is watching. Reach for the stars. Teach a man to fish. Never give up. Live each day like it is your last. Be kind to your web-footed friends. And keep telling your stories!

THE EN-

Well.

I suppose there is one more story I *could* tell. Though please don't feel obligated to read on. It's not for everyone. If you prefer to think of me (as I hope you do) as an unemotional, unfeeling, un-vulnerable, unsentimental old curmudgeon, this is the perfect place to stop.

For the rest of you, take heed. What follows is rather sappy.

You have been warned.

WE'VE BEEN HAVING FUN EVER SINCE.

19

A Love Story

It all started with a text message. I was sit -- *Wait*...

She's telling me that it was *not* a text message, it was a Facebook message.

It all started with a Facebook message, sent to my cellphone, which appeared to me to be a text message. The date was February 8, 2014. I--

2015! I'm told it was 2015. (As you can see, my special Guest Editor has taken a keen interest in this particular story.)

The date was February 8, 2015. I was sitting at my desk on the 43rd floor of my office building in downtown Chicago on a Sunday afternoon, trying to keep up with an ever-growing number of assignments at work. The message on my phone said:

"Our parents are plotting."

I stared for a moment. Then did what I often do when I'm lost in thought, or nervous, or in this case, both. I started pacing.

The night before I had been alone in my apartment. Floor-to-ceiling windows surrounded the room on three sides, showing off spectacular views of the city and Lake Michigan. I was working for a top law firm, living in a great city, making good money. But despite these "accomplishments," I was not happy. I had worked too much the week before, then drank too much the night before, and felt pretty rotten about the entire state of things.

700 miles away, my parents were in Washington, D.C. for a Hillsdale College alumni event. They were joined by their long-time friends, Mark and Jeannette Donovan.[1] I was not expecting to hear from them until they

---

[1] You should be familiar with their work by now. If not, you've skipped ahead. Return to the Introduction. Do not pass GO, do not collect $200.

got home, so was surprised to see my phone light up with a message from Dad.

"Your mother is trying to set you up with the Donovan girl."

Oh, is she?

I knew of this Donovan girl. A year earlier I had run into Mark and Jeannette in Chicago, and we chatted for a while. I learned that their only daughter, recently out of college, was a teacher and lived in New York City. I looked her up on Facebook, judged her to be physically attractive, and sent a friend request. (*I would have sent the friend request anyway*—she also just happened to be attractive.) She accepted the request and went about her life without giving me a second thought.

I replied to Dad that I would go along with whatever arrangements Mom wanted to make. Why not? I trusted that she would not try to set me up with someone miserable. The endgame was unclear—the Donovan girl lived in New York, after all—but if some sort of meeting could be worked out, I would participate.

So, as I was sitting in my offic--

Sigh ... now the special Guest Editor is saying I skipped one of the best parts. She's absolutely insistent that I include this. Very well. The following paragraph is provided *under protest.*

As I mentioned, the Donovan girl did not give our Facebook "friendship" a second thought. I, on the other hand, before any of the scheming in our nation's Capitol, *did* give her a second thought, maybe even a third. It seemed to me that we should meet. Re-meet, actually, since we had known each other as kids. I sometimes saw her brothers in Chicago and we had great times. She was probably just like them, I reasoned, only better looking. I figured our paths might cross if she was home for a visit, or maybe I could find some reason to go to New York. So, she *was* on my radar.

Be that as it may, it must be noted that I was not just sitting around thinking about her 24 hours a day like some chump. If the special Guest Editor tells you otherwise, she's lying. I had dozens of thoughts over the course of my day and most were totally unrelated to her. I had plenty to think about.

250

I am hungry. I have to pick up my dry-cleaning. Should I go for a run? Mom's birthday is coming up. The plaintiff's motion should be denied. The game starts at 7:00. Whatever happened to Ross Perot? I think the Donovan girl is cute. I am hungry again.

Still, it is true that *on occasion* I imagined a scenario where I could meet the now grown-up Donovan girl, and it was an exciting surprise when my dad informed me that a hypothetical arrangement was being discussed. It's completely embarrassing and now the WHOLE WORLD knows it. Can you tell I'm uncomfortable with love stories? Moving on!

Back in my office, I pondered the message from the Donovan girl. *"Our parents are plotting."* This was a most interesting development. It almost certainly meant she was single, and she wasn't completely repulsed by whatever plot was being hatched. She could have said, "Our parents are plotting. Have you ever heard anything more ridiculous? What are you, 40 years old?!"

But she didn't. She just tossed the bait out there. A most interesting development indeed.

Now came the tricky part: the response message. The ideal reply would suggest interest in the alleged plot—but couldn't come off too eager. The response should be humorous, charming, but not too goofy so as to scare her away.

I decided to play it casual. After sufficient time had passed, I replied: "Cool story, bro."

Okay, okay, it wasn't quite like that. I don't recall the exact phrasing but suffice it to say that I conveyed an interest in meeting her at some uncertain date in the future, threw in a witty one-liner just so she knew I am a funny fellow, and left it there.

She replied almost immediately (quite eager, if you ask me) and so began, as those horrible reality TV dating shows like to say, "our journey." Facebook banter begat text message threads, which begat phone calls, which begat video calls, and finally, the plans for a date. She would be back home in Illinois for Easter and the long-awaited plotting would materialize.

In my post-law school, pre-marriage days, I spent many of my free nights in the city with a group of my cousins, all of them younger and hipper than I. They were kind enough to let me tag along to bars and the occasional club, though I never stayed longer than fifteen minutes at the latter. I liked to think of myself as the wise, elder statesman of the group. Looking back, I think I was more of a mascot. A coworker once told me that he had spotted me at some posh bar over the weekend and was stunned by what he saw.

"Dude! I saw you roll into the bar with like eight chicks on Friday. That was epic!"

"Yeah, I'm related to all of them."

"Oh, okay. That makes a lot more sense."

Since my parents had already approved the Donovan girl, I knew the next most important endorsement I needed was from the cousins, specifically, the girl cousins. All Murphys have strong opinions on—well, everything—including each other's love lives. Not just opinions, but ferocious honesty. Woe to the outsider who makes a bad first impression with the Murphy cousins.

As the big day approached, I met with some of my consulting group, cousins Kerry, Lauren, and Cara for brunch. They could tell I was anxious about the impending date, so we walked through some of my concerns.

First, it was important to me that I not give the wrong impression. I'm not a man of refinement. I like dive bars and cheap beer. I still wear clothes I wore in middle school. My prized possession is a record player from the 1950s. I suggested to the brain trust that I take the Donovan girl somewhere to watch the NCAA basketball tournament. Cara had a less stupid idea and suggested a nice restaurant called The Library. It had a classic, speakeasy feel with vintage booths and chandeliers. I also appreciated the collection of antique books that lined the walls, figuring I could thumb through those if the conversation dried up. It was classy but not flashy. So, the Library was the choice.

Next up were sartorial questions.

"Okay, what are you going to wear, Claus?"[2]

"Jeans. Collared shirt?"

"No ... no. You need to get some nice chinos, or khakis at least."

---

2 Some people call me Claus. Eh? Ehh?

"I feel like it's false advertising. I don't want her to think I'm a fashionista."

"She is *not* going to think you're a fashionista, I promise you. Get some khakis."

When Date Night finally arrived, I slid into my hip new khakis (unpleated—the cousins were very adamant about that) and greeted the Donovan girl at the door. Cortney looked beautiful, of course. I was surprised to see how short she was. She was surprised at how gray my hair was. The Library was the perfect spot, even without the basketball games. It helped that we had already chatted on the phone for several months. No need for that brutal first-date small talk:

"So, you're a teacher? ... How do you like it? ... Neat. ... Me? No, I don't care for children. ..."

The conversation flowed effortlessly. We shared many laughs and old stories of Donovan family trips to visit the Clauses. Once it became clear that the date was going well, I learned there is something the kids call "DTR." That is, it was time to Define The Relationship.

I'm a lawyer, so I know the importance of clearly defining terms. My proposal was that we enter into an informal mutual understanding, whereby we continued to see each other as often as practicable, with terms and conditions to be finalized at a later date. My proposal was summarily rejected. Before I could blink, we were dating. Going steady, as it were. "Exclusive."

With that settled and dinner completed, we were off to our next stop. For some reason, I thought our first date would be a fine time to visit some of my cousins. Kerry and Lauren were in the neighborhood, so we bounced into a local restaurant and met them for a drink. We may as well have shouted, *"Hey guys! Look how much fun we're having on this date!"* In fact, I think I did shout that. Afterward, we went to visit Cortney's brother Jake and his girlfriend, Liz, to show off for them. We were parading around the city as if we had won the Stanley Cup, having too much fun to care how ridiculous we must have looked.

We've been having fun ever since. Cortney flew back to New Y--

The special Guest Editor says I skipped another part. I'm well aware and I'm going to come back to it! It's part of my narrative structure. *I* will handle the storytelling duties. You can read it when it's finished, just like everyone else. *Go away!*

As I said, *we've been having fun ever since.* Cortney flew back to New York, and with everything neatly DTR'd, we continued to visit each other as much as possible until she moved back to Chicago following the school year.

I proposed on New Year's Eve, nine months after our first date. The chosen spot was a small stone bench that sits outside St. David's Episcopal Church in Glenview, where Cortney's beloved grandmother, Ginny Donovan, had been a member for many years. A few months earlier, we had attended Ginny's funeral there. Ginny's own engagement also happened on a stone bench, at Hillsdale College. It was my attempt at an homage, but I think it might have just been confusing. I sat Cortney down on the bench and explained the significance of the scene and that I hoped she would spend her life with me. After five straight minutes of uncontrollable weeping (a very curious reaction to my speech, I thought), she nodded in agreement. Notwithstanding the sobbing, she claimed she was happy. Our parents and many of our siblings were waiting for us at her brother Ross' and his wife Corrie's house for a New Year's celebration we would never forget.

Faith, family, and fun—three elements woven into that day that we have tried to maintain during our young marriage. Our philosophy is that if you can get roughly in sync on those three items, the rest should fall into place.

We've had our differences of course, a few memorable enough to recount, if only to show how trivial a married couple's arguments can be. There was the time we bickered—fought, actually—over *how the game of golf is scored.* (You know Cortney, that golf aficionado.) It was as weird as it sounds. Her position was that the only way to express a golf score was in relation to par. I calmly educated her, explaining that the total number of strokes is the more common way to state your score. Somewhere along the way I must have said something wrong, though as I sit here today, I could not tell you what. Shouting ensued. Shouting led to screaming. Screaming led to silent fuming. But eventually we calmed down, and we promised each other that from that moment on, we would never, *ever*, talk about golf.

Then there was the time I volunteered to wash some dishes.

We were brand new members at our church in Chicago and barely knew anyone. Hoping to make some friends, we attended an Easter brunch in the basement of the church. The tiny group of volunteers was busy cooking and serving, and plainly could not keep up with the dirty dishes and silverware as people finished their meals. The stack of pots and pans piled higher and higher in the sink. I had finished my meal, so left my seat and went back into the kitchen area to help out. I cheerfully rinsed a pan and was about to turn my attention to a dirty spatula when I happened look over at Cortney.

There was a five-alarm fire in her eyes. She appeared to be hyperventilating.

"*What are you doing?* I don't think they want you back there. Did someone ask you to help? I don't think they want you back there. Come back! *MIKE. I don't think they want you back there!*"

I handed Cortney a paper bag to breathe into and explained that no one was going to mind some extra help washing up. And wouldn't you know it? The volunteers were grateful for the assistance! Who could have predicted that?? We ended up making some good friends and Cortney found it in her heart to forgive my selfishness.

You may be noticing a theme to these stories. Somehow, I end up smelling like roses in all of them. For the sake of maintaining a balanced account, there was one occasion that people familiar with the tale have suggested I was less than a model husband.

We had just brought our firstborn child, Sally, home from the hospital. It was her second night at home, and everything seemed to be going as scripted. She didn't do much but lay around and eat. So, when a friend called and invited me to join his trivia team that night, I asked Cortney if it would be alright if I went out. She said it would be "fine." Though I did note there was none of the usual twinkle in her eye when she said it.

What a night it was! Maybe it was the adrenaline of new fatherhood, but I have never had a stronger round of trivia. I couldn't miss. The synapses were firing on all cylinders as one answer after another shot to my brain.

Dostoyevsky.

Heinz 57.

Admiral James Stockdale.

A Spanish mandolin.

The limit does not exist.

Victory was secured when I correctly identified the theme song from the television show, *Dr. Quinn, Medicine Woman*. A wild celebration followed. We laughed and sang and posed with the trophy. I sent Cortney a picture of the champions and let her know what a terrific time I was having.

When I got home (still embracing the trophy), I found Cortney holding Sally. Both were crying something fierce, and from the looks of it, had been for a while. This is a good lesson for any new fathers out there. If your wife says it's "fine" that you go play trivia while she cares for your newborn, it might not actually be "fine"—and if you do leave to play trivia, *do not* send her a message telling her how much fun you have are having. And under no circumstances should you carry the trophy home and expect a hero's welcome.

So, we both have our faults. I can be an inconsiderate dolt. Cortney can be a touch irrational. I refuse to let her know what I'm thinking. She insists on interrupting when I'm telling a story. We're working on it. As my Grandma Murphy used to say, if you're annoyed with your spouse, just remember you're no saint either.

Before a proposal and wedding, before a honeymoon and children, before a mortgage and minivan—there was a first date at the Library restaurant. We walked in, hoping all those things might happen someday. We walked out certain they would.

I'm not quite sure why I brought it up on that first date. We weren't discussing religion or anything of the sort. It was near the end of dinner and something compelled me to just come right out with it.

"So, here's the thing." I told her. "Sorry if this is weird, but when my dad told me you all were in DC together, I said a prayer that night."

Cortney dropped her fork. She looked astonished.

"I said a prayer too," she said. "What was your prayer?"

I told the truth—that it was a sort of wishy-washy, "if it be Thy will, I would like an opportunity to meet this girl when the time is right, etc. etc."

"What was your prayer?" I asked.

"Oh," said Cortney. "I said, 'I pray that I marry Mike Claus.'"

It was my turn to drop my fork. That certainly was direct. She explained that she too was feeling pretty lonely and lost that February. Somehow, she knew that the Claus boy was right for her.

"Your prayer was better than mine," I admitted.

From that moment, there was no question in either of our minds that it was going to happen.

None of this proves the existence of God. It might be considered circumstantial evidence at best. I am very mindful of the prayers that seemingly go unanswered. A sick loved one who does not recover. The couple unable to have children. A prayer for peace in a world of endless wars. Why should only some prayers get results? I don't have any answers, believe me. Those things cause us to doubt or lose our faith completely. It's one reason why more and more people these days consider the whole thing a lot of hocus-pocus.

By now you know where I come down on the issue. I believe that God answered our prayers. But even if it was just a happy coincidence, it's still a heck of a love story, isn't it? And since it's my book, I get to end it my way.

Here goes nothing.

I was wrong. It did not all start with a text message. It started with two prayers, whispered 700 miles apart. The date was *February 7,* 2015. God heard those prayers then. But the Almighty is infinite, unbounded by time or space, the first and the last, so it is even more epic than that. God heard our prayers in 2015, but also on New Year's Eve in the German village of Tuningen in 1827, and a hundred generations before that. God heard our prayers in Caherciveen, Ireland, and Pomerania, Prussia. He heard them on crowded steamers crossing the Atlantic Ocean. He heard them in the quiet woods of Northern Michigan and on the crowded streets of Chicago. In an apartment on 34th Street in Queens and in a medical tent on a battlefield in Virginia. God heard those prayers as a young girl cried over the death of her father and when she played tennis with her grandson seventy years later.

He heard them at picnics at Whipple Lake in Michigan and class reunions at Clear Lake in Indiana. He heard them when a mother told her son to "do the best you can with what you have" and when a young pastor and his new wife heard the news that the war that had engulfed the world was finally over.

Those prayers bind Cortney and me every day. It's an unspoken bond but is always present. It bound us when we celebrated the births of our children and when we mourned the lost pregnancies. With each first step, first word, and first day of school. The routine times too—when I leave the house and walk to the train station. When she makes breakfast for the kids. When we stay up too late watching 90's music videos. On Christmas Eve, surrounded by four generations of Donovans, and in the warm confines of the Claus House at Thanksgiving.

A somber lesson of these family stories is that life on Earth is fleeting—oftentimes tragically so. There are no guarantees. Still, we hope. My hope, my prayer, is that Cortney and I grow old and gray (gray-er, in my case) together. We'll sit with our grandchildren and teach them. Teach them about the extraordinary people their great-grandparents were, and that their parents are, and that their children's children's children can be. And with faith, family, and fun to bind them, they can find someone who makes them as happy as the person we each found.

Amen.

EPILOGUE
The (Next) First Chapter

All that ink spilled, yet four of the most important Clauses are barely mentioned. I'm not happy about it either, but hopefully you will understand. At ages 5, 4, 2, and three-days-old, drafting meaningful biographies of my children would be premature. Nevertheless, eventually someone is going to have to write the kids' stories, as is our obligation to future generations. I might as well get a head start.

Chapter One. They are born.

Childbirth stories are a bit like your buddy's retelling of how he almost made eagle on that short Par 4 at Oak Tree. It's never quite as interesting to the listener as it is to the teller. There are exceptions, of course. My sister-in-law, Mary, delivered her own baby in the passenger seat of a speeding pickup truck. Now that's a birth story worth telling! But usually, the details of contractions and drives to the hospital and which relative the baby resembled the most—while precious memories for the parents—are of passing interest to the rest of us.[1] With that in mind, while these stories technically involve the births of the Claus children, this chapter is really about becoming a family, and loving mothers, and insane grandfathers, and how Batman made me cry.

Sally Anne Claus was born March 16, 2018, but if she had her way, it would have been more like November 20. She was apparently having a fine time in the comfort of the womb and had no immediate plans on vacating, so the doctor decided to induce.

---

[1] Or me, at least. Your mileage may vary.

We were told to arrive at the hospital the evening of the 15th. The nurses hooked Cortney to the usual accouterments and began injecting her with some drug that would "ease her into the labor process." They promised her that a relaxing evening lay ahead while the drug slowly went to work. Cortney downloaded some shows to watch, and I brought snacks and put the NCAA basketball tournament on TV. The doc said that we would start to see some movement around noon the next day.

"Just try to get some sleep!" they told her.

Perhaps they inadvertently doubled the dose of the drug, or maybe it was a particularly potent batch. Whatever it was, Cortney's pain went from zero to ten in about as many seconds. She put on a brave face, but with my keen eye I could tell something was up. (The tortured cries and repeated vomiting were good clues). She told the nurses that things were not as relaxing as we had been led to expect.

"Try to get some sleep!" was the response.

"Ma'am," I said, stepping in as the Man of the Family. "She's spent the last four hours throwing up, sweating through her gown, and writhing in agony. Could you try something else?"

"Oh, my. Well, try to get some sleep!"

Useless.

Cortney's parents arrived in the morning, expecting to find the labor process about to commence, when in fact, it had been going like gangbusters for twelve hours.

"How are you doing, Sweetie?" Jeanette asked tenderly.

"Not great," was the honest reply.

Then Mark joined the conversation.

Now, I'm what is known as a Mark Donovan Apologist. If someone has the nerve to criticize my father-in-law, I am the first to rise to his defense. The man can do no wrong in my eyes. But even I cannot defend his remarks to his daughter, my wife, following twelve hours of labor pains, vomiting, and no sleep. He looked at her and said:

"Ohhh, are you being cranky, *already?*"

(Pausing to let the gasps of female readers die down).

Not exactly words to meet the moment. I like to think he was aiming to provide some comic relief and just misfired. With gritted teeth and as politely as she could, Cortney asked Mark to leave the room and he quickly scampered out.

23 hours into it, the doctors decided to go ahead with a C-section, a little before midnight. And after a successful procedure, a nurse carried the baby around the curtain to give us our first look at our daughter.

My parents arrived at the recovery room later, Dad carrying his trusty camera. He took pictures of Sally and the proud mother and father. He took pictures of the glowing grandmothers. Then ... he started taking pictures of other things. He took a picture of the view from the window. He took a picture of the television. He took a picture of the IV bags. He took a picture of the bathroom. Cortney shot me a look, as if to say, *what is he doing?* When he took a picture of—I am not making this up—*the garbage can*, an extremely confused Cortney flew into a fit of laughter. A horribly painful fit of laughter, given that her stomach was being held together by a couple of safety pins. Chuck and his camera were banished to the hallway to join the other Loony Toon—Daffy Dad and the Tazmanian Father-in-Law run amok at the hospital.

The birth of Winston Charles Claus on April 25, 2019, was an entirely different kind of story. His was a "planned" C-section—but nothing went according to plan. From the moment he emerged he was having trouble breathing, and he had a nasty rash, almost a bruise, running across his entire body. After an all-too-brief glance at our baby boy, they rushed him down to the NICU.

Cortney, meanwhile, was out of surgery but losing blood, and fast. The looks on the faces of the nurses went from cheerful, to perplexed, to anxious. Over and over, they pushed down on her abdomen as blood cascaded down to the floor. One doctor worked on Cortney when another arrived from the NICU to give us an update.

"What's the baby's name?"

"It's Winston."

"Okay, well, Winston . . . Winston is a bit of a puzzle."

That was it. The doctor declaring our baby "a puzzle" as I stood in a pool of my wife's blood while she lay helpless on a gurney in horrible pain, and me just as helpless next to her. After 35 years, that was the moment I officially grew up.

They eventually got the bleeding under control and I made my way to the NICU. It's a heartbreaking place to visit, filled with miniature hospital beds and worried parents. The nurse reassured me that everything would be fine, Winston just needed some time to get stronger.

On one of many subsequent trips to the NICU, I ran into some unexpected visitors: Captain America and Batman. It was the day the highly anticipated movie *Avengers: Endgame* was released, and the country was packing the theatres and celebrating, "National Superhero's Day." At Central DuPage Hospital, a group of "superheroes" came to visit the kids in the pediatric unit while a television crew filmed for the nightly news. Then they stopped by the NICU to hand out stuffed animals to the newborns.

Captain America and the Caped Crusader arrived at Winston's room, and I waved them in. I snapped a picture with my phone and the Captain placed a stuffed Donald Duck on the chair.

"Thanks, guys." I whispered.

Batman nodded at me, stepped forward, and we shared a manly handshake. And after managing to contain my emotions with everything that had happened in the last 48 hours, this was the moment I began sobbing. Full waterworks. All the fear and uncertainty and worry spilled out of me with one handshake from Batman.

What is wrong with me? I wondered. I'm not a crier by nature, and I certainly don't cry when I shake hands with men in silly costumes. It's not like he was a real superhero.

On second thought, here was a guy spending his day cheering up sick kids in the hospital. Maybe he *was* a real superhero.

Batman patted me on the shoulder. He didn't speak, but he may as well have said, "Stay strong, Citizen. Everything will be okay."

Batman was right. The doctors eventually determined that a tiny hole had developed in Winston's tiny lungs which was causing the breathing difficulties. It healed up as he grew stronger, and the rash eventually disappeared as well. We took him home eight days later.

Compared to our first two experiences, the birth of Peter Murphy Claus on May 17, 2021, was an absolute breeze.[2] No trips to the NICU or emergency blood transfusions. No long discussions with the doctors about when we might take the baby home. Plus, it was during the COVID-19 pandemic and visitors were restricted, so no danger of troublesome grandfathers wreaking havoc.

Cortney was positively loopy with joy as she held Peter for the first time (a large helping of painkillers may have played a role, too).

"I'b so habby," she repeated again and again. "I'b just sooo habby."

I was so habby too.

Now another tiny new human is sleeping next to me. Arthur Hungerford Claus, born just three days ago, on January 8, 2024. A very healthy nine pounds, seven ounces of cuteness, and his entire existence in front of him. Our full family of six, and grandchildren after that, with a thousand memories to make and stories to tell. "And so make Life, and Death, and that For Ever, one grand sweet song."[3]

Life might be one grand sweet song, but somebody else really should write the next book. I can't concentrate right now. Sally is whining that she wants a cupcake. Winston needs help with a puzzle. Peter is trying to steal the puzzle from Winston. And now Arthur is starting to cry for the twentieth time today. These are not writing conditions. With all this chaos in the house, I think I need a new hobby for a while.

You know, this seems like the perfect time to get serious about improving my golf game. Did I ever tell you about the time I almost made eagle on the short Par 4 at Oak Tree?

---

2 Easy for me to say.
3 Kingsley, Charles. "A Farewell" (1858).

ABOUT THE AUTHORS

Mike Claus is a lawyer by day and amateur author by night and morning train commute. He graduated from DePauw University in 2007 and the University of Notre Dame Law School in 2013. A dedicated husband and father, he lives with his wife and four children in Wheaton, Illinois.

Jake Donovan is an illustrator and elementary art teacher. He studied Fine Art at Hillsdale College and Art Education at Northern Illinois University. Jake resides in Arlington Heights, Illinois, with his winsome wife and daughters.